Living *in the* Land *of* Death

Native American Series

Clifford Trafzer, *Series Editor*

To Be the Main Leaders of Our People: A History of Minnesota Ojibwe Politics, 1825–1898
Rebecca Kugel

Indian Summers
Eric Gansworth

The Feathered Heart
Mark Turcotte

Tortured Skins
Maurice Kenny

Nickel Eclipse: Iroquois Moon
Eric Gansworth

In the Time of the Present
Maurice Kenny

"We Are Not Savages": Native Americans in Southern California and the Pala Reservation, 1840–1920
Joel R. Hyer

Combing the Snakes from His Hair
James Thomas Stephens

Empty Beds: Indian Student Health at Sherman Institute, 1902–1922
Jean A. Keller

Living *in the* Land *of* Death

THE CHOCTAW NATION, 1830–1860

Donna L. Akers

Michigan State University Press • *East Lansing*

⊗ The paper used in this publication meets the minimum requirements of ANSI/NISO Z39.48-1992 (R 1997) (Permanence of Paper).

Michigan State University Press
East Lansing, Michigan 48823-5245
Printed and bound in the United States of America.

10 09 08 07 06 05 04   1 2 3 4 5 6 7 8 9 10

LIBRARY OF CONGRESS CATALOGING-IN-PUBLICATION DATA
Akers, Donna.
Living in the Land of Death : the Choctaw Nation, 1830–1860 / Donna Akers.
p. cm. — (Native American series)
Includes bibliographical references and index.
ISBN 0-87013-684-4 (pbk. : alk. paper)
1. Choctaw Indians—Relocation. 2. Choctaw Indians—Social conditions. 3. Indians, Treatment of—Southern States—History—19th century. 4. Jackson, Andrew, 1767–1845—Relations with Choctaw Indians. 5. United States. Act to Provide for an Exchange of Lands with the Indians Residing in any of the States or Territories, and for Their Removal West of the River Mississippi. 6. Indians of North America—Government relations—1789–1869. 7. United States—Race relations. 8. United States—Politics and government—19th century. 9. United States—Social conditions—19th century. I. Title. II. Native American series (East Lansing, Mich.)
E99.C9A34 2004
976.004'97387—dc22
2004000274

Cover and interior design by Sharp Des!gns, Inc.

Cover painting is *Choctaw Immigrants* by Valjean Hessing. Image was provided by the Heard Museum and is used with permission of the artist.

g green press INITIATIVE Michigan State University Press is a member of the Green Press Initiative and is committed to developing and encouraging ecologically responsible publishing practices. For more information about the Green Press Initiative and the use of recycled paper in book publishing, please visit *www.greenpressinitiative.org*.

Visit Michigan State University Press on the World Wide Web at *www.msupress.msu.edu*

Contents

Acknowledgments

T HIS MANUSCRIPT HAS BEEN POSSIBLE ONLY THROUGH THE KIND-ness and assistance of numerous people and organizations. I would especially like to thank my family and friends of the Choctaw Nation, Clifford E. Trafzer (Wyandot) and William T. Hagan, respected mentors and friends. The Oklahoma Historical Society's priceless collections of archives and the staff at the Society helped immeasurably in the research and editing phases of this manuscript. I would like to thank Sarah Evans, archivist at the Thomas Gilcrease Museum, and the staff at the Western History Collection at the University of Oklahoma for their assistance and for making the research for this work a pleasant and enjoyable experience. Special thanks to Sarah and Michael Whitt and Mary Ellen Dodd Leftwich for their love and encouragement through the years.

Preface

URING THE 1830S, THE AMERICAN GOVERNMENT UNDER PRESIDENT
Andrew Jackson implemented a policy called "Indian Removal."
It was, perhaps, a time in American history that modern historians would love to make disappear. Not only was this policy a disaster for
the Indian people affected, it was one of the most disgraceful events in
U.S. history. "Indian Removal" was a deliberate, thinly veiled confiscation
of Native American lands for very little compensation, and no apologies
were offered to the Indian people. It was simply the only way white
America could take possession of the Indian lands in the eastern half of
the United States without bringing in the army and killing every native
man, woman, and child. The Indians refused to give up their lands voluntarily, so the American government devised the policy of removal, a
remarkable and contradictory rhetorical justification that failed to convince either the Indians or many white Americans. Part and parcel of the
conquest of North America, Indian removal has been mischaracterized
and downplayed in the annals of American history because it belied all of
the ideals on which the American nation was founded. For the past 175
years, therefore, Western historians have spun a myth of American history that simply does not reflect the truth.

The Choctaw people personally experienced the process called
"Indian Removal." This book is the story of the years immediately preceding and following the forcible removal of the Choctaw people in the

1830s from their homelands in the East to present-day Oklahoma, a place they called "the Land of Death." Come, then, with me to an old place, another time, one that still lives and breathes in the memories and traditions of the People. Come with me to the Land of Death.

DONNA L. AKERS
September 2003

Introduction

T HE HISTORICAL LITERATURE SPECIFICALLY REGARDING THE CHOCTAW people is very thin, and most is written from the perspective of outsiders. Almost without exception, historians of the Choctaw people exclude sources written in Choctaw, and do not examine the Choctaw language from a sociolinguistic perspective. Scholars almost invariably omit from consideration oral traditions and Choctaw history as related by the Choctaw people themselves. Even the most astute researchers neglect these significant and valuable sources. Because of this omission, the Choctaw perspective is missing from most historical accounts.

In addition, most works on the Choctaw people focus on their relationship with the government and citizens of the United States, rather than being Choctaw-centered. For example, many historians treat the removal of the Choctaw people from their Mississippi homelands as a mere footnote in the struggle over States' rights, nullification, and the bank during the Jackson administration, rather than as a major episode of American history in and of itself. Other scholars mention "removal" as illustrative of the process of American "westward expansion," or the "frontier."[1]

In addition to scholarship that assigns peripheral and secondary positions to major historical events involving native people, American historical works still omit altogether major portions of history when the main actors happened to be native. For example, most historical accounts of

INDIAN TERRITORY, 1830–1855

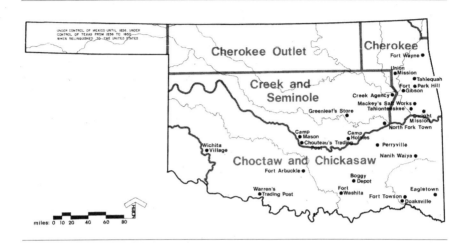

the American Civil War omit mention of the war in Indian Territory. Those few that include this theater minimize its import and often exhibit a startling ignorance of the events and participants of the Civil War in this region. Often, maps of the battles or geographical locations of participants in the Civil War exclude any mention of battles and units located in Indian Territory. Those that do include coverage of this theater look superficially, if at all, at the impact of the Civil War on the Choctaw people and other Indian nations. Scholars often treat Indian history as incidental to the "main" story, which is, of course, the history of the dominant white society.[2]

Exploration and analysis of the history and culture of native peoples *in and of themselves* constitute an important, relevant part of the greater history of the people of North America. Yet certainly, the glaring omission of huge numbers of people, much less prominent historical figures and events, indicates a continuing bias on the part of U.S. historians. Even in their coverage of the Civil War, which has been termed the "central event in the life of the nation," American mainstream scholars continue to employ an ethnocentric selectivity, excluding native people from view, in effect making them "vanish."

In addition to the problem posed by this Eurocentric approach to U.S. history, scholars continue to view native people as "victims"—either of "progress" or of omnipotent, avaricious whites.[3] In divesting native people of power in this way, historians trivialize native responses, since struggle against "omniscient" power inevitably leads to failure. This approach stereotypes both native and non-native people, providing a power/powerless dichotomy that is superficial and predictable. It oversimplifies the complexity and diversity of native responses and renders them futile. As Choctaws and other native people struggled to survive the negative impact of increasingly intrusive relations with whites and their government(s), they alternately innovated, adapted, maintained, incorporated, rejected, submitted, and defied Euroamericans and their civilization. In these responses one finds a rich variety of cultural, linguistic, religious, and political formations and re-formations. Yet, instead of exploring this complexity, some scholars classify, generalize, and stereotype responses and relationships in order to confirm their perspectives. It is far simpler to portray an unvarying descent from power to powerlessness, from independence to dependence, than it is to explore the ebb and flow of a subject that is continuously in motion. The ethnocentric perspective of some scholars infuses their historical accounts with expectations of the triumph and dominance of white America. Not only is presentism a problem in such an analysis, but, even worse, an underlying sense of "inevitability," "progress," and the triumph of "civilization over barbarism" begins to pervade the historical record. Viewing history from a Eurocentric, colonialist perspective narrows inquiries and lines of analysis that might be forthcoming from a less Western-biased perspective.

The United States formed the so-called Indian Territory from lands obtained as a result of treaties with many different native groups. As has been generally acknowledged, many of these agreements occurred as a result of chicanery, deceit, or downright fraud.[4] Often the United States negotiated these treaties with puppet governments—"leaders" who did not represent the thousands of native people by whom they claimed to be empowered. When the southeastern native people began arriving in Indian Territory, they met with enormous hostility and anger on the part of the indigenous peoples of this area. The story of the relationships between the "prairie" Indians and the emigrating southeasterners has been almost entirely omitted from past accounts. Yet, the Kiowas' most sacred places, including Rainy Mountain, "became" Choctaw without Kiowa consent. The livestock, farms, and residences of the sixty thousand southeastern emigrants intruded on the hunting grounds of the Comanches and Osages, lands containing the buffalo herds of central and eastern Oklahoma. These fierce, independent Plains warriors and hunters did not abandon their claims at the behest of the United States. What, then, was the nature of the interaction between these groups of native peoples? How extensive were the hostilities? What happened to the Plains peoples' east-west trade networks and routes which were blocked by the presence of newly arrived southeasterners? Questions such as these have not been examined or often asked in the past, perhaps because they were irrelevant to the narrowly focused interest in the history of U.S.-Indian relations.

The history of the native people of Indian Territory was the subject of much of the work of historians Grant Foreman and Angie Debo. Their perspective reflected the early-twentieth-century generation of progressive historians. They pronounced the Choctaws and other members of the "Five Civilized Tribes" (Cherokees, Chickasaws, Choctaws, Muscogees, and Seminoles) victims of an irresistible, inevitable force. Debo, in particular, related the history of the Choctaw people as a sad decline over many years, culminating in their "disappearance." From her academic vantage point, she reviewed primarily official government records. Her questions reflected the era's interest in the public and official, the famous and the rich.

Debo did not see the Choctaws as adapting to their new lands and continuing to develop their native society. Rather she described them as "assimilating" and "progressing up the ladder of civilization," thus "becoming white." Indeed, Debo's ethnocentricity informed even the melodramatic conclusion of her major Choctaw work. In 1907, as a result of laws passed by the United States that unilaterally dissolved the tribal governments of the Five Civilized Tribes, the Choctaws, according to Debo, "became fused" with the white people of the new state of Oklahoma. This corporate view was not one intended to be inclusive, however; instead, Debo and her contemporaries thought they had witnessed the actual disappearance of the Choctaw Nation and people. According to Debo, the history of the Choctaw Nation simply "passed out of existence."[5]

Debo sympathized with native people and felt that whites imposed upon them, or worse. She viewed American actions in the early years of the twentieth century as unworthy of a "civilized nation." Yet she also apparently shared the relief of many early Oklahoma non-Indians that the Indians had "dropped from [white] sight" in the early years of Oklahoma statehood. Debo, among many others, may have preferred not to look too closely at the results of the Century of Betrayal.

Grant Foreman also wrote extensively on the Choctaws and their close neighbors, the Chickasaws, the Muskogees, and the Cherokees. In his book *Indian Removal: The Emigration of the Five Civilized Tribes of Indians,* he indicts white America collectively for the entire "removal" process, and for the "cruelty, sordidness, and rapacity" that inspired it. According to Foreman, the Choctaws, Cherokees, Chickasaws, Seminoles, and Muskogees, the so-called Five Civilized Tribes, differed from many other native groups at this time in that they were "aware of their rights under prior possession and treaty guarantees." He felt that to dispossess people who were clearly capable of peaceful coexistence and even integration within the greater community was clearly an act based on avarice and prejudice. What so many historians have euphemistically called the "removal" of the southern Indians, Foreman saw as "the forcible uprooting and expulsion of sixty thousand people" who were "stubbornly resist[ing] the aggressions of the whites."[6]

Both Debo and Foreman reflected the thinking of their times. Writing in the early to mid-twentieth century, they focused on leading men, prominent institutions, and political events. Though empathetic to the plight of their subjects, they were blinded by their ethnocentric assumptions, which subconsciously attributed any change in Choctaw culture to acculturation. To Debo and Foreman, this was the struggle of native people to find their place within white society. The sources used by Debo and Foreman were primarily the official records of institutions of government and church. Although presented with amazingly rich opportunities in oral history sources and the availability of firsthand observers, neither incorporated the oral traditions of the native people. Instead, both historians relied heavily and somewhat uncritically on records written by government and church officials, which reflected the perspective of white society. Neither scholar spoke or read native languages. In some respects, they accepted their mission as defined by their contemporaries, to define "history" as accounts primarily of political and economic events and of "great" men. One can sense, however, and in some cases plainly detect, that both Debo and Foreman harbored great interest in the human aspects of history. Unfortunately, these stories were not considered the proper province of historians at that time. Still, each plainly revealed a critical perspective on the actions of the American government in regard to native people.

In *Indian Removal*, Foreman used sources "in the main" from the official United States government records held in the files of the Office of Indians Affairs and the War Department.[7] His other major primary sources were letters and correspondence of Presbyterian missionaries, in addition to manuscript collections in the Library of Congress, the Draper Collection, the Newberry Library's Ayer Collection, and the John Ross Manuscript collections in Colorado and Oklahoma. Years after the publication of this work, Foreman became director of the Oklahoma Works Progress Administration's Indian-Pioneer History Collection. In this capacity, he interviewed or edited the interviews of hundreds of people who had lived in Indian Territory in the 1800s. This research probably informed his scholarship, but he did not cite these important sources in most of his work. As with other historians of his age, Foreman may not have viewed oral accounts as valid historical sources.[8]

The Choctaws were only one of five groups of southern Indians about whom Foreman wrote. Angie Debo, however, wrote extensively about the Choctaw people. Published in 1934, her book *The Rise and Fall of the Choctaw Republic* remains the definitive work on the Choctaw people and is consulted extensively today. As was common at the time, Debo's book employed an assimilationist framework in which the Choctaw people progressively acculturated into the white world of (present-day) Oklahoma. In Debo's view, a homogeneous group of Choctaw "mixed-bloods," with the assistance of Christian missionaries and schools, led the nation in a one-way journey of "progress," which meant, of course, becoming more and more like whites in the States. She acknowledged that the people she called the "full-bloods" did not become absorbed into the white society of Oklahoma, but rather lived on the fringes of civilization, slowly but surely disappearing, both culturally and racially.

Debo and Foreman reflected notions about race that were common to this era. They invoked "race" as an explanation and causation for decisions and actions. Foreman argued that the Indians of the North were "weaker and more primitive" than the southern tribes and thus "yielded with comparatively small resistance to the power and chicane of the white man."[9] Debo described the Choctaws as "a people strangely gifted in thought and speech but slow in action and practical judgment . . . inclined to violent deeds." She related how Choctaw boys hunted birds and animals with their blowguns while "tormenting" dogs and other animals "with the innate cruelty of little savages." Choctaw freedmen, she asserted, were "generally more thrifty and self-assertive than most members of their race . . . living apart from whites and Choctaws but to a certain extent holding themselves superior to Negro immigrants for the 'States.'" In fact, Debo charged that it was the "increasing difficulty of this racial situation," in addition to political and legal complications, that caused the United States "to decide to end tribal government."[10]

Foreman's writings reflected his era's assumptions that the adoption of white political institutions and lifestyles by the Indians was evidence of "progress." For example, he wrote that the Choctaw Nation, in 1830, included a few "leading men who entertained advanced ideas on the subject of education and industry." The Choctaws had "acquired the rudiments of the white man's culture and were making amazing progress in civilized ways at the time of 'removal.'" The language and word choices of both Debo and Foreman clearly reflected their ethnocentricity and worldview.[11] They found "race" when it was not there; they saw "classes" determined by race; and they believed that individual and group behavior was dictated by mutual *racial* interest rather than economic or market interests (or cultural, ethnic, or societal unity).

Debo and Foreman emphasized that relationships of power were contingent on the racial makeup of the actors. There was, according to this view, a "mixed-blood aristocracy" that governed the nonaristocracy and dictated their assimilation and the future of the nation. "Whiter" individuals dominated politics in the nation, hoarded educational and business opportunities, and used the "ignorant full-bloods" to further their own ends, according to this view. Political alignment, personal and public decisions, and the desire to assimilate were all predicated upon, and dictated by, race.

This highly race-conscious worldview unfortunately resonates with that of more recent literature. David Baird's *Peter Pitchlynn: Chief of the Choctaws* and Richard White's *The Roots of Dependency* continue to categorize the Choctaws and their actions by race, linking their decisions to their genetic makeup. "Mixed-bloods" act as a group and generally are portrayed as progressive, educated, and often wealthy. Ignorant, conservative "full-bloods," it seems, also spontaneously agree with one another because they are "full-bloods."[12]

White argues that, "virtually all of the mixed-bloods not in the direct employ of the American government opposed the cession [of 1820]."[13] The mixed-bloods "were, for all their patriotism, different from their countrymen. Their interests and attitudes reflected their position as the children of white fathers, the settlers of borderlands, the owners and heirs of the cattle herds and later the cotton plantations.[14] . . . Conflict between values and reality had developed which tradition could neither resolve nor halt. The mixed-bloods' solution to the dilemma was simple enough: dispense with tradition. They were people of property and their concerns were with property. . . . . The mixed-bloods took the individual pursuit of wealth and accumulation of property for granted in a manner their countrymen did not."[15] White argues that an alliance between the mixed-bloods and missionaries formed as a result of their similar secular values. He remarks that, "In 1820 the mixed-bloods, while rising quickly in the nation, were in no position to compel obedience to their program."[16] However, "temperance, which in fact meant prohibition, was critical on two levels to the new order of the mixed-bloods. . . . It was a critical part of the political program of the mixed-bloods and they pushed it vigorously."[17]

White echoes Debo's work of a half century ago in finding that the mixed-bloods formed an elite group that sought to direct the affairs of the Nation in the manner of mixed-bloods. "Riding a wave of resistance to the treaty and fear of eventual removal, the mixed-bloods adroitly moved to depose the chiefs and achieve what David Folsom frankly called a revolution in the affairs of the nation. . . . At the end of the 'revolution' the mixed-bloods were the most influential group in the nation."[18]

Some scholars depict "mixed-blood" Choctaws as fitting into neither white nor Indian society. Historian David Baird argues that Peter P. Pitchlynn, Principal Chief of the Choctaw Nation during the American Civil War, was "more white than Choctaw," but that he was "at home" in neither society. Pitchlynn, however, consistently asserted his identity as Choctaw. Baird's assessment seems to reflect the racial ambivalence and discomfort of the early 1970s rather than the reality of Pitchlynn's 19th century world. One might argue that Pitchlynn was indeed uncomfortable, and sometimes his loyalties were suspect by either "full-bloods" or "whites" but all of his writings reflect an unquestioning identity as Choctaw that does not seem to support Baird's contention. Baird also reflects the either-or dichotomy of Debo and White, except he sees it as Choctaw v. white instead of full-blood v. mixed-blood. By viewing identity as a clear dichotomy, Baird, Debo, and White, miss the more subtle and pervasive cultural and ethnic variations that abounded in border societies. Pitchlynn was able to navigate both white and Indian worlds.

This study argues that "race" was a less important factor in Choctaw society than it was in white society. The American hierarchy of race established and promulgated in many manifestations over the course of the nineteenth century did not transfer to Indian Territory, where the majority of people were those that white society deemed inferior. Since native people owned the land and lived in relative isolation from white society, a completely unique society flourished in the Choctaw Nation, with stratifications only occasionally related to race. Unaffected by categories determined by white society outside the Choctaw Nation, most Choctaws defined people in a more traditional manner. If one lived like a Choctaw, acted like a Choctaw, and spoke Choctaw, then one was included in the community of Choctaw people. This category could and did include people of solely Choctaw heritage, of mixed Indian heritage, of mixed Indian and white heritage, and of mixed Indian and black heritage. One's racial heritage did not always dictate lifestyle. Ethnicity here overrode considerations of "race."

Some of the conflicts identified by Debo, Foreman, Baird, and others that superficially indicated division by "race" were, in actuality, invested with divisions springing from ethnicity, lifestyle, and economic class. Sometimes race overlapped with other causative factors, leading some scholars to ascribe certain behaviors and groupings to race when it was not, in fact, a major aspect or defining category of those behaviors or groupings at all. Although in some respects white perspectives on race infiltrated the Choctaw Nation, ethnicity and lifestyle appeared to be more important to the Choctaw people.

Clearly, racial heritage was but a minor factor in relations among Choctaw people. Political coalitions formed not as a result of racial identity or degree of Indian "blood," but rather as a reflection of perspectives that were not directly related to race. A cohesive "aristocracy" of people of mixed heritage did not exist in the Choctaw Nation. Race did not define one's rights, privileges, or responsibilities as a Choctaw. For example, many white men married to Choctaw women enjoyed citizenship in the Nation. Race was more a coincidental factor than a determinant one. The repeated use of terms such as "mixed-blood," "full-blood," and "aristocracy" to explain individual behavior, success, or failure, then, indicate an inherently racist perspective of history and culture that certain scholars brought to their scholarship. This work will demonstrate that the activities, behaviors, successes, and failures of individuals were predicated on lifestyles and worldviews shaped by language, culture, identity, values, and beliefs, and had little to do with culturally constructed definitions of race. "Race" paled in importance next to culture, language, and economic class in influencing or determining the behavior, worldview, and self-identity of Choctaw people in Indian Territory during the nineteenth century. Interpretations that find "mixed-bloods" versus "full-bloods" as meaningful groupings constitute a misreading of the historical record, reflecting the racially imbued worldview of American historians rather than the reality of life in the Choctaw Nation and Indian Territory.

Racist paradigms, combined with a great empathy and compassion for the native people, resulted in a tone of pathos, a sense of inevitable doom, which pervaded the writings of Debo and Foreman. This, in turn, led to a view of Choctaws not as actors, but rather as victims, unable to stave off the inevitable triumph of white civilization and "progress." "Victimization," while inherently empathetic, also suggests incompetence and powerlessness. The Choctaw people were no less active in shaping their futures than were any other people. They actively and aggressively worked to shape their lives and their society.

Although there were some problems with their perspectives and theoretical frameworks, however, Debo and Foreman remain the preeminent authorities on Indian "removal" and the history of the Choctaw people in the nineteenth century. Their scholarship was path breaking. It laid the foundation for future scholars of the southeastern peoples and of Indian Territory and legitimized the field of native history. Debo and Foreman were among the first historians whose major subjects were Native Americans. Their scholarship still provides valuable analyses and extensive bibliographical resources for current researchers. Yet, by failing to enter Native American communities, and by objectifying Indians as "victims," Debo and Foreman limited their understanding of the people about whom they wrote. Their failings, however, must be ascribed to the prevailing theoretical and methodological limitations of the era in which they wrote, rather than to any deficiency of scholarship, for Debo and Foreman produced scholarship that was head and shoulders above that of most scholars of their time, and of many who have since followed.

In a similar but distinctly modern vein, historian Richard White has utilized the "dependency thesis" in his work entitled *The Roots of Dependency: Subsistence, Environment, and Social Change among the Choctaws, Pawnees, and Navajos.* White places the historical experience of the Choctaws within the theoretical framework of world systems theory originally outlined by Immanuel Wallerstein. He argues that the combination of social, cultural, political, and economic factors, occurring under an increasingly asymmetrical relationship between the government and the economy of the United States, drew the Choctaws inevitably toward a position of dependency, in which native economic activities were increasingly shaped, and responses increasingly dictated, by forces outside their control. This process of integration into the global capitalist system was accompanied by social, cultural, and political changes and distortions, in addition to alterations in the Choctaw economy.[19]

According to White, beginning in the early eighteenth century, the Choctaws played off the interests of the French against the English, and by maintaining a superior and intimidating military prowess the Choctaws were able to resist the intrusion of the market for generations. However, when this system collapsed with the defeat and expulsion of the French in 1763, the English and the Americans were then able to use the market system to draw the Choctaws into an inescapable cycle of indebtedness and insobriety. They became hopelessly entrapped, succumbing in the 1820s to a state of dependency and dispossession, according to White. He concludes that the Indians were "rendered utterly superfluous—a population without control over resources, sustained in its poverty by payments controlled by the larger society, and subject to increasing pressure to lose their group identity and disappear."[20]

Although White concedes that culture played a role in historical change, he argues that market forces so overwhelmed cultural responses and adaptations that these efforts were irrelevant. Although White recognizes that the changes occurring in the Choctaw Nation were interdependent and reciprocal, resulting not from a single economic process but rather "from a complex interchange of environmental, economic, political, and cultural influence,"[21] he dilutes this argument by emphasizing that the increasingly intrusive world market economy dictated change from outside the Choctaw Nation, in essence rendering the Choctaws powerless. In arguing that the market was the single factor most responsible for change in the Choctaw Nation, White concludes that for the Choctaws, "trade and market meant not wealth but impoverishment, not well-being but dependency, and not progress but exile and dispossession. . . . They were never [militarily] conquered. Instead, through the market they were made dependent and dispossessed."[22]

Thus, White joins Debo and Foreman in taking the perspective of an outsider "looking in." Instead of entering into the community and viewing events through the perspective of the subjects of his analysis, White oversimplifies, generalizes, and forces events and people to fit his predetermined model of dependency. In this manner, White passes through and around the Choctaw people and culture, basing his understanding on broad theoretical constructs, not on the historical evidence.

While it is true that by the late 1820s the Choctaws had lost much of their former self-sufficiency and were struggling through a period of uncertainty and massive change, White's Choctaw obituary is very premature. White fails to recognize the temporary nature of this period of chaos. He looks at the state of the Choctaws in 1820 and assumes that this was the end of the story. Had this been accurate, it certainly would have fit his dependency framework well. Yet his argument is oversimplified and his conclusions are, therefore, erroneous. White freezes the Choctaws in a "snapshot" in time in order to validate his presuppositions about the Choctaw people and to fit his theoretical framework. As is true of many other scholars, White's theoretical framework drives his analysis; when he reaches the point in time in which the Choctaws seem to conform to his preconceived paradigm, he looks no further. Yet the Choctaw people's odyssey did not abruptly end in 1820, and because White's theory drives his findings, he misses the Choctaws' subsequent recovery and their achievements in reconstructing their society and attaining prosperity in the post-1820 period. White grossly underestimates the cultural persistence and adaptability of Choctaw culture.

There are other problems with White's argument. Not surprisingly, White's description of the demise of the Choctaws could comprise a very neat linear graph, an invariably straight descent from independence and vigorous strength as a people to a state of dependence and weakness. Yet not much in human history fits such a neat and uniform description. White argues that the Choctaws slid into dependency when they had hunted out the game that provided them with access to the market system on which they had become dependent. Their inability to adapt to the absence of game (for example, by turning to pastoralism or market agriculture), combined with their descent into a state of almost constant inebriation, thus ensnared them in a hopeless cycle of debt and despair. In fairness to White, there is certainly some validity in his assessment of the situation in Choctaw Nation in the period from 1810 to 1820. However, White's assessment of the Choctaw people is far too neat and predictable. White fails to understand this period within its proper context. He extracts a period of chaos out of context, pronouncing the "story" as finished. In these years the Choctaw people experienced the apex of American economic, political, and social aggression, which resulted in a period of widespread social pathology. Choctaw society and culture came close to being overwhelmed by the problems they were encountering. This was a period of readjustment, of experimentation, and of trial and error in which a strong and enduring culture attempted to find solutions to a cacophony of cultural enemies whom it had taken to its breast.

As American interests eroded traditional practices and social and cultural foundations, the Choctaw people desperately engaged in a contest to preserve themselves and their society. In some places, and at some times, they totally failed. Yet through the amazing resiliency of Choctaw culture and the determination and courage of the Choctaw people, they did survive this period and lived to prosper once again as a people and a nation.

In this study, the author will argue that the Choctaws devised successful responses to the complex challenges that they faced. For example, the Choctaws met the complex and far-reaching problems created by the illegal importation of alcohol into the Nation by creating new institutions with which to compensate for the broken treaty promises of the U.S. government and its failure to expel intruding white whiskey dealers from the bounds of the Choctaw Nation. Choctaw leaders created an enforcement organization called the Lighthorse and passed laws against the consumption or possession of alcohol within their territories, thus devising new cultural institutions to fight destructive forces promoted by white traders and profiteers.[23]

Secondly, White's conclusion that through the market the Choctaws "were made dependent and dispossessed" is grossly oversimplified and easily refuted.[24] Although it is arguable that in 1820 the Choctaws suffered greatly from the disruptions caused by rapid cultural and economic change, the aberrations they were experiencing were not symptomatic of the end of the Choctaw Nation, but rather were indicative of a temporary state of cultural flux and transition. This was a transitory period in which the Choctaws searched for accommodation and sought cultural solutions that would assure their survival as a viable and distinct society. The cultural flexibility, resiliency, and adaptability of the Choctaws and other southeastern native groups during these especially trying times illustrates their will to cohere as a distinct people, and demonstrates not failure, but a successful era of struggle against very strong opponents.

As historian Clifford E. Trafzer has argued, societies experiencing times in which they are threatened on multiple levels, with fundamental assaults upon their integrity and identity as a people, commonly find themselves in a state of "social anomie." Social scientists note that social anomie is a temporary state from which many societies recover. This was the case with the Choctaw people. This study will illustrate how the Choctaws incorporated necessary adaptations to meet a succession of challenges to their existence and how they successfully overcame those threats and retained their identity and cohesion as a distinct Nation.[25] Not only did the Choctaws recover from the chaos of the 1820s and 1830s, they clearly demonstrated self-sufficiency, adaptability, and integrity as a people and as a nation as they built a new life in Indian Territory.

White's major error is that he tries to make the history of the Choctaw people conform to world systems theory and to a neat theoretical framework. Choctaw history, like that of white America, is messy and must be viewed as an ongoing phenomenon. Just as American history, for example, does not end with the chaos and ineffectual defense evident during the bombing of Pearl Harbor, the story of the Choctaw people did not end in a permanent state of dependency in 1820. Had White followed the subsequent history of the Choctaw Nation in Indian Territory, he would have found ample evidence to completely refute his main thesis.

Richard White, like Angie Debo and Grant Foreman, makes victims of the Choctaws. The "fate" of the Choctaws, as related by White, is similar to the "victimology" pervading the works of Debo and Foreman. In the latter, the "march of civilization," and especially the relentless linear "progress" that pervades every aspect of Euro-American scholarship and worldview, infuses the future of the Choctaw people with certain demise. White sees the same inexorable movement, in reverse—the decline of the Choctaw people into a permanent state of dependency—but he credits the world market system, rather than the now politically incorrect but still extant cultural and economic "superiority" of earlier white historiography. In Choctaw history as written by Debo, Foreman, and White, among many others, Choctaws are not actors who create, choose, and shape their own destiny, but rather victims of "fate," controlled by the forces of racial determinism or the invisible hand of the world market.

White's perspective also conforms neatly to the "vanishing Indian" myth of earlier scholarship and of American popular culture. Historian Jack Forbes has written that American scholars are always "losing Indians and finding blacks." Debo, Grant, and White all promulgate this same fantasy. Not only did the Choctaws succumb to the market, according to White, but they also "were made dependent and dispossessed," thus, in a very real sense, they vanished as a nation and an independent people. The subsequent history of the Choctaw Nation in Indian Territory is made into a coda, an irrelevant postscript that is insignificant in White's telling.

Both of these approaches—the view of Choctaws as succumbing to an unavoidable fate and that of the Choctaws as a vanishing people—fail to see that the history of the Choctaws is a continuing story, one in which these snapshots in time are simply that: a still frame, a tiny slice of the whole.[26] When taken out of the context of the longue dureé (long term), a transitory state may be perceived as permanent.[27]

In this work, the history of the Choctaw people is viewed as a continuing process alive in space and time. In addition to a focus on the theme of continuity, this analysis will examine the persistence of culture—how and why the Choctaw people viewed themselves as distinct from other peoples, and the attributes that comprised the essence of being Choctaw. Among these factors are language, lifestyle, gender roles and division of labor, kinship patterns, values, and beliefs. Race is not viewed here as an essential basis for determining a person's identity, as discussed previously.

The other major theme of this work is the importance of viewing the people of southern Indian Territory in *context*. Although this may appear at first blush to be an obviously necessary objective of any historical effort, few, if any, efforts have been made to examine the interrelationships between the Plains Indians (and indigenous agriculturists, such as the Caddos, the Wichitas, and so on) and the people of the Choctaw Nation. To see the Choctaw people in context also requires an understanding of their relationships with whites living in surrounding states and with those living among them. The Choctaw people were influenced not only by neighboring whites, but also by the people of African origins living and working among them. Even as the Choctaw culture evolved to accommodate and adapt to changing circumstances, other native people, Euro-Americans, and blacks, along with their cultures, languages, and worldviews, felt the impact of the Choctaw society.

Viewing the history of the people of the Choctaw Nation in the context of their interrelationships with other peoples is still not enough, however. In order to gain an understanding of the Choctaw people, we must view them within the context of the land, the wind, water, and fire. We must understand Choctaw views of nature and their attitudes toward wild animals and plants. Native cultures generally viewed the natural world in a manner different from that of people of European origin.[28] Yet even among native peoples, the land of southern Indian Territory had diverse significance. For example, the Wichita Mountain range, especially Rainy Mountain, held deep spiritual significance to the Kiowa people. In 1830, the United States "ceded" this area to the Choctaw Nation without consulting the Kiowas.[29] The Comanche and Osage hunting grounds were likewise "given" by the United States to the displaced southeastern peoples despite the prior claims of the former. This behavior demonstrates the contempt in which the United States held native people and their relationship with the ecosystem. It led to innumerable conflicts between the indigenous peoples of this area and the emigrant nations.

Those other nomads of the Plains, the bison, were also disturbed by the arrival of sixty thousand southeastern peoples. Their wintering areas, where the southern Plains people allowed them to replenish themselves and rest without human interference, were occupied and invaded by southeastern natives. How did this intrusion affect the sharp decline of the bison herds on which the southern Plains people depended for their very lives? Other wildlife was forced to adjust to these immense changes.

The great chain of nature was radically altered in accommodating the arrival of great numbers of emigrants.

As the nineteenth century grew older, the expansion of the world market system had a profound impact on the people of Indian Territory and their ecosystem. The increasing participation of the people with the world market and its demand for coal, cattle, and timber, produced behavioral, cultural, and material responses and change.

This, then, is the ongoing story of the Choctaw Nation of the nineteenth century. It is a story of relationships—of the people to the land, and of the Choctaws to other people. It is about men and women, parents and children, villages and clans. It is a story of Choctaw continuity—the persistence of culture, language, values, and identity. Without taking our eyes from this continuity, we will also examine change, adaptation, and evolution. Furthermore, since no group of people ever exists in a vacuum, we will place this story of relationships within the context of space, time, and events. This author will construct a history that is processed through the eyes of native people, unlike many of the early efforts in Indian history. Now, let the story begin.

1 A Brief History of the Choctaw People to 1817

T HE OLD CHOCTAW MAN CLOSED HIS RHEUMY EYES, RETREATING to a place and time that no one else could see. Asked to tell of the origin of the Choctaw people, he cleared his throat, and in an aged, shaky voice began to speak:

Long ago, in a place near the setting sun, the Choctaw Nation was in turmoil. Threats from enemies caused the people to have to flee their homeland. Gathering the bones of the ancestors and placing them in packs on their backs, the Okla Chahta moved out in long columns of old and young, well and unwell. Young mothers with suckling babes keened the mourning cries; solemn, quiet warriors urged everyone forward, silencing misbehaving children with a single glance.

Days turned into weeks, then months of walking, walking. Trudging forward, the aged grew bone-weary, the sick began to die. But still they walked. Each night the Leader planted the great stake in the ground; each dawn he arose to find it leaning in the direction they were to travel that day. The years passed; the People walked on. Babies were born, the young grew old, the aged passed away. Their bones were added to the packs. The burdens of the ancestral bones increased with each passing year. Forty-three long years passed in this manner, with thousands of living Choctaws bearing their ever-increasing sacred burdens. Finally, a day came when a few began to murmur that they could go no further.

Many had spent their entire lives on the migration, bearing the relics of the dead they had never known. One of the Isht ahullos, an old man and secret-teacher, feared for the people when he heard the complaints, and reminded them that the Spirits required the living to take care of the bones of the departed. Were the People to fail in this sacred compact, the hunters would kill no more meat, hunger and disease would walk with the Choctaws, then confusion and death would come, and wild dogs would feast on the carcasses of a nation that remembered not the dead. The vengeance of the spirits would be poured out upon the nation.

The next dawn at the moment of sunrise, the Leader's pole danced and punched itself deeper into the ground, settling in a perpendicular position, without having nodded or bowed in any direction. The Leader called all the people together and announced with joy the end of their long migration, saying, "We are now in the land of tall trees and running waters, of fruit, of game of many kinds and fish and fowl, which was spoken of by our good chief, who is missing, in the far off country towards the setting sun. His words have come to pass. Our journey is at an end, and we shall grow to be a nation of happy people in this fruitful land."[1]

The place of journey's end was called Nanih Waiya, and it was to be the permanent home of the Choctaw Nation. There the sacred bones of the dead were respectfully brought together in a great pile, then thickly covered with cypress bark. Then, to manifest their respect for the spirits of the dead, everyone carried earth to cover the bones until a great mound was built. From that day to this, the Choctaw people, when asked from whence they came, answer "Nanih Waiya," as it is the home for all time.

The old man's head sunk on his chest, and for a moment everyone stared, silently wondering if death had taken the Storyteller. But then, as though waking from a momentary dream, the old man's eyes opened wide. He looked around at the gathered crowd of people, then slowly he arose and walked away.

Choctaw elders have thus passed down the traditions and history of the Nation from time immemorial. Choctaw children grew up hearing these stories, knowing them by heart. Choctaws believed that they were led out of a place in the far west, a place of death, on a forty-three-year journey toward the rising sun. Eventually, they reached the land of Nanih Waiya, the Great Mother Mound, in what is now the state of Mississippi.

This place is sacred; it is the place that was destined to be their homeland. There, from ancient times, they made their homes, believing that the Great Spirit drew them there and would provide for them. Choctaw spiritual teachings reinforced this idea of Nanih Waiya as the center of the Choctaw universe, where the earth was actually part of the Choctaw, the living and the dead. Choctaws in later years, when passing by Nanih Waiya, would ascend to the top and drop offerings down into the sacred interior—trinkets, a venison ham or turkey, or other valuables—in token of their respect and veneration. Nanih Waiya is still known to many Choctaws as *Iholitopa Ishki,* or "Beloved Mother."

Not only did Choctaws believe that they were one with the earth of Nanih Waiya, the spiritual teachings also conveyed the consequences that would follow if they ever should leave these lands. Choctaws believed that there was a sacred compact between the living and the dead. Those who went before were to be remembered, their remains treated with great respect. One of each person's two souls—the *shilombish*—stayed with the body's remains, watching, waiting, to see that the person was remembered and the remains were properly treated by their descendents. The spirits of the dead lived with the Choctaws, sending messages to their descendents and interceding with other spirits.

The Choctaw people lived for untold generations in their traditional homelands. They grew up with the plants and animals and spirits, part of one vast organism of life. They were as the herbs of the forest, roots buried deep into the earth where they were planted.[2] They could not imagine leaving their homelands, and very few Choctaw people ventured away, until the conquest of their lands by Europeans and their American descendants.

The white invasion began abruptly with the landing of Hernando de Soto at Tampa Bay in 1539. He led an army of 600 men, 220 horses, a herd of hogs to serve as meat on the hoof, and several large, vicious Irish wolfhounds for use against the native people. De Soto's intentions were not peaceful. He had no interest in the peoples of North America. His sole purpose was to find wealth, preferably in the form of gold. In the years following Cortez's invasion of Mexico and his success in wresting vast supplies of gold and silver from the Aztecs and others, several expeditions pierced the lands of North America, similarly seeking wealth.

The expedition landed on the west coast of Florida in May 1539. De Soto and his men marched through the southeastern part of what is now the United States, burning and plundering their way through native villages and demanding information on indigenous sources of gold. They appropriated food and took slaves wherever they went, taking them by force when they were not readily forthcoming. They impressed hundreds of native people into service as bearers, chained together so that they would not flee. Their cooperation was usually assured by the capture and imprisonment of native leaders. De Soto roamed from Florida north into Georgia, west through Alabama and Mississippi, into Arkansas, and eventually south through Louisiana to the Mississippi River. By the time de Soto and his men reached Mabila, near modern-day Mobile, the natives united in a great battle to expel the intruders. Hundreds were killed on both sides, but the native people suffered by far the largest number of casualties.

De Soto and his men met with uniform hostility in their invasion of the American Southeast, with one or two exceptions. The southeastern people proved impossible to intimidate, and they ceaselessly harassed the invaders, using the tactics of guerilla warfare. Finally, de Soto succumbed to fever in May 1542, leaving his men without his leadership somewhere in Arkansas. They managed to find their way to the Mississippi River, and fled as the native southeasterners threw six-foot javelins, chasing the three hundred surviving invaders down the Mississippi in canoes.

Subsequent to the de Soto invasion, few Europeans came into contact with the Choctaw people until the eighteenth century. During this time, however, Europeans were rapidly expanding their colonies elsewhere on the continent. In 1607, the English planted colonies on the northeastern coast, expanding in both westerly and southerly directions. The French entered from the Gulf Coast region, spreading their influence throughout the Southeast from the southern Mississippi River. The Spanish imposed missions in Florida, vying for influence with the local peoples.

During the eighteenth century, the Choctaws allied themselves primarily with the French, although factions loyal to the British and the Spanish also formed. Contact with Europeans during this period introduced the Choctaws to new tactics and objectives in warfare, to new technologies, and to horrendous diseases. In addition, many new cultural concepts accompanied the material imports. Europeans bore a huge array of alien concepts, beliefs, and values. Their worldviews, colored by alien languages, religions, and heritages, differed profoundly from those of the indigenous peoples. Disease among the native peoples caused demographic and societal collapse, prompting innovation and adaptation for survival. Southeastern scholar Patricia Galloway shows that disease, warfare, and the world market system caused such disruption and dislocation in the southeastern chiefdoms prior to 1700 that the Choctaws were formed from groups of refugees who created a new nation from the substantial numbers of fragmented polities.[3] By the time that Europeans in any number were coming into contact with the Choctaws, however, they had formed themselves into a reasonably cohesive whole, which the Europeans took for a single entity.

By the mid-1700s, the Choctaw people were familiar with European ideals, values, and beliefs. The intrusion of the market system began to take a toll on Choctaw hunting grounds and the availability of game. Nevertheless, the primary dislocation of Choctaw society was caused by the English slavers of Carolina, who paid the Chickasaws to capture Choctaws and other native peoples for export to the Caribbean slave market.

Chickasaw slaving expeditions into Choctaw territory instigated a brutal and long lasting cycle of total warfare, unknown in earlier times. The Choctaws and other southeastern peoples had long had a form of slavery—captives of warfare were frequently adopted into the clans to replenish numbers lost in warfare. Yet this new threat was slavery of a different genre. Chickasaws captured hundreds of Choctaw women and children, killing the men who tried to defend them. The world market drove the slave hunters, reaching into the hinterlands of remote regions of the world to supply the demands of the marketplace.

Anthropologist Charles Hudson relates that the Indians were "cheated, beaten, enslaved, embroiled in conflict caused by the traders," and that, "having their goods stolen and their women molested and raped, the Indians had had enough. In 1711 one estimate was that the Indians were in debt to the traders to the amount of 100,000 deerskins. Putting it in other terms, this meant that each and every adult male Indian was in debt for about two years of his labor."[4] In 1715, in the Yamasee War, the Choctaws, Creeks, some Cherokees, and the Savannah River peoples rose up against the Charleston English slave traders in an orchestrated rebellion intent on their destruction. The English Carolinians won in the end, using the time-tested device of turning the native peoples against one another.

In 1750, however, the Choctaws and other southeastern native nations were still very strong. Although they were surrounded on three sides by encroaching European invaders, they nevertheless outnumbered their enemies. The enormous territory occupied by the southeasterners prevented any one group of Europeans from gaining clear advantage over their rivals until after the Seven Years' War. At the conclusion of this war, however, Britain gained sole hegemony over North America east of the Mississippi, including the southeastern territory of the Choctaws. The Choctaws saw their French allies beaten in this conflict, and watched with great unease as the French withdrew from the posts and settlements in and near the Choctaw homeland.

Enormous changes rocked the Choctaw Nation in the last quarter of the eighteenth century. Physical and spiritual assaults weakened its foundations. Alien concepts, new ways and means of warfare, a culture based on the exploitation of the land and resources, and bitter, deadly competition for material advantage gradually invaded the Choctaw culture. Private ownership of land, individual accumulation of wealth at the expense of others, and ideas of acquisition, domination, and colonization entered the Choctaw Nation along with their European proponents, disrupting lifeways developed over thousands of years, causing strife, sowing discord, and altering fundamental beliefs.

Aside from the disruption caused by the importation of alien ways, the Choctaws suffered dreadfully from European illness and disease. From the earliest contacts came dreaded diseases: smallpox, cholera, whooping cough, tuberculosis, and fevers. In the second half of the eighteenth century, these diseases returned with cyclical regularity—visiting each new generation with a reminder of the failure of traditional cures in fighting the invaders. The destruction of the physical bodies of the Choctaws through disease was greatly magnified in its effects on the mental welfare of the society and individuals. The failure of Choctaw healing to successfully deal with these new illnesses resulted in psychological effects that weakened fundamental beliefs and concepts undergirding the Choctaw worldview. Searching in vain for traditional ways to understand the horror and devastation caused by sudden onslaughts of epidemics, the Choctaws and other indigenous peoples began to doubt their leaders, their powers, and their ability to cope with the world. In the face of the continual defeat of their bodies by foreign disease, Choctaws looked to innovate, to accommodate, to change, and to evolve to meet the new world.

The world market system, driving the European invasion and conquest of North America, made inroads into Choctaw culture in diverse and seemingly disconnected ways. The demand for furs and pelts continued, inciting overhunting and erosion of the fundamental concepts of balance and harmony. Game became increasingly scarce, markedly so in the post-1750 era. Participation in the European trade system assaulted beliefs about community sharing and the fundamental aversion to hoarding or private accumulation. Desire for European goods outstripped the take of the hunt, leading to indebtedness and dissatisfaction. Since hunting was a male activity and procured increasingly desirable European goods, distortion of the traditional balance of gender roles crept into Choctaw society. Hunting prowess thus rewarded and encouraged declension of native concepts of communal and clan identity.

By the beginning of the nineteenth century, the availability of game had decreased in the land of the Choctaws. The hunting men were forced to venture further and further from home in their search for good hunting grounds. This led to long periods of absence of many of the men, which, in turn, impacted Choctaw communities in many negative ways. The complex social system of the Choctaws relied upon the balance of male and female roles in subtle but essential ways. Men served as elders, enforced the laws of the clans, and were essential in the gender-balanced everyday functions of life. Rituals were postponed or delayed by their absence. The manufacture of tools and weapons declined further, since men spent less time at home. This, in turn, increased Choctaw reliance on Europeans for trade goods, and contributed to the vicious cycle of indebtedness that provided a weakness seized upon by Americans when they wanted to force the Choctaws to cede valuable lands.

The long hunts left adolescent boys without mature males to teach hunting and warfare skills and knowledge of the spirits and traditions that regulated Choctaw life. The absence of most of the men left the villages relatively unprotected from enemies. Clan and village functions suffered without mature men in their prime, since they guided and sometimes controlled the boys who were just emerging into manhood. The men's duties also included the enforcing of clan law. In their absence, important conflict resolution was delayed, and aberrant behavior by young men went unchecked. Most critically, long male absences led to the disruption of social and peer controls that hastened the decline of clan law. Since clan law regulated Choctaw society and was essential to its functioning, erosion of this critical element portended significant societal dysfunction in the future.

White traders began to enter the Nation with more frequency during the latter half of the eighteenth century. Some married Choctaw women and lived their lives out among the Choctaws. Some of these men, John Pitchlynn, Nathaniel Folsom, Pierre Juzan, and others, became influential in the cross-cultural communications and negotiations between Americans and Choctaws, especially after the Revolutionary War. These men, often on the payroll of the Americans, performed essential services to both the Americans and the Choctaws as interpreters and cultural brokers, but their loyalties were always a major question. In early years, it appears that John Pitchlynn, who entered the Nation about 1773, leaned decidedly in favor of his American employers in American-Choctaw negotiations. Later, however, in his old age, after rearing a family and living for dozens of years with the Choctaw people, he expressed great bitterness and disgust with Americans and their interactions with the Choctaws. In a letter to his son, who had already moved to the West, Pitchlynn wrote, "The longer I stay the worse I despise white people for I see that none but a few is friends to the Red Man." He described to his son how whites were overrunning the old Choctaw Nation, stealing cattle, horses, and hogs and "whipping Indians for claiming their own property." Whites and Indians, he said, could not live together, because the whites were so bad.[5]

The white men who intermarried with Choctaw women cannot be stereotyped. They varied in their beliefs and their reasons for living on the frontier with native people. Some of them adopted Choctaw ways, lived as Choctaws, and rejected their American or European heritage. Others were minimally involved with the Choctaw culture. More commonly, these white intruders lived lives that reflected both Choctaw and Euro-American lifestyles and beliefs. Conversant in Choctaw, they still taught their children some English. Selective in their adoption of Choctaw beliefs, they provide interesting and complex examples of the blending of cultures. John Pitchlynn was a white man with a large Choctaw family. He was fluent in Choctaw, but also taught his children English and sent them to school in the States. He identified closely with the Choctaws and thought much more highly of them than of whites.

These intermarried whites brought changes to the Choctaw Nation. They imported cattle; they established more isolated homesteads; and they oftentimes engaged in commerce, such as ferry stations, trading posts, or inns. These activities attracted other whites, exposing the Choctaws to more Euro-American influences. Their Choctaw families were introduced to white ways and society through the visitors and travelers their fathers entertained. One of the most important impacts of these intermarried whites on Choctaw society was the introduction of pastoralism as an economic activity. Cattle were almost unknown before 1770 in the Choctaw Nation. Their introduction inspired imitation, and even some of the "full-bloods" were raising cattle by the turn of the century. During this period of the steep decline of game in the Choctaw Nation, cattle farming provided a viable economic alternative.[6]

White men brought other goods into the Nation that led to terrible problems. The most deleterious impact of white culture on the Choctaws surely was the importation of alcohol. In both subtle and obvious ways, whiskey and rum eroded the foundations of Choctaw culture and life. Inebriation became a common method of escape from the chaos that resulted from the onslaught of changes inflicted on the Nation. Aside from its fundamentally disruptive influence, alcohol as a trade item led to the economic ruin of the Choctaws. The problems assailing the Nation, especially the decline of game, caused many to try to lessen their pain by the consumption of whiskey. Illegal white traders entered the Nation with the explicit design of cheating the Choctaws after plying them with rum and whiskey.

The legal trade in alcohol was encouraged and abetted by the U.S. government. Traders were urged to sell goods on credit to native people unused to white commerce. As their debts mounted and the value and supply of skins and pelts declined precipitously, many of the less sophisticated Choctaws fell into a cycle of debt that quickly spiraled out of control. President Jefferson urged American agents to use the indebtedness of Choctaws as a way to procure native land. When native debts amounted to more than they could ever hope to pay, the U.S. government would step in and relieve Choctaws of their trade debts in exchange for native lands. In fact, Jefferson saw this as a legitimate instrument for procurement of their lands, and delighted in the entrapment of ignorant tribesmen in the foreign world of Euro-Americans.[7]

Changes also came as a result of the American Revolution. The Choctaws supported the French during the French and Indian War. A decade after their traditional allies, the French, were expelled from North America by the British, when enmities mounted between the British and the American colonists, the Choctaws watched warily, trying to decide the best course of action. Both sides solicited the political and military involvement of the Choctaws, but neither side offered the comfortable relations enjoyed between the French and Choctaws. With the triumph of the Americans over their former British masters, the Choctaws were dismayed to find the arrogance of Americans to be greater than that of the British. Aside from the diplomatic and political implications of the American victory, the Americans' reputation of avariciousness and dishonesty was well-known throughout Indian Country.

When the Revolutionary War ended, Americans began intruding in greater numbers on Choctaw lands. Tories fled persecution at the hands of their Patriot neighbors, causing an influx of people into the backwoods of the Choctaws and other southeastern nations. Other refugees from the war included deserters, criminals, adventurers, and veterans looking for a way of life outside American "civilization." Oftentimes these men did not enjoy the highest character, and frequently they caused problems for native people.

The political, diplomatic, and military ramifications of these enormous changes rocked the foundation of the Choctaw society. The Choctaw Nation had dealt from a position of strength with Europeans in the years prior to the French and Indian War. They were virtuosos at playing the Americans and Europeans against each other. For much of the eighteenth century, the Choctaws allied themselves primarily with the French. Their relationship was generally comfortable, and it was familiar. When the French were expelled at the end of the French and Indian War, the Choctaws were simultaneously experiencing a steep decline in their general well-being. In the last quarter of the eighteenth century, the Choctaws came to know hunger. Their villages suffered disruption due to the long absences of the men on hunts, the escalating use of alcohol, the scarcity of game, the weakening of social systems, and a six-year war with the Creeks. Just as they were getting used to dealing with the British, the American Revolution changed everything.

From the beginning of American-Choctaw relations, the Choctaws tried to deal with the Americans in the same way they had worked with the French. Yet these tactics and assumptions did not produce the same effect when dealing with the Americans. The latter not only assumed a cultural and an economic superiority but also expounded a belief in their own destiny and right to native lands. In treaties procured from the Choctaws, the U.S. government demanded recognition of the political hegemony of the Americans, causing important differences in their dealings with native nations as compared to those of European nations. The Choctaws were forced to acknowledge a status of reduced sovereignty and some degree of dependence on the United States in these treaties. These clauses of diminished sovereignty marked an important distinction, the "principle of preemption"—the sole and exclusive right claimed by the U.S. government to purchase native lands whenever they were willing to sell. Both the principle of preemption and the acknowledgment of reduced sovereignty led inevitably to other legal instruments and policies engendering an unequal relationship of power between the United States and the native nations. These rather subtle distinctions became increasingly crucial as the desire for Indian lands escalated and the value of these lands increased. The principle of preemption and diminished sovereignty set legal precedence for later Supreme Court decisions that enshrined this unequal relationship into American law. Within a mere half century, the United States would use its laws to force native people to appear to willingly dispossess themselves, an amazing accomplishment in and of itself.

These unequal power relationships were exemplified in the duplicitous politics of Thomas Jefferson in his dealings with the Choctaws and other native people. Publicly, Jefferson hoped to adopt a policy that would lead to peaceful relations between the native people and Americans. He was fascinated by native people and wrote extensively on the subject in his *Notes on Virginia*. Philosophically, Jefferson espoused progressive and humane ideals in white and Indian relations. He believed that Indians would become "civilized," which would then allow them to join with whites and "become one people."[8] However, as historian Arthur DeRosier Jr. argues, Jefferson "never actually intended to allow his wiser and more humane policies to prevail." Jefferson's letters to Indian agents and others conceptualized the making of farmers of the Indians not as a benefit for the native people, but as a method of "confining the Indians to a small plot of land so that the government could buy up the large surplus and sell it cheaply to frontier settlers." He wrote to Andrew Jackson in 1803 that the "basic reason for keeping agents among the Indians was to obtain their land." He encouraged unjust dealings with the Indians in his instructions to U.S. agents in their negotiations with the Indians. He wrote William Henry Harrison, for example, that he cared little about how Indian land was obtained, but rather "that he was solely concerned with the result."[9]

Jefferson was the earliest proponent of Indian "removal." He saw the U.S. colonization of North America metaphorically as an ocean wave before which the Indian populations should flee. In a letter dated 12 August 1803, he wrote, "When we shall be full on this side [of the Mississippi River], we may lay off a range of States on the western bank from the head to the mouth, and so, range after range, advancing compactly as we multiply."[10] As mentioned earlier, Jefferson also was the first to advocate a policy of getting native people to run up debts at U.S. trading houses, so that when "good and influential individuals among them run in debt . . . they become willing to lop them off by a cession of lands." Jefferson even openly advocated a policy of bribery to obtain land cessions from corrupt native leaders, and stated that if this policy failed, he would "propose a constitutional amendment which by force would move the Indians to the West."[11] Indebtedness was used as a snare to catch unsuspecting native peoples in a web of market relations alien to their worldview. It struck at the heart of native society—the system of communal land tenure. This became one of the most effective weapons in the American arsenal of conquest. Using individual indebtedness—debts incurred by individuals, not the nation—to force the surrender of the communal land holdings of Indian nations was an extralegal process of conquest.

U.S. government agents met with several southeastern Indian nations, including the Choctaws, to negotiate a treaty for the first time in 1785 at Hopewell, South Carolina. This treaty vividly illustrated the intentions of the Americans in the establishment of an unequal power relationship between the two nations. For example, in Article 3, the Treaty of Hopewell defined "the boundaries of the lands *allotted* to the Choctaw nation to live and hunt on, *within the limits of the United States of America.*" The Choctaws agreed in Article 2 that the tribes, towns, and lands of the Choctaws were "*to be under the protection of the United States of America, and of no other sovereign whosoever."* Construction of this grossly unequal relationship belied the reality of the times. The United States in 1785 was not able to compel the Choctaws to give up their independence and sovereignty, but they set up a system from this early date that later allowed the U.S. government to legally justify doing so. This treaty further required that the Choctaws report any activity "against the peace, trade, or interest of the United States" of which the Choctaws suspected or knew. It imposed an agreement that U.S. law would take precedence over Choctaw law, even in the Choctaw Nation in cases involving U.S. citizens, and it reserved to the United States the "sole and exclusive right of regulating the trade with the Indians, and managing all their affairs in such manner as they think proper." In this treaty, then, the Choctaws gave up enormous power to the United States, wittingly or not, laying the framework for future U.S. aggression and formalizing an unequal relationship based in U.S. law of which the native people would have not been cognizant. The Treaty of Hopewell, signed on 6 January 1786, sowed the seeds of conquest in an alien legal process that would ultimately lead to the dispossession of the Choctaw Nation.[12]

The results of Jefferson's countenance of unfair dealings with Indians are exemplified in the Treaty of Fort Adams, signed on 17 December 1801. In this lopsided affair, the Choctaws ceded more than 2.5 million acres of extremely valuable land, including Natchez and more than one hundred miles of the eastern bank of the Mississippi River in what is now the state of Mississippi. In exchange, the U.S. government agreed to give the Choctaws "the value of two thousand dollars in goods and merchandise, net cost of Philadelphia," and "three sets of blacksmith's tools." The Choctaws hoped to appease the Americans with this huge land cession, and made it clear they did not expect to cede any more land. However, only six months later, the U.S. negotiators reappeared.

This time the Americans wanted to survey the eastern and northern boundaries of the Choctaw Nation, they said, in order to keep whites from settling on Choctaw lands. Three months of negotiations ensued, resulting in the Treaty of Fort Confederation. In this treaty, the Choctaws allowed the United States to run a boundary line, but they conceded no land. However, at the completion of the survey, the United States took Choctaw land that today comprises a portion of Jefferson County on the Mississippi River.[13]

President Jefferson's policy of using Indian trade debts to coerce land cessions bore fruit again at the Treaty of Hoe Buckintoopa. Individual Choctaws had accumulated debts with the British trading firm of Panton, Leslie and Company. General James Wilkerson met with the Choctaws and demanded immediate payment of this debt. On 31 August 1803, the Choctaw leaders signed the treaty, ceding more than 850,000 acres of land to the United States, who would then discharge the Choctaws' debts to Panton, Leslie and Company. In this remarkable case, U.S. agents intervened in private business transactions between individual native people and a private British trading house, acting as an accounts receivable factor in paying off debts incurred by Choctaw individuals, forcing the entire Nation to pay debts owed by individuals. In this treaty, and the subsequent Treaty of Mount Dexter, the U.S. government dropped any pretense to just relations between sovereign nations and moved into the private sector to further the effects of the world market system in commodifying lands far removed from the world marketplace and ensnaring unwilling participants in market relations they did not understand. In addition, this treaty made explicit the incorporation of bribery of Indian leaders as standard fare. As a "consideration" for ceding 853,760 acres to the United States, the Choctaw leaders who signed this treaty received "fifteen pieces of stroud, three rifles, one hundred and fifty blankets, two hundred and fifty pounds of powder, one bridle, one man's saddle, and one black silk handkerchief." These goods were either kept for the personal use of the Choctaw leaders who signed the treaty or were used by them to reward their followers. At any rate, the value of these goods was miniscule as an exchange for the cessions made.[14]

By 1805, individual Choctaws had once again incurred debts amounting to $46,000 to Panton, Leslie and Company. DeRosier argues that the U.S. government responded to American citizens' demands for more Choctaw land by opening more trading houses for the Choctaws so that they would become indebted more quickly. Panton, Leslie demanded payment in May 1805, and within months the Choctaws had angrily ceded over four million acres of rich Mississippi Delta land for $50,500 in cash, of which $48,000 was paid directly to Panton, Leslie. The remaining $2,500 was paid to the U.S. interpreter, an intermarried white by the name of John Pitchlynn, "to compensate him for certain losses sustained in the Choctaw country, and as a grateful testimonial of the nation's esteem." In addition, the U.S. government was to pay an annuity to the Choctaws of $3,000 in trade goods. Once again, the United States bribed Choctaw leaders, enumerating their reward for services rendered in Article 3, which states that "the three great Medal Mingoes, Pukshunbbee-Mingo, Hoomastubbee, and Pooshamattaha" were each to receive $500 plus an annuity of $150 for as long as they held office. This time, however, Jefferson's negotiators exceeded the level of dishonesty he could tolerate. He thought the Indians had received too little compensation for the rich farmlands the United States coerced them to cede. Therefore, he declined to present the treaty to Congress until two years later. In 1808, however, when the United States and Spain were close to war over the possession of Florida, Jefferson finally sent the treaty to the Senate for ratification without altering the terms.[15]

Rather than sponsoring the commercial rape of the Choctaw Nation through the extension of credit to consumers who were ignorant of the ways of the market, the United States could have discharged its duty to protect the native people, prohibiting the extension of credit unlikely to be repaid. Instead, the U.S. government colluded with private-sector firms to coerce the divestiture of native community wealth to meet the private debts of individuals. The Choctaws were "under the protection of the United States," which through its own treaties had "the sole and exclusive right of regulating the trade with the Indians." Unfortunately, the United States chose to subject Indians to dishonorable means to obtain the ancient Indian homelands.[16]

The Choctaws that continued to rely on hunting for pelts to trade to Americans for manufactured goods were caught in an unending cycle of debt. The cost of the trade goods the Choctaws needed exceeded the value of their income from hunting and so each year they went deeper into debt. The more progressive Choctaws avoided this trap by shifting to herding cattle. They could count on a steady income from herding cattle, unlike the hunters, who each year found less game and lower prices for the pelts they could produce.

Jefferson's Indian policy promoted the liquidation of these debts through cessions of land. Yet the land to be ceded belonged to the whole Nation and was their national wealth. Thus, those individuals who clung to the dying hunting economy had their debts expunged in a manner that charged everyone in the Nation. The herders and hunters alike thus paid for the debts run up by a few. Furthermore, the herders lost valuable pastureland in these cessions, so they were doubly dunned. The division in economic interests among the Choctaws was a very new and significant change for these native people. Previously, they had shared the same pursuits, with the exception in the last quarter of the eighteenth century of the intermarried whites (some of whom owned inns or ferries or participated in other ways in the American market economy). The United States, then, by this method gained enormous amounts of land for next to nothing, and also succeeded in creating a serious rift among the Choctaws.

This process illustrates the hypocrisy of the U.S. Indian policy. During the first quarter of the nineteenth century, official American policy encompassed the idea that if the Indians could become "civilized," or more like the whites, then they could eventually be absorbed into the Union and become full-fledged citizens of the United States. The Americans charged the Indians with uncivilized ways primarily based on their reliance on the hunt. Americans urged Native Americans to abandon the hunt and to become good yeoman farmers. This was part and parcel of Jefferson's vision. The horrendous policy of Indian Removal that was instituted in the early 1830s was based in large part on the false accusation that the native people were nomadic hunters, and thus were not attached to the land and could easily "remove" west of the Mississippi and give up their good farmlands to white American yeoman farmers. In 1805, however, the United States delightedly used the hunters to lever huge concessions of land from entire Indian nations.

The Choctaw economy had long been a mixed economy. Primarily agriculturalists, the Choctaw women grew large crops, working in the fields communally. The men hunted and helped with the crops only when heavy labor was needed, as when new fields were being cleared. Women also gathered all kinds of wild plants for food and medicine, and the men also fished. Occasionally they would trade for foods not grown in the Nation. This multifaceted economy had served the Choctaws well for generations. In the last half of the eighteenth century, however, the economy became seriously impaired, for two primary reasons.

The first was that the Choctaws became increasingly reliant on the trade of deer and buffalo hides for manufactured goods made in Europe or the United States. Items such as axes, knives, and pots and pans—things made of metal that the Choctaws could not make themselves—replaced less efficacious native-made goods. Trade cloth, beads, and some luxuries also found their way into Choctaw life. These trade goods, first procured in the early eighteenth century, became a necessity to the Choctaws as the old skills were gradually forgotten as time went by. Thus, trade goods that were initially luxuries had, by the 1800s, become necessities.

The second reason for the decline of the Choctaw economy was the decrease in game in the lands of the Choctaws. Game had been plentiful at one time, but as the white traders encouraged Indians to produce the maximum possible number of deer hides, overhunting swiftly became a factor. Where before, the hunters had been very careful not to overhunt, with the rising reliance on trade goods, many of them increased their yearly take without regard for the consequences. In addition, the invasion of whites and displaced Indians to the Choctaw lands contributed to the decline in game. By 1800, the scarcity of game mandated that the Choctaws leave their homelands and travel long distances to what is now the state of Oklahoma. There they found plentiful game, deer, bear, and buffalo, but they also ran into hostile Osages and others, on whose hunting grounds the Choctaws trespassed. The price of the hides also fluctuated, causing unpredictable fluctuations in the number of hides each individual hunter needed to procure in order to meet basic needs. Of course, liquor also entered the Nation at this time. Many men, and increasingly women, too, became overly fond of alcohol and used it to excess. Some people succumbed to alcoholism and others came to enjoy and expect periodic drunken revelries, leading to a "need" for an ever-increasing number of hides to use to procure whiskey.

These changes, of course, occurred over several decades, but in the life of a people, this was a blink of an eye. The changes were substantial and impacted the daily lives of all the Choctaws. By 1800, when the Americans entered the picture and started using Choctaw weaknesses to obtain their land in a manner that seemed very complex and perhaps inexplicable to the native people, the Choctaws had a very difficult time defending themselves from American avarice. The "treaties" with the United States came to be primarily instruments of American conquest. They had less and less to do with good relations or military truces, and more and more to do with forcing Indians to give up their homelands in processes they barely understood.

For eleven years after the Treaty of Mount Dexter was signed in 1805, the Choctaws were not asked to cede more land to the United States. These were fateful years for the Nation, as the winds of change continued to blow across the region. The Choctaw economy continued to erode, with game becoming increasingly scarce. Many of the old traditionalists saw their subsistence decline precipitously, and they were seemingly unable to make the transition from hunting to herding. Many of these folks turned increasingly to alcohol. They found an antidote to their despair in the message of the Shawnee Prophet and his brother, Tecumseh.

In 1811, Tecumseh traveled throughout the Southeast, including an important stop in the Choctaw Nation, where he tried to convince the Choctaws to join his Pan-Indian Movement. Tecumseh envisioned a great military and political alliance that would drive the whites back across the Ohio River and keep them out of Indian country. Tecumseh was a great orator and excited a number of young Choctaws. Many warriors wanted to join his great alliance. Then the renowned Choctaw chief and war leader, Pushmataha, rose. He acknowledged the appeal of Tecumseh's vision. However, he argued that even with a great intertribal alliance the Americans would ultimately win. He feared that if the People took up arms against the United States, the Americans would annihilate the survivors.

Pushmataha was a stirring speaker, a fearless warrior, and a leader held in the highest esteem. He swayed many of the Choctaws to his point of view. Still, the council could not reach consensus. The deadlocked council called upon a renowned Choctaw *hopaii* (prophet) to break the deadlock. The *hopaii* ordered the Choctaws to reconvene at dawn the next morning and build a scaffold, saying that the Great Spirit would decide the issue for them. After slaying a flawless red heifer, the *hopaii* ordered all who were present to prostrate themselves on the ground before the scaffold, and to remain there until told to do otherwise. The *hopaii* set on fire the heifer's carcass and the scaffold. He then rolled himself up in the skin of the sacrificial calf, uttering prayers and exhortations. After the fire had consumed the scaffold, the *hopaii* rose up, shouting, *"Osh Ho-chi-to Shilup anumpulih hakloh!"* (The Great Spirit has spoken. Hear his words.) All the Choctaws jumped to their feet as the *hopaii* pointed to the sky, exclaiming, "The Great Spirit tells me to warn you against the dark and evil designs of Tecumseh, and not to be deceived by his words; that his schemes are unwise, and if entered into by you, will bring you trouble. You will bring sorrow and desolation upon yourselves and the nation."[17] This decided the issue. Although some Choctaw warriors did join Tecumseh's movement, the majority remained neutral.

In August 1813, the Creek followers of Tecumseh—called the Red Sticks—attacked Fort Mims in Alabama, killing many of its citizens and touching off the Creek War. Still most Choctaw warriors remained neutral, but the great chief Pushmataha offered to bring several hundred warriors in on the side of the Americans. General Ferdinand Claiborne and his force of Mississippians entered the Choctaw Nation in November 1813, where he then consulted with Pushmataha and they jointly planned their campaign against the Creeks. During December and January, about seven hundred Choctaws fought alongside Claiborne's American forces, with Pushmataha leading two successful attacks on the Creeks at Black River Creek.

The defeat of the Upper Creeks occurred on 27 March 1814. The Choctaws under Pushmataha joined with Andrew Jackson's American forces and warriors from the Cherokees and an opposing Creek faction against the Upper Creeks. They massacred the Upper Creeks—killing more than eight hundred of them, and leaving only twenty alive. This battle is often overlooked in American history. Yet it was an extremely important defeat for all Native Americans. In the peace treaty negotiations that followed, Jackson betrayed his Lower Creek allies—those who had fought on the American side during the Creek War, against their own people. Jackson demanded that the entire Creek Nation cede twenty million acres of their most valuable lands. This betrayal was bitter enough. Unfortunately, the defeat had even larger ramifications. It signaled the end of the southern nations' ability to resist the Americans militarily, and more importantly, the Americans knew this and were determined to exploit the relative weakness of the Indians and press home their dispossession. When the Indians were strong enough to be a threat to the Americans, they were dealt with more fairly. As soon as the Americans perceived themselves to be stronger than the Indians, however, even the appearance of justice or fair dealing evaporated in U.S. Indian policy. From the end of the Creek War onward, the huge native nations of the South were treated like a subjugated people. Despite the alliance of many

Choctaws, Cherokees, and Creeks, who sincerely believed they were the respected allies of the Americans, the U.S. government clarified almost immediately that its policy toward Indians would undergo an enormous change.

The Choctaws also allied with the Americans in defeating the British at the Battle of New Orleans. Mingo (head leader) Pushmataha was commissioned a brigadier general. He led hundreds of Choctaw warriors at the battle, executing a key flanking movement that directly contributed to the success of the battle. With the defeat of the British, Andrew Jackson became wildly popular. He saw that the extermination of the Indians was what Americans of the South and West wanted. Jackson realized that the time was ripe for a major shift in dealings with Indians. He wrote and spoke repeatedly about what he saw as a ridiculous charade, pointing out that in dealing with Indian nations the United States no longer had to pretend that they were sovereign states or that they deserved any sort of consideration. Instead he called for the dispossession of all native peoples to some undetermined point in the West, and demanded that the American government begin dictating terms to Indians, instead of following the protocol of treaty-making and its legal niceties.

Jackson played into the naivete of the Choctaws, who up to this point actually thought they were a valued ally and friend to the United States. Jackson praised the Choctaws for their assistance in the Battle of New Orleans, and the Choctaws received formal recognition and thanks from the U.S. government. Even the Mississippi Territory legislature passed a resolution praising the Choctaw warriors and presenting them with gifts. The following year, 1816, the Choctaws met with American agents to negotiate the Treaty of Fort Stephens. The Choctaws and the Americans met with much good feeling. The United States promised the Choctaws that they would always remain their friends and "that never again would the United States allow them to be mistreated."[18] The Choctaws ceded a small area of land straddling the Mississippi-Alabama border. In return, the United States paid them an annuity of $6,000 for twenty years, and gave the Choctaws merchandise valued at $10,000. This era of good feelings and peace was short-lived, however. In 1817 Mississippi became a new American state, and the lull in American demands for Choctaw lands ended.[19]

2　History, Change, and Tradition

"It is our duty to make new efforts for the preservation, improvement, and civilization of the native inhabitants. The hunter state can exist only in the vast uncultivated desert. It yields to the more dense and compact form and greater force of civilized population; and of right it ought to yield, for the earth was given to mankind to support the greatest number of which it is capable, and no tribe of people have a right to withhold from the want of others more than is necessary for their own support and comfort."[1]

James Monroe, president of the United States

P RESIDENT MONROE'S FIRST ANNUAL MESSAGE TO CONGRESS ON 2 December 1817 presaged the complete reorganization of American Indian policy. After extensive review, the new secretary of war, John C. Calhoun, recommended three important changes in American policy. First, he suggested that the United States drop the pretense of treating native tribal groups as sovereign nations. Secondly, he recommended that the United States try to prevent the complete extinction of the native people through education and "civilization," although he clarified that native people were not ready for instruction in reading, writing, and arithmetic, but should instead be instructed in manual arts— farming and homemaking. Last, and most importantly, he proposed that the United States force native people to adopt the concept of private ownership of land by confiscating their homelands, then giving individual Indians small plots of land west of the Mississippi River. Native compliance with this new policy was to be voluntary, and military force would not be used to force Indians off their lands. If the Indians refused to move, the states would extend their laws over them and they would be granted only such rights as each state decided to offer, and the native nations would, of course, cease to exist.[2] The alternative to this creative form of second-class citizenship was termed "removal," a euphemism that implies the native people voluntarily elected their own dispossession and permanent exile to the West.

Calhoun's policy was too gradual for American land speculators and others who wanted land. They demanded the immediate dispossession of all native people east of the Mississippi. The price of cotton on the world market had doubled from 1814 to 1816, old cotton lands were exhausted, and plantation owners needed new land on which to deploy their slaves and expand cotton production.[3] Recent immigrants and American citizens without land sought farmland to support themselves and their families.

Andrew Jackson led the clamor for Indian dispossession, inspired by his personal ambition for wealth, and also with an eye toward the presidency. Jackson had become a national hero due to his fame as a military leader and "Indian fighter" during the War of 1812 and the Creek War. His increasing demands for the dispossession of the native people living east of the Mississippi began early in the second decade of the nineteenth century. His great public support and his experience in dealing with Indians gave him influence far in excess of his political status. The American public trusted his judgment as he called for change in American Indian policies. The fact that he was calling for the dispossession and expulsion of the huge Indian population east of the Mississippi, which would clear title to millions of acres of land uniquely suited to growing cotton, endeared him to the land speculators and others calling for immediate removal. Jackson demanded that the government end its policy of using treaties to negotiate with Indians. Instead, he argued that the United States should unilaterally dictate the course of the future for native peoples. As Jackson saw it, the days were gone when the United States had to consider the native peoples as a military threat, and thus treat with them as though they were sovereign nations. In previous years, when the United States had been weak, the treaty process had been a necessity, but now that the American nation was stronger than any single native nation, Jackson felt that she should use her strength, "to affect any object which its wisdome [*sic*], humanity, and justice may please to adopt with regard to these unfortunate people."[4]

In response to these growing political demands, Secretary of War Calhoun sent American negotiators to meet with the Choctaws in October 1818. Almost as soon as the commissioners made it clear that the Americans wanted more land cessions, the Choctaw leaders shut down the negotiations. The Choctaws had not only grown weary of the unending demands of whites, they also had become more adept and unified in their opposition to further compromise.[5]

From 1815 to 1820, economic conditions in the Choctaw Nation continued in a precipitous decline. The end of the War of 1812, the defeat of the Creek Red Sticks, and the growth in the demand for cheap land resulted in masses of white intruders moving onto Choctaw lands.[6] The United States did little to expel the intruders, and did even less to try to control the illegal importation of alcohol into the Choctaw Nation, even though it was bound by treaty to do so. The territorial and state courts would not enforce the many laws against whites selling liquor to Indians in Mississippi and elsewhere. The U.S. government even issued a daily ration of whiskey to the Choctaws who were gathered for treaty negotiations at Doak's Stand in 1820, despite the vehement protests of Choctaw leaders. (The U.S. government paid William Eastin and William B. Lewis nine cents per Choctaw to supply them with all the liquor they could drink. Eastin and Lewis were close friends of Andrew Jackson, the chief U.S. treaty negotiator.)[7] The United States used whiskey as an agent of conquest. They hoped the Indians would get drunk and would be then less able to deal intelligently with the U.S. negotiators. These unconscionable tactics, as well as blatant bribery and fraud, were routinely employed by the United States in their dealings with Native Americans.[8]

By 1818, hundreds of whites had intruded into the Choctaw Nation. Some had moved into native houses and fields. Many were building shelters and clearing fields, enlisting the precedent of squatters' rights. Others were running liquor into the Nation, selling it through middlemen who were sometimes native but more often white entrepreneurs. Intruders became an increasingly urgent problem as their numbers grew. They were illegally residing in the Nation, many to sell liquor or other goods, some as refugees from the law and white "civilization," others seeking land. The U.S. government turned a blind eye to their activities, especially as it became apparent that their presence and troublemaking might help persuade the Choctaws that it was impossible to remain in their homelands.

The Choctaw hunting economy by this time had completely collapsed, and many of the Choctaws were living in dire circumstances, since the game had disappeared. Each year, more and more Choctaws took up herding, which necessitated that they move out of their villages and into more open prairie land with room for pasturage of their livestock. The social and demographic changes accompanying these moves contributed enormously to the decline of traditional lifeways. The clans were weakened as their authority declined, and the social constraints that regulated Choctaw life decreased with the dispersion of the population.[9]

Pastoralism also exposed the Choctaw people to the concept of individual private property. Each animal, though it ran in the open range, belonged to someone, not to the clan or village. Furthermore, pastoralism weakened sanctions against the accumulation of individual wealth. Thus, although herding provided an alternative to hunting, it also contributed enormously to the breakdown of Choctaw society.

In another change to their traditional lifeways, Choctaws also increasingly went to the farms of white men to pick cotton after they had gathered their own crops. The white farmers paid them in cash, one of the rare occasions on which the Choctaws of this period found themselves in possession of cash. This practice increased their interaction with the market and drew them into more complex market relations than they had ever before experienced. With hundreds of men, women, and children going outside the Nation to pick cotton, and the steady increase in herding, many societal changes occurred. Individual behavior was less tightly constrained and social and cultural norms were less assiduously enforced in the absence of close tribal community. Without the traditional watching eyes of the clan elders and the social regulation engendered by proximity, individuals began to abuse alcohol and to engage in personal acts of violence that would have been controlled in the villages.[10]

During these years, Choctaw leaders searched for a course that would preserve the Nation and allow them to continue their own way of life without American interference. Given the decline in the relative strength of the Choctaws as compared to the Americans, however, their options were quite limited. Three courses of action did suggest themselves. The first was to do nothing—to remain in the traditional homelands and endure the disintegration of Choctaw society, hoping for some sort of miracle. The second course of action open to the Choctaws was to migrate, to agree to exchange their homelands for land west of the Mississippi. Many problems attended this idea, however. First, many more traditional Choctaws steadfastly refused to leave the bones of the dead. The oral traditions taught that if they left their homelands, the Nation would die. Second, the vast majority of Choctaws, who were uninvolved in negotiations with the Americans, could not believe that the Americans would actually dispossess them. The more sophisticated also rejected emigration, since they would, in all likelihood, lose much of their accumulated wealth if they abandoned their homelands. The largest point of resistance to migration, however, was inspired by the fundamental injustice of the concept. The Choctaw people had been in their homelands forever; what right did the United States have to force them off of their lands? Across the entire socioeconomic spectrum, Choctaws stubbornly and adamantly refused to leave their homelands.[11]

The third option open to the Choctaw leaders appeared to be the best alternative. The Choctaw people could gradually adopt some of the concepts and institutions of Euro-Americans, while simultaneously preserving their native traditions and beliefs. This was a very delicate and difficult road to follow. If changes were implemented too slowly, the Americans would move to force the Choctaws into exile, based on the argument that they were still too "uncivilized" to live in proximity with whites. If changes occurred too quickly, however, the traditional Choctaws would accuse their leaders of betraying them and siding with the whites in their war of cultural aggression. What the Choctaw leadership did not fully appreciate, however, was the fact that no matter how much they assimilated they would still be forced off their lands. The crux of the problem was not a question of "civilization" but rather a thinly disguised, increasingly urgent desire among whites to possess the rich agricultural lands of the Choctaws.

Land was wealth in the early republic, and native claims and rights formed a barrier to white demands for land. White Americans could tolerate the injustice of white men having different levels of material wealth, but they could not abide the thought of native people enjoying land that whites wanted. Increasingly, white Americans constructed a racially inspired body of legal and moral reasoning that justified depriving native people of the fundamental property rights that formed the basis of the world and American market economies. Conveniently borrowing from the arguments of proponents of African slavery, many Americans constructed inherently illogical arguments in an attempt to justify the dispossession and exile of a huge body of people based solely on their differences from white Americans, thus creating yet another racial class in America unprotected by the "inalienable" natural rights of man that formed the basis of American political and social thought.

However, at this early date, the Choctaw leadership still listened to the white friends of the Indian who deluded themselves into believing that native people would be absorbed into the dominant culture as full citizens, if they would only "progress" in civilization and education to the level already attained by Euro-American culture.[12] An important line of defense developed among native leaders who saw no alternative but to carry this logic out on the outside chance that by "progressing" native people would then be given the constitutional protection enjoyed by white American citizens. However, reckoning which areas of culture to change or modify and which to leave alone was a very difficult undertaking. For example, Choctaw leaders sought instruction in reading, writing, and arithmetic for children. The only way to obtain teachers, though, was to allow Christian missionaries to open missions within the Nation. As they learned their ABCs, students would be proselytized in Christian beliefs and urged to give up the Choctaw belief system and way of life. Yet, formal education proved so important to the Choctaws that they allowed the Christian missionaries to open schools. Still, the Choctaws clearly resented the cultural and religious messages of their missionary tutors. Regardless of the difficult and complex choices involved in selective adaptation, however, this clearly was the road most Choctaws chose to try to preserve their country and their homelands.

Choctaws fought the mounting American calls for their dispossession through this elaborate system of accommodation and adaptation. They employed a time-honored process of resistance, negotiation, and compromise that had many antecedents in Choctaw history. They adapted some white ways in order to appear to be "progressing," while leaving intact the core Choctaw culture. This strategy worked for many years, delaying their dispossession. The Choctaws had an inherent cultural flexibility that allowed gradual changes to be imported without endangering the survival of core beliefs. Southeastern scholar Patricia Galloway, in her study of early Choctaw cultural heritage and traditions, found that the Choctaws "could organize and reorganize in complex ways that they themselves invented. They could choose to honor some among them or not; they could expand, stressing their environment until it failed them, and then fall back on older subsistence activities that had remained in their repertoire for bad crop years. . . . These people were themselves innovators . . . who had confronted and accomplished change many times; they were in no sense passive victims."[13]

An excellent illustration of Choctaw innovation appears in regard to American demands that they outlaw the execution of witches. Within the Choctaw culture, witches were malevolent persons who appeared to be innocent bystanders; their design was to injure the community and to cause death and destruction. Witches were not human, and so could have no clan affiliation, and thus they were not protected by clan law, which commonly restrained assault and homicide among the Choctaws. There was no prohibition in Choctaw law against killing a witch, and indeed this activity was seen as a duty or service to the community. White missionaries loudly condemned the practice of killing witches and clamored for the Choctaw leaders to stop this barbaric practice. The Choctaws passed a law in 1829 to address this concern, and herein we see a clear illustration of the outward appearance of "progress," with core traditional beliefs remaining intact. The new law gave any person accused of being a witch the benefit of a trial. The amalgamation and adaptation of Choctaw traditional beliefs in and about witches and the effort to comply with demands for cultural and political "progress" are strikingly illustrated in the wording of this law:

COUNCIL HOUSE, SEPT. 18, 1829

Whereas, it has been an old custom of the Choctaws to punish persons said to be wizards or witches with death, without giving them any fair trial by any disinterested persons; and many have fallen victims under the influence of this habit—

We do hereby resolve, in general council of the north, east, and southern districts, that, in future, all persons who shall be accused of being a wizard or witch, shall be tried before the chiefs and committees,

or by any four captains; and if they be found guilty, they shall be punished at the discretion of the court.

Be it further resolved, that if any person or persons shall find at any
place the entrails of a wizard or witch, the said entrails going from or
returning to the body, the said body shall be put to death at the place
where it may be discovered; and the said body shall be cut open, by a
proper person, and an examination be made to see whether it has in it
any entrails, and a report be made of said body.[14]

The Choctaw leadership clearly did not intend to force the traditional
Choctaws to give up their beliefs in witches or the idea that they were deserv-
ing of punishment. The change they were making was that the witch or wizard was to be given a *trial* to determine his or her guilt or innocence. Note
particularly the wording in the law that "the said *body* shall be put to death
at the place where it may be discovered." This clearly conveyed the Choctaw
belief that a witch or wizard was not human, but merely inhabited a "body."
This law also affirmed the traditional Choctaw belief that witches threw their
entrails over the limbs of a tree during their malevolent activities.

The Choctaws thus complied with the form of American jurispru-
dence only to encode traditional beliefs inimical to the Euro-American
society. They therefore appeared to be "progressing," but one can make
the case that they were fundamentally not changing at all.[15] They adopted the American ideal of a "fair" trial while simultaneously sustaining
their belief in witches. In this manner, they appeased the missionaries and
others calling for cultural "progress" but kept traditional beliefs relatively
intact. Articles in the white press touted the fact that the Choctaws had
outlawed witchcraft and used this in the fight to prove they were making
progress toward civilization and should not be dispossessed. The Choctaw
leaders became quite skilled in these tactics and were able to make a reasonably good case for progress, even as they knew the deeply rooted
Choctaw cosmology could not be truly changed within the time frame
necessary to avoid dispossession. They therefore wisely tried to create an
illusion of progress, and thereby bought time against American aggression. The missionaries and others praised them for enacting this law, so
they effectively appeared to be "progressing." In this way, many Choctaw
cultural norms continued well into the twentieth century, even after their
expulsion from Mississippi.[16]

In the meantime, the political campaign by those interested in obtaining Choctaw lands continued to escalate. Andrew Jackson continued to criticize the Monroe administration's moderate Indian policy. Finally Secretary of War Calhoun attempted to co-opt his critics by appointing Andrew Jackson to try to negotiate a land cession with the Choctaws. In August 1819, Jackson and two other American treaty commissioners met with the Choctaw delegation on the Yazoo River. Jackson argued that the Choctaws should trade their homelands, which the whites wanted and were destined to have, for land west of the Mississippi. He promised that they would receive "fair compensation" for their improvements: a gun, a blanket, and a trap or a kettle, and that the United States would supply them with food until they could raise their first crop. However, the Choctaws refused to negotiate and Jackson became increasingly enraged.

He resorted to threats, telling the Choctaws that if they did not agree to exchange their eastern homelands for land in the West, the United States would force the Choctaws who lived west of the Mississippi back into the eastern Nation and would also prohibit Choctaw hunting parties from going to the western lands to hunt. Several hundred Choctaws had moved to present-day Oklahoma to get away from whites and to take advantage of the plentiful game. They had left the old Choctaw Nation despite their chiefs' opposition and therefore were looked upon as outsiders. The Choctaw leaders did not want them to return. Jackson's threat to prohibit Choctaw hunting in the West would have caused starvation. The many Choctaws who still relied on the hunt for their subsistence would starve, since the Choctaws' lands had little game left; they would have no alternative but to join another native tribe. This, Jackson averred, would be the end of the Choctaw Nation. The great Chief Pushmataha answered Jackson for the Choctaws. He told him that the Choctaws living in the West were not there as members of the Nation, that they were not considered Choctaws, and that the United States could do with them as it pleased. Negotiations broke down as Pushmataha made it clear that no agreement could be made.[17]

Jackson was enraged at his failure to procure a treaty. He railed against John McKee, one of his fellow American treaty commissioners, complaining that McKee favored the Choctaws and was false to the American interests. Jackson was also angry at what he considered

Calhoun's timidity in dealing with the Indians. He raged that the Indians were weak and therefore subject to the demands of the United States, and that it was "high time" that the U.S. Congress asserted control over them. Jackson's anger was in part due to the high expectations his followers had that he would succeed in expelling the Choctaws from their rich homelands. Land fever was running high in the surrounding white settlements, and land speculators were poised to make a fortune in the Indian lands. When it all came to naught, Jackson's fury was exceeded only by their own. According to the *Mississippi State Gazette,* the Mississippi governor, legislature, and people were infuriated at the failure to procure Indian consent to their removal from the lands "which they hold to the great detriment of this state."[18]

In 1820, Calhoun once again sent Jackson and two other treaty commissioners to the Choctaws. Jackson's preparations included making sure that the Choctaws were plied with food and liquor. Their daily ration was to include one and a half pounds of beef, one pint of corn, salt, and liquor. Despite their preparations, the Americans almost immediately encountered stiff opposition from the united Choctaw leaders. In response, Jackson threatened to negotiate with the handful of Choctaws living west of the Mississippi, letting them speak for *all* the Choctaws. Pushmataha again bluntly informed Jackson that the hunters who had gone west of the Mississippi and stayed were no longer recognized as members of the Choctaw Nation.[19] Jackson then argued that the president would be forced, through their recalcitrance, to withdraw his protection from the Choctaws, leaving them at the mercy of the Mississippians. Jackson made what he thought was a generous offer: the Choctaws would cede about one-third of their remaining domain in Mississippi—over five million acres—in exchange for more than thirteen million acres in the Arkansas territory. In addition, each man would receive a blanket, a kettle, a rifle, a gun, bullet molds and wipers, ammunition, and enough corn to last each family one year. The United States would also provide the Choctaws with blacksmiths, schools, and agents.[20]

Yet Mingo Pushmataha was suspicious of Americans offering a "bargain." He accused Jackson of deliberately misrepresenting the lands in Arkansas, telling him he was well acquainted with these lands from the many hunting expeditions he had made there. He told the negotiators that he knew the country well and that a vast amount of it is poor and sterile, trackless and sandy deserts; nude of vegetation of any kind. As to tall trees, there is no timber anywhere, except on the bottom lands, and it is low and brushy even there. The grass is everywhere short; as for the game, it is not plenty, except buffalo and deer. . . . There are, however, but few beaver, and fruit and honey are a rare thing. The bottoms on the river are generally good soil, but liable to inundation during the spring season, and in summer the rivers and creeks dry up or become so salty that the water is unfit for use. It is not at these times always salty, but often bitter and will purge a man like medicine.

He allowed that Jackson did not have firsthand knowledge of the lands he was proposing to exchange, but he still thought it surprising that Jackson proposed to swap "an undefined portion of Mexican territory" for the eastern lands of the Choctaws. The boundaries of the land Jackson proposed for the new Choctaw land would have included land in the Mexican territory southwest of the Red River. Further, Pushmataha said, "there is an objectionable difficulty in the way. What I ask to know in the stipulations of the present treaty is, whether the American settlers you propose to turn over to us in this exchange of countries are, when we get them in possession, to be considered Indians or white people?"[21]

At a momentary loss for words, Jackson then responded that Pushmataha was mistaken, that there were only a few hunters on those lands. The Choctaw leader replied that there were indeed many, many Americans settled in that area, who were "substantial, well-to-do settlers, with good houses and productive farms," who would not be easily ordered off. Jackson countered that the American military would drive them out, so Pushmataha dropped the subject. In fact, there were more than five thousand American settlers on these lands, evidently unknown to Jackson. As soon as the treaty was signed, however, they made their presence known, causing the American government much embarrassment.[22]

Jackson continued to threaten and harangue the Choctaw leaders, and with resistance weakening on the last day of negotiations, Jackson made clear the American determination to acquire Choctaw land at any cost, threatening that, "If the Choctaw children of your father the president will adopt the measures here recommended, they will be happy; if they should not, they may be lost forever. This is the last attempt, we repeat it, that will be made to treat on this side of the Mississippi." He suggested that the Choctaws living in the West "might be found to be a 'majority' of the nation, and would make an exchange that might not suit those living here."[23]

Mingo Pukshunbbee of the Western District, the area that held the land sought by the Americans, continued to block the negotiations, even in the face of threats. Jackson repeated that the Choctaws would lose all their land if they did not trade part of it for land in the West, and then he added a new threat—that the U.S. Congress would seize control of the Choctaw government and then would cede the land of the Choctaws to the United States. At this, the opposition of the chiefs and captains not directly affected by the cession began to crumble. Mingo Pukshunbbee, "unable to agree with the emerging consensus," left the council meeting, in the traditional Choctaw expression of disagreement.[24]

The next day the American negotiators again submitted the treaty. On 19 October, the Choctaws signed, ceding six million acres of prime Mississippi Delta lands in exchange for thirteen million unimproved and mostly unexplored acres in the Arkansas Territory. In private, threats, bribes, and fraud were used to procure the Treaty of Doak's Stand, but the American public saw none of this. The preamble to the Treaty of Doak's Stand embodies this hypocrisy:

> Whereas, it is an important object with the President of the United States, to promote the civilization of the Choctaw Indians, by the establishment of schools amongst them; and to perpetuate them as a nation, by exchanging, for a small part of their land here, a country beyond the Mississippi . . . and whereas, it is desirable to the State of Mississippi to obtain a small part of the land belonging to said nation; for the mutual accommodation of the parties, and for securing the happiness and protection of the whole Choctaw nation, as well as preserving that harmony and friendship which so happily subsists between them and the United States . . ."[25]

Anger and resentment over the treaty exacerbated the already widening divisions between the Choctaw people. There was no firm consensus on how the Choctaws should proceed, and the complexities involved were enormous. Animated by a myriad of motives, individuals sided first with one and then another leader, but nothing seemed effective and many despaired. Agent Edmond Folsom, who was appointed to assist those who wanted to emigrate under the terms of the treaty, found that "his efforts had achieved nothing but the bitter hostility of the Indians: that he was opposed by the full-bloods, the headmen, and the whites living among them."[26] Fewer than fifty Choctaws emigrated under this treaty. For many, the land in the West was simply insurance in case the Americans seized the rest of their homelands east of the Mississippi. Should this occur, they knew that they would have territory of their own in the West. They did not want leave their homelands and would do so only under the greatest duress.[27]

Virtual unanimity against leaving the traditional homelands continued, while the Nation's leaders struggled to derail the growing American movement for their dispossession. The adopted, intermarried whites and some of their offspring encouraged the Nation to adopt some of the legal and institutional forms of the Americans, if for no other reason than the possibility that this could deter the takeover of their lands. Their American opponents were seeking excuses to precipitate action, but the Choctaw leaders employing this strategy guessed correctly that for the time being, the Americans would not blatantly take their lands without first trying to veil the process in humanitarian concerns for the Indians' welfare.

The leaders willing to incorporate change in a strategy to keep the Choctaw homeland intact first had to introduce a new concept of "law," as differentiated from kinship. Sociologist Duane Champagne explains that the Choctaws had an overlapping kinship and political organization in which "social and political solidarity were synonymous."[28] Crime and every other form of antisocial behavior was punishable by the clans— everything was personal. Individuals were not autonomous, but were defined solely by their clan membership. The law of revenge set up the clans as the arbiters of all behavior. The clans were the judges, juries, and executioners, and the most important, fundamental social contract of these tribal people was that clans—not individuals, and certainly not an impartial political institution—ruled.

Prior to this time, clan laws—unwritten, traditional laws known to all and enforced by the clans—had governed the nation. Yet, although inherently flexible, traditional clan law was ill adapted to regulating market relations and addressing the problems raised by the market economy.

With the intrusion of the world market, the accumulation of private property, especially in the form of livestock as pastoralism became a way of life, and the importation of slavery and other market-based institutions, a concomitant need for legal devices capable of dealing with private property law arose.

All Choctaws—whether of mixed heritage or not—struggled to find ways to continue their way of life that would also deal with the problems that seemed to be overwhelming the Choctaw society. Traditional mechanisms for maintaining societal order and harmony—the complex system of clan and tribal law—appeared to be inadequate. Choctaw leaders thus began selectively adapting and implementing laws within their districts. For example, Aboha Kullo Humma, the chief of the Six Towns District, of the Okla Hunnali clan, outlawed the importation of whiskey and the practice of infanticide and instituted severe punishment for theft.[29]

Many traditional practices abhorred by the Christian missionaries continued, however, and with the exception of new laws governing market relations—that is, private property—the Choctaws continued with their traditional ways. For example, sororal polygyny (the custom of a man marrying two or more sisters) was common among the Choctaws, and it continued to be practiced well into the late 1800s. Each woman had her own home, and the husband visited for a period of time in rotation. The Armstrong Census of 1830—the count the Americans took of the Choctaws for removal—showed that many households were still headed by women, a result of the practice of polygyny. The Choctaws did not outlaw the practice until 1849, and even then the law was not enforced.[30]

Missionaries were exasperated with many Choctaw ways. To these Christian evangelists, Christianity and Euro-American culture were indivisible. Time and again over the nineteenth and twentieth centuries, Euro-Americans were not satisfied with native spiritual or religious conversion. Native people, in order to be "saved," had to adopt the culture, values, and language of the dominant white society. In the mission schools, for example, the missionaries taught not only Christian doctrine and beliefs but also insisted that Choctaws cut their hair, change their names, dress in Euro-American styles, adapt the gender roles of the Euro-American culture, and reject everything that was Choctaw, including their own language. In these early years, the missionaries failed miserably in their quest to convert Choctaws into white people, but they nonetheless persevered.

By the end of the 1820s, only 360 Choctaws had been "saved," and many of these were African-American slaves. Only 538 Choctaws attended the mission schools in the first decade of their existence.[31]

Choctaw leaders and the American missionaries did agree about one thing, however. Alcohol was destroying the Choctaw people, and some way of controlling it had to be found. The presence of white men was always accompanied by liquor. Their intrusion into Choctaw lands in growing numbers in the early nineteenth century meant a huge increase in the supply of alcohol imported illegally into the Choctaw Nation. The incentive of enormous profits and low risks led many whites to run whiskey into the Nation, oftentimes as a sideline to their usual subsistence activities. As change assaulted the Choctaw Nation on every front, hard liquor poured in. Demand on the part of the Choctaws rose as they reacted to the fear and dislocation brought on by rapid economic and political change. White peddlers plied the Choctaws with whiskey, often intercepting hunters coming home from a long hunt, laden with the season's haul of pelts. Some would later arrive at their home villages with nothing but bad hangovers to show for their season's work, having traded away their entire cache for alcohol. As a consequence, families were reduced to dire poverty, children went hungry, and the agony of the Nation increased.

Choctaw leaders repeatedly tried to stem the supply of liquor coming into the Nation. As early as 1770 the Spanish official in charge of the Arkansas Post wrote his superiors that the Choctaw "Grand Chief" had requested that the Spanish government not give any liquor to Choctaws who came to the trading post. During treaty negotiations at Fort Adams in 1801, the Choctaw leaders stated, "We came here sober, and we wish to go away so—We therefore request that the strong drink, which we understand our brothers have brought here, may not be distributed." They petitioned the U.S. government to enforce the Intercourse Acts that barred unlicensed traders from the Nation.[32]

Yet the Americans made little effort to stem the tide of alcohol, as historian Richard White informs us, because the trade in whiskey, while appalling, "served their [the Americans'] own interests so well."[33] When the United States and the Choctaws tried to stop the illegal trade, their efforts met with fierce resistance from whites who saw this trade as legitimate entrepreneurial activity. The use of alcohol within the Euro-American culture in the backwoods regions near native populations was endemic. Alcohol abuse was part and parcel of white frontier life. Whiskey was the beverage of choice for whites living in the backwoods. Water, milk, and other alternative beverages were inconsistent in quality and availability. Whiskey did not spoil, was believed to aid in digestion, and could be easily transported. Backwoods whites saw the United States distribute liquor as part of the daily rations given to Native Americans at treaty negotiations; they also saw the U.S. Army dole out a daily supply of whiskey to all soldiers. The use of alcohol was ingrained in the fabric of everyday life in white society, so whiskey was not considered a vice by many whites, and its abuse was seen as a matter of personal choice and an indication of faulty moral character.[34]

Even though they were the major suppliers of this liquid nightmare, whites living in the backwoods condemned the Choctaws as "lazy drunkards" who were attached more to alcohol than to their "most sacred cultural duties." One American, writing to the editor of the *Natchez*, invited him to "Shew me an Indian in the street and I could buy all the bones of his forefathers . . . for a pint of whiskey." He expressed the sentiments of many whites living in close proximity to the Choctaws when he continued, "I look upon the introduction of whiskey as a great point: it has already done a great deal in facilitating the acquisition of Indian lands all over the United States."[35]

Choctaw leaders tried to control the importation of alcohol into the Nation, but tribal institutions could not address this scourge. In order to control the illegal importation of liquor, a centralized government authority was necessary, one with enforcement capabilities, but such authority was unknown in traditional Choctaw society. The traditional clan law and its mechanisms of enforcement could not address the problem adequately. Choctaw leaders insisted that the U.S. government include a provision in the Treaty of Doak's Stand to try to deal with this enormous problem. Article 12 accordingly empowered the U.S. agent "to seize and confiscate all the whiskey which may be introduced into said nation." The United States demonstrated its approbation by providing a permanent annuity for the expenses of maintaining a unit of Lighthorsemen. The Lighthorse was a group of five to twenty mounted men who patrolled the Choctaw Nation to try to curb the importation of alcohol onto Indian lands.[36]

The creation of the Lighthorse by the Choctaws was a radical innovation. The Lighthorse constituted an institution external to the clan rule
of law, and was unprecedented in Choctaw history. The creation of a
police force was the first effort by the Choctaws to differentiate their
social and political systems, but it was also shaped to conform to Choctaw
tradition. The Lighthorse was created by the more acculturated Choctaws
to address problems primarily originating with white intruders, including
the illegal trade in whiskey and theft of livestock. Since under the Trade
and Intercourse Acts the United States was supposed to expel white
intruders from the Nation and arrest and prosecute non-native criminals,
the Choctaw Nation theoretically had no jurisdiction over crimes involving whites. The increasing incidence of white intruders, squatters, and
criminals, however, made it necessary for the Choctaws to find a new way
to address these problems. The creation of the Lighthorse provided a
potent new force to deal with crimes against property and the illegal trade
in alcohol. The Lighthorse was also frequently used by the Mingos
(chiefs) to expel white squatters and other interlopers.

The primary purpose of the Lighthorse, however, was to continue the
Choctaw leaders' war on alcohol. An example of its use came when
District Mingo Mushulatubbee left the Nation to go to Washington, D.C.,
for a meeting with the president. He instructed his nephew, who was head
of the Lighthorse, that during his absence he was to "take and destroy all
Liquor that may be unlawfully brought in to my district" with the help of
all headmen and warriors. "It is to be distinctly understood that no
whiskey is to be Drank that may be confiscated by any of the Light
Horsemen, but to be destroyed publickly [sic]."[37] Missionary Cyrus
Kingsbury reported in 1829 that although the missionaries had had a part
in the "progress" of the Choctaws, most of the credit had to go to "the
enlightened chiefs [who] have taken the lead in the work of reformation
and it is through their word that some of the most important changes
have been made. . . . Eight years ago intemperance prevailed from one
end of the land to the other. . . . At this time, intemperance within the
nation is hardly known."[38]

The creation of the Lighthorse is important in the light of cultural
change and adaptation. Some scholars have suggested that its creation was
evidence that the Choctaw clans and traditional society were breaking
down and that Choctaws were assimilating. On the contrary, the Choctaw

police force strengthened the traditional power of Choctaw leaders, restoring efficacy to the Choctaws in dealing with the problem of whites who were external to their traditional laws and creating a new mechanism by which to deal with changing realities. The creation of the Lighthorse bolstered the power of the Choctaw district chiefs and stemmed the erosion of Choctaw sovereignty that the U.S. government seemed eager to affect.

In 1825 and 1826, the Choctaws watched in dismay as a leading planter and headman of the Creek Nation illegally sold all Creek lands within Georgia to the United States. Determined to avoid a similar fate, the Choctaws moved to centralize their government and to make the district chiefs less autonomous. In the traditional Choctaw culture, social and political realms were undifferentiated. The office of chief, or Mingo, was hereditary, passing down the matrilineal line, and tenure was for life. As American demands for Choctaw land grew to a crescendo, and with the example of the Creek Nation before them, the Choctaws moved to centralize government power and to install leaders whom they thought would be able to stand fast against American demands for land. Two of the greatest, legendary chiefs had died on a trip to Washington in 1824 and had been succeeded by young, inexperienced men who were next in line. In the third district, the older chief, Mushulatubbee, remained headman.

Choctaw factions united to depose these leaders and install a trio of men whom they thought could best deal with the American threat to the Nation. They passed a constitution, which stipulated that the three district chiefs would be elected, and would serve four-year terms.[39] The national council was comprised of all the headmen of the clans (iksas), who had traditionally held similar power. In this way, although the Choctaw Nation adopted the American legal form of a constitution and elected chief executives, the essence of Choctaw government remained decentralized, through three chief executives and a national council composed of hereditary representatives of the clans.

Thus, many aspects of Choctaw society changed, but much also remained the same. The distinguishing factors of this period in Choctaw history were the unrelenting and ever-strengthening white calls for Choctaw dispossession and exile and the incredible range of changes on every front—economic, diplomatic, political, military, and cultural. Many forces were at work simultaneously, uniting in a critical confluence that weakened Choctaw unity and their ability to stave off American demands for their dispossession. As change assaulted the Nation from every possible direction, Choctaw leaders valiantly attempted to find ways to adapt and accommodate, but in the late 1820s, the changes began to be accompanied by a new strain of American aggression that would not deal with equanimity toward the Choctaws. Andrew Jackson was coming to power, and the Choctaws knew that upon his ascendancy to the presidency, he would not yield until the Choctaws were forced out of their homelands.

The Choctaws saw themselves as exceptional, and they did not believe that the Americans would betray them until Andrew Jackson began to be taken seriously. The Choctaws little understood the pressures of the market and the animating force of world cotton prices on the demands for their dispossession. Being loyal and steadfast allies, they were lulled into complacency until the Treaty of Doak's Stand, when Andrew Jackson made it clear that, regardless of past alliances, regardless of the so-called progress that Choctaw society had made toward assimilating American culture, the United States would hear no reason and would see no crime in seizing their homelands and forcing the Choctaws into the West.

It is truly amazing that the Choctaws and the other southeastern native peoples were able to avoid dispossession as long as they did. They did so through a series of concessions and compromises that left fundamental native beliefs and traditions intact. Conceding only when they had no other choice, even on minor matters, the Choctaws and their fellow southeastern native people delayed American dispossession at times through feinting, tactics of obstruction, and every other ploy they could devise. At last, however, with the election of Andrew Jackson to the presidency in 1828, the state governments joined hands with the federal government to finally and summarily expel native people from their ancient homelands.

3 The Physical and Spiritual World of the Choctaw People

T HE WORLD EURO-AMERICANS CALLED "INDIAN TERRITORY" WAS A living, breathing, feeling being—an enormously complex, self-sustaining system that encompassed an infinite number of creatures, people, and spirits. The physical and spiritual worlds overlapped more extensively in the native conceptualization of the world than in that of western Euro-Americans. For example, native people believed that spirits were literally all around them, that they heard and monitored the behavior of men, and that they actively affected their lives. They believed that spirits communicated with humans through dreams and visions, and therefore they paid careful attention to the spirit world, knowing that it profoundly affected the physical. Fundamentally, this giant, all-encompassing system of life proceeded with order and reasonable predictability as long as two essential properties were maintained: balance and harmony. If either attribute were breached, the gigantic system of life would be thrown off, with unpredictable results of unknowable proportions.

Balance was understood as the avoidance of excess in all things, as the maintenance of equilibrium, and as the careful separation of forces of opposition. As anthropologist Charles Hudson explains, "The cosmos was conceived of as consisting of parts which were in opposition to each other, so that, for example, the forces of the north were opposed to the forces of the south . . . the forces of the Upper World were opposed to the forces of the Under World, men were opposed to women, and some people were opposed to other people, as white is opposed to red . . . [and] misfortunes were often interpreted as having been caused by one force prevailing over its opposite."[1] Opposing forces not only had to be kept separate, but also had to balance one another, to maintain the equilibrium of the world. If one polluted the other, or if, for example, man subjugated woman, the balance of the world would be affected. Were man to overhunt or disrespect the sacrifice animals made in providing man with sustenance, he could be sure that there would be consequences. The contamination of opposing forces was also understood as potentially catastrophic, so that southeastern native peoples exhibited a keen interest in maintaining purity, in carefully guarding the separate-ness of opposite concepts, beings, and objects.

Differences found in Western philosophy between the abstract and concrete were not present in the belief systems of the southeastern natives. The concrete and the abstract merged inextricably, as seen in the belief that individual misbehavior polluted the purity of the village Sacred Fire over time. Thus the most important ceremonial observance of the year was the Green Corn Ceremony, in which several days were spent purifying, decontaminating, and reseparating, in order to restore the world of the village to its proper balance. Abodes were swept clean, bedding was replaced, garments were changed, old grudges were settled and forgotten, ritual and ceremonial purification reigned, and, finally, the Sacred Fire was newly lit and each villager took a light from it to kindle his or her home fire.

The importance of keeping categories separate is clearly illustrated in the Muskogean languages, which were spoken by many southeasterners. These languages have a built-in and continually used system of classification of different things, grouped by conceptual similarity. For example, in Choctaw, pencils, logs, fingers, and other cylindrical objects were in the same category. Dissimilar objects were kept separate, so that they would not pollute each other.[2] There was a clear logic to this system of separation, and it served to regulate the material and spiritual lives of the people. The Choctaws saw fire and water as opposites, unalterably dissimilar, and disastrous if mixed. When pork was first introduced, Choctaws rejected the assimilation of this type of meat into their diets because pigs were cloven-hoofed, and did not therefore fit into the categories of the ancient language. Anything that did not fit concisely into a predefined category was viewed as an abomination, a freak that would pollute any category into which it was placed, and therefore unable to be recognized or used. Keeping these unlike objects from mixing with and polluting one another served to provide order and thus preserve balance in their world.

The second great organizing force of the native universe was harmony. Harmony was the absence of conflict and the avoidance of excess. In order for the great system of life to function, harmony was essential. Conflict provoked and resulted in imbalances, which, as we have seen, threatened the well-being of all. Elements of nature, other beings, animals, rivers—everything—had a spirit and were part of the whole. All other beings, therefore, had to be considered in one's actions and behavior. If trespassed upon, or wronged, these other elements of the world could retaliate, upsetting the desired state of balance and risking unknowable potential disasters. One of the most important ways of maintaining harmony was through the definition of relationships between people, animals, plants, and things.[3]

Relationships formed the fundamental order in the Choctaw world. Relationships defined each and every person, place, and thing. Because the Choctaws saw the world as one huge, complex whole, everything within their world was related. The most basic type of relationship was that of kinship. Kinship provided identity to the individual, the family, the clan, and the village. It defined all Choctaw people and, therefore, all people who were *not* Choctaw. Kinship dictated behavior and ordered the way each human related to all others. Clans were the basic unit of kinship within the Choctaw Nation. They were matrilineal, relating each Choctaw individual through his or her maternal line.[4]

Outside of kinship, relationships were defined in ways that brought others into the world system. Fictive relationships abounded in Native America and were established between peoples to define their relationship to the satisfaction of all. For example, many southeasterners called the Delawares their "elder brothers," despite the literal contraindication. U.S. agents understood this system imperfectly, but still tried to use it in establishing a hegemonic relationship with Indian peoples: the U.S. government referred to its president as the "Great Father" of the Indians, and native people were deemed "children." In doing this, the United States was trying to establish a relationship modeled upon Western European patriarchal society. Whites understood the relationship between father and child as that of benevolent dictator and subject. In the Southeast, however, most Indian nations practiced matrilineal kinship, in which the relationship that Europeans assigned to father and child was, in fact, that found between maternal uncle and child. To native southeasterners, "fathers" were outside the child's clan, whose identity was taken from the mother's line. The father was not considered to be as closely related as any member of the child's clan, and so had little authority over the children he sired. The maternal uncle provided discipline and participated in major decisions affecting his sisters' children. He was the "father." So, while U.S. agents were smugly implying one role defined by their understanding of the relationship between fathers and children, the native people of the Southeast understood these implied relationships entirely differently.[5]

People outside of the clans and the Nation often were defined through relationships using fictive kinship. Applying a kinship label to one who was not literally related established a pattern of behavior and set expectations for the relationship. Using fictive kinship, native people were able to bring others into their universe and to define them as having a legitimate relationship and humanity.[6]

Rituals of gift giving and reciprocity were practiced extensively to establish and maintain fictive relationships between groups of unrelated native peoples, especially political and diplomatic relationships. The importance of relationships cannot be overstated in understanding the belief systems of the native people of the Southeast. The fundamental ideal of the interrelatedness of all beings, creatures, and objects of the native world caused them to behave in ways that differed profoundly from the Western Europeans who invaded and eventually conquered Native America.

For example, the native people of North America carefully maintained relationships with the flora and fauna of their universe. Taboos and strong cultural censures existed to prohibit excesses such as overhunting or the careless infliction of damage to rivers, trees, or animals. This concern for maintaining balance and harmony, and a recognition of the interrelatedness of all things, resulted in environmentally sound practices and the maintenance of a sustainable relationship between man and animal and man and the ecosystem.

Choctaw people knew that the spirits in nature would retaliate against humans if proper relations—that is, harmony—were not maintained.

Animals could not be killed for sport, and the earth could not be trans-
formed or manipulated for human profit. To do these things meant suffering dire consequences, because they believed that the forces of nature
were much more powerful than mere human beings, and if they inter-
fered with these contending, powerful forces, they would suffer retalia-
tion and punishment.

The native world was one whole, in which the sacred and the secular
were inextricably intertwined. Spirits were ever present, and manifestations of their being constantly intruded into the world of humans. The
spirits of the dead, the spirits of the animals, the water, inanimate objects,
and all else communicated with man through dreams, signs, and deeds.
Man demonstrated and acknowledged his understanding through ritual,
ceremony, prayer, and action. The spiritual beliefs of the native people
were so intertwined with all else in their universe that one cannot understand their lives or behavior separate from these beliefs.

Choctaws and other southeastern native peoples viewed themselves as
part of the great system of life. They conceived of themselves as an inex-
tricable part of what Euro-Americans might call an ecosystem. Yet built
into their conceptualization were ideas encompassing spiritual concepts,
other forms of life that could change physical properties and defy
European "laws" of nature. The Choctaw believed that the very air was
peopled with good and evil spirits. They were there in the shadows, watching, waiting. Their whispers could be heard among the trees. An old
Choctaw man told U.S. commissioners in 1842 that "the Great Spirit talks
—we hear him in the thunder—in the rushing winds and the mighty
waters." The spirits of the dead, he went on, could be heard in the pine
trees. These spirits were active and living participants in the world of the
Choctaws. One of the Choctaw told U.S. commissioners that when the
Choctaws met with U.S. treaty negotiators in 1830, "every warrior you see
here was opposed to the treaty. If the dead could but have been counted,
it would never have been made; but, alas! Though they stood around,
they could not be seen nor heard [by the white man]. Their tears came
in the rain-drops and their voices in the wailing wind, but the pale faces
knew it not, and our land was taken away."[7]

Choctaws believed that the spirits communicated with them through
nature. The spirits "[made] known their presence through both animate
and inanimate nature. The sighing of the winds; the flight of the birds;

the howl of the lone wolf; the midnight hoot of the owl" and all other sounds heard throughout the forests during the day and at night "had to him most potent signification; by which he so governed all his actions that he never went upon any enterprise before consulting the signs and omens; then he acted in conformity thereto." The Great Spirit communicated his will through various natural phenomena—"in dreams, in thunder and lightning, eclipses, meteors, comets, in all the prodigies of nature, and the thousands of unexpected incidents that occur to man."[8]

To the Choctaws the Earth was the Mother—*chashki yakni* or *Iholitopa Ishki* [beloved mother]. As discussed in chapter one, the Choctaw people emerged from *Nanih Waiya,* the sacred mound, the Mother of the Choctaw people. One day in 1810, the renowned mingo Pushmataha met U.S. agent George S. Gaines traveling on a road that passed *Nanih Waiya.* Pushmataha, seeing that Gaines had just come down from the top of the mound, said, "Well, friend Gaines, I see you have been up to pay your compliments to our good mother." Gaines replied that he had decided to pay her a visit as he passed by. "Well, what did she say to you?" asked the chief. "She said," responded Mr. Gaines, "that her Choctaw children had become too numerous to longer be prosperous, contented and happy in their present country, and therefore, she thought it best for them to exchange their old country and lands for a new country and lands west of the Mississippi River, where the game was much more abundant, and the hunting grounds far more extensive." To this Pushmataha jokingly replied, "Holobih! Holubit ish nohowa nih! (It's a lie.) Do not go about telling lies. Our good old mother never could have spoken such words to you."[9]

The Choctaws believed that the Great Spirit had given their homelands to them and that dire consequences would result if they left their lands. In the migration tradition discussed in chapter one, the Choctaws were warned never to leave their homelands, the lands around *Nanih Waiya,* or the Nation would die—the hunters would be unable to find game, the crops would fail, sickness would invade the villages, and all would die. Frequently, as U.S. agents urged the Choctaw leaders to "exchange" their Mississippi homelands for lands in Indian Territory, the elders tried to explain their attachment to their home, as one old man did in the removal years, telling a U.S. agent, "We wish to remain here where we have grown up as the herbs of the woods, and do not wish to be transplanted into another soil."[10] Choctaws saw themselves as part of the soil, an integral element of the ecosystem, tied inextricably to the Earth and everything in it. Mingo Pushmataha, lying on his deathbed in Washington, D.C., in 1824, told those attending him that his death would be like "a mighty oak falling in the solitude of the woods."[11]

The spiritual dimension of Choctaw life imbued all practical activities with a sense of the sacred. During the so-called Indian removals, when the U.S. government confiscated the homelands of the Choctaws and other southeasterners and forced them into permanent exile in Indian Territory, the Choctaws underwent a terrible travail. Their physical world changed profoundly and, with this relocation in space, their spiritual world changed also. Separating the physical from the spiritual was impossible in the Choctaw worldview, but was and is typical for Euro-Americans and their forebears. Not only is land a commodity in the latter's belief system, it is also merely a physical entity, quite separate from the spiritual world.

From the Euro-American point of view, the region known as Indian Territory was a world long inhabited by man, intimately known to countless generations of human beings. However, native people saw this space as being part of a large, intimately interrelated system. In the earliest times, this vast system of living space formed into mountains and plains, forest and prairie. Rivers and lakes arose, all part of a great system that functioned smoothly and ceaselessly, set in motion by eternal forces. Into these lands came fauna; human beings; and the spirits of the land, water, and sky. This area was home to many native peoples over the centuries, people who understood the rhythms of life and death, of birth and rebirth, of the visible and invisible worlds surrounding and entwined with us all.

"Indian Territory," as whites would eventually call it, sat in the middle of the continent, where one can see and feel the dramatic meeting of the arid West with the humid East. At roughly the one hundredth meridian, Mother Earth changes from well-watered, bounteous, productive agricultural lands to the increasing aridity of the western reaches, which are not conducive to agriculture without the use of extensive irrigation. In fact, this region was called the "Great American Desert," and labeled unfit for agriculture and therefore of little worth to the expansion of white America and her legions of farmers. That it was so labeled accounts for the lateness of the conquest of the region by white invaders. It was explored and exploited a full two centuries after the conquest of the eastern coastal areas of the United States, and was taken then only because it was the last "available" land.[12]

This region forms an important zone of transition, a physical crossroads where the Eastern Woodlands meet the Great Plains. Here the earth undergoes a metamorphosis from the humid forestlands of the East into the arid, barren lands of the West. As one moves west, increasing aridity alters every living thing. Luscious vegetation gradually contracts into scrub brush and bunch grass. The stumpy, twisted post oaks and mesquite of the dry lands displace the beautiful broad-leafed shade trees of the East. Living creeks and lazy flowing rivers give way to endless horizons over which the ever-present sighing and howling winds blow. Here, the humid air of the eastern half of the continent meets the dry air of the High Plains, producing fantastic lightning storms as angry air masses collide.

The land of the Southern Plains forms a huge plane, draining from northwest to southeast. This enormous graded slope originates in the Rocky Mountains, its soils formed through stream deposit or aggradation. As rain and winds wore down the mountains, soil was spread out along the surface, creating enormous foot slopes. Rivers and streams flowing southeast helped soil and rock fan out to form a great apron of debris, creating the soil of the plains and prairies of the American West. This great apron stretches unbroken from the Rocky Mountains to the Mississippi River valley. In the far northwestern corner of present-day Oklahoma, the Black Mesa rises 5,000 feet above sea level, sloping downward at an average rate of six to eight feet per mile toward the Southeast, reaching only 325 feet above sea level where the Red River leaves Oklahoma's eastern border.

In some areas, great spaces lie unrelieved by sources of water. Limestone, gypsum, salt, and other minerals inhabit some of the streams, leeching into the water, making it unpalatable. In 1853, Captain R. B. Marcy of the U.S. Army remarked that the water of the Red River had a "very bitter and disagreeable taste because it passed through a gypsum formation for one hundred miles." Thirty years prior to the Marcy expedition, Choctaw chief Pushmataha told Andrew Jackson that in the summers the rivers and creeks dried up or became so salty that the water was unfit to drink. It was not always salty, but was, at these times, "often bitter," and "would purge a man like medicine."[13]

Aridity shaped the interaction between man and earth in this region. Forcing a constancy known only by dedicated lovers, man had to think of water incessantly. In the centuries immediately preceding the arrival of the Choctaws in the Southern Plains, mankind had adapted to the scarcity and inconstancy of water in this area. Large villages did not exist in these arid regions. Instead, a nomadic lifestyle evolved that fostered a whole way of life adapted to aridity. Horse, buffalo, and man danced to this never-ending silent tune, a song heard by every living creature.

Seventeenth-century invaders were the first Europeans to report the great desert lying to the west of the humid lands of the Mississippi Valley. De Soto feared that he and his invasion force would perish from the lack of water when they crossed into this area from the American Southeast. Later explorers also reported the barren stretches of arid lands and flatly stated that these lands were unfit for human habitation. The U.S. exploration party commanded by Captain S. H. Long in 1819 reported that this area "was almost wholly unfit for cultivation, and, of course, uninhabitable by a people depending upon agriculture for their subsistence." American maps labeled the area the "Great American Desert." History and geography texts used in nineteenth-century schools across the eastern seaboard helped fix this vision in the minds of most Americans.[14]

The Choctaws knew that the lands the Americans wanted them to move to in the West varied tremendously in regard to aridity. Rainfall declines dramatically from east to west in what is now the state of Oklahoma. In the eastern third of the Indian Territory, rainfall averages between twenty and forty inches per year, forming a moderately humid climate in which trees, plants, and grasses flourish. However, in the western third of the Choctaw land, aridity affects the lives of every living thing. Rainfall tapers off to less than twenty inches per year in the far western portion of this area, an amount insufficient to grow crops without the use of irrigation.[15]

In the eastern half of this region, sufficient amounts of rain fall during normal years to allow the production of the same crops that Choctaws grew in their eastern homelands. In the east, the Choctaw lands received far more precipitation than the lands in the west—fifty to sixty inches of rainfall per year. In Indian Territory, in the months critical to crop production (April through September), twenty to twenty-four inches of rain falls, of an annual total of thirty-six to fifty-two inches. At the center of the western Choctaw lands, the Cross Timbers region marks the transition from a subtropical humidity to the dry lands of the plains. The Cross Timbers is an area of short, wind-whipped post oaks and mesquite trees extending southwesterly from the Arkansas River to the Brazos in Texas for about four hundred miles. From this point west, trees, undergrowth, and tall grasses disappear, giving way to mixed and short grass prairies and then to the bunch grass typical of the Great Plains.[16]

Annual temperatures in the Southern Plains average sixty degrees Fahrenheit, but this mild reading is misleading. On many summer days, temperatures reach or exceed one hundred degrees, discomforting flora and fauna alike. One missionary's wife reported in 1860 to her mother back East that it was a very, very hot August: "The mercury is from 98 to 100 degrees every day and has not been below 80 in a month."[17]

These high temperatures contribute to a high rate of evaporation, which also affects the growth of plants. Over the almost level surface, and in the absence of trees, wind blows almost constantly over what were the plains of the western and central Choctaw Nation. The high temperatures of July, August, and September bring extremely hot, dry air gusting in off the High Plains. Highly destructive, these winds are capable of destroying green crops almost overnight. From about the center of the Indian Territory westward, the lack of rainfall combine with a high level of evaporation to make farming problematic at best. The high wind velocity and the intense heat and aridity of the air sweeping over the Southern Plains region caused frequent crop failures before the advent of irrigation systems.[18] "Everything goes before the blast furnace," historian Walter Prescott Webb relates. "It has been reported that over 10 million bushels of corn were destroyed in Kansas in one season. It is not uncommon for fine fields of dark-green to be destroyed in two days."[19]

Hot, dry winds coming off the plains were not the only new climatic phenomenon the Choctaws experienced in Indian Territory. "Northers," the rapid invasion of a cold air mass into a warmer area, were also quite common in the new Choctaw lands. Generally, these air masses moved very quickly, sometimes dropping the temperature from twenty-five to fifty degrees, often in a matter of minutes. A missionary living among the Choctaws in 1859 wrote to her mother in New York that one night, "the weather was very hot but that night the wind changed and within minutes the temperature had dropped from 70 to 30 degrees." Enormous dark clouds accompanied by rain often followed the cold winds. During these storms, people often looked to the skies for the telltale signs of twisters descending from the sky. Tornadoes occurred with frightening frequency. In May 1854, a tornado destroyed many of the buildings at Fort Towson. This tornado demolished the commissary storehouse and two buildings housing troops, among other structures, and uprooted all the shade trees in the area.[20]

The Choctaws were familiar with grass prairies. In their homelands in Mississippi, tall grass prairies were used in the budding pastoralism practiced by a growing number of Choctaws. In Indian Territory, some tall grasses grew in the eastern portion of the new Choctaw lands, but the predominant types of grasses were blue-stem gramma prairie grass and buffalo grass, in areas that were later classified as "mixed-grass" prairies. Buffalo grass attained full growth in the spring months that comprised the rainy season, and when the dry, hot months of summer approached, it "cured," or dried up, but still retained all the nutritious qualities originally possessed, making it an excellent source of forage over winter months.[21]

These mixed-grass prairies provided prime grazing lands for horses, cattle, buffalo, and other herbivores, highly prized by both whites and native peoples. The Comanches and Kiowas grazed their herds of horses on these lands to fatten them up for their summer incursions against encroaching whites in Mexico and Texas. The Choctaw people had for many years increasingly engaged in raising stock, and recognized the excellence of the mixed-grass prairie as pasture. Later in the century, white intruders and "boomers" touted the values of this pastureland. It was especially valuable in that stock could winter over without the expense and labor required to supply fodder such as hay or corn. In a pamphlet promoting white settlement of the Choctaw Nation in 1884, Reginald Aldridge wrote that throughout this region, "buffalo grass cures naturally on the ground, affording nutritious feed during the winter" for stock. This source of feed saved the rancher from having to supply food to his herds over four to five months of winter, thus making cattle ranching much more profitable. As one missionary wrote, "Cattle get their own living summer and winter and though they get very poor in the winter, so rich is the pasture in the spring that by the middle of May there are plenty of beeves so fat as any one need wish to see or to eat and this without their eating a kernel of corn or other grain." In fact, these lands became well known among Texas cattlemen, who, later in the century, leased hundreds of acres from the Choctaws for grazing their herds being driven from ranches in Texas to the railheads in Kansas and Missouri.[22]

The eastern lands of the Choctaw were also much more wooded than those in the west. In Indian Territory, grasslands developed in large part from a lack of trees. West of the one hundredth meridian, trees did not naturally occur, other than drought-tolerant varieties such as mesquite. This climate favors the growth of grass and not trees. Trees must have soil conditions conducive to their growth, along with adequate drainage, and an adequate supply of moisture. Trees also suffer from high winds and the repeated fires typical of this region.[23]

Fire is an integral component of the natural ecology of grassland prairies. Texas cattlemen and others encountered fires that consumed large stretches of prairie land, set off by lightning flashes that accompanied spring thunderstorms. This process continues today, but was especially important when natural grasslands were relatively undisturbed by human hands. As an important part of the larger ecosystem, fire "was the natural catalyst for diversity that provided stability in those ecosystems. In the absence of fire, trees and shrubs begin to invade the prairies, diversity becomes monoculture, and the presence of wildlife declines precipitously."[24]

Monstrous prairie fires swept across the lands of Indian Territory. Pushing all that was living before them, these fires came roaring out of the horizon, often catching people and animals unawares. Parties of white settlers, hunters, and other newcomers to Indian Territory often recounted the terror of narrow escapes and lost possessions, harrowing experiences remembered for a lifetime. Vivid memories of the smell of smoke and burning cinders, of the terrifying quickness of the fire, and of its deafening roar lived forever in the waking dreams of those who barely escaped.

Naturalist and artist George Catlin experienced these fires on a trip to Indian Territory in 1832. He recalled two types of prairie fires. "Over the elevated lands and prairie bluffs, where the grass is thin and short, the fire slowly creeps with a feeble flame, which one can easily step over; where the animals often rest in their lairs until the flames almost burn their noses, when they will reluctantly rise, and leap over it, and trot off amongst the cinders, where the fire has passed and left the ground as black as jet." Yet there was another kind of fire, one that allowed no living thing to rest before it—animals, insects, birds, and humans, all animate beings fled in sheer panic before these roaring flames. This kind of fire was "the war, or hell of fires where grass is seven or eight feet high, as is often the case for many miles altogether . . . the flames are driven forward by hurricanes, which often sweep over the vast prairies. . . . The fire in these [meadows] travels at such an immense and frightful rate, and often destroys, on their fleetest horses, parties of Indians, who are so unlucky as to be overtaken by it."[25] Another explorer wrote that "huge waves of flame, with a roaring sound like that of the ocean, were rolling over the rank grass, and rushing onward with fearful rapidity." Hunters, travelers, and explorers could be suddenly endangered, as when the Whipple exploration party was forced to march "double quick time" to escape flames from tall grass burning in their path.[26]

Wild pea vines and other vegetation impeded the rider's progress and complicated his flight from the flames, forcing him to follow the zigzag paths of the deer and buffaloes. In some instances, a rider's progress was so slowed by this vegetation that the smoke that was swept before the fire would overtake him, causing his horse to stop and stand still and terrified, "till the burning grass which is wafted in the wind, falls about him, kindling up in a moment a thousand new fires, which are instantly wrapped in the swelling flood of smoke that is mobbing on like a black thundercloud, rolling on the earth, with its lightening glare, and its thunder rumbling as it goes." Yet, this living flight was the cause of many a hunter's celebration. Wild animals fled before the flames, sometimes finding security in a deep ravine. Catlin described how one afternoon when the prairie was on fire for several miles, the wind was blowing the flames before him. Grouse flew before the flames, "which seemed to extend from horizon to horizon," in "flocks that would almost fill the air." The birds lit in great numbers in every tree, where Catlin's party shot them down, "sometimes killing five or six at a time."[27]

Terror was only one of the emotions inspired by the flames. Many travelers remarked on the exquisite beauty of prairie fires at night, one reporting that they were indescribably beautiful, "appearing to be sparkling and brilliant chains of liquid fire . . . hanging suspended in graceful festoons from the skies." Yet, the great beauty of the fires belied their desolate aftermath. Miles upon miles of charred cinders would greet travelers with "waterless, woodless, desolate fields of black ashes," where here and there, "clumps of grass [were] still burning."[28]

Choctaws had a long history and intimate knowledge of the use of fire in the ecosystem. Native people had employed slash and burn agriculture for centuries. The parklike appearance of much of the eastern coast of North America at the time of the European invasions arose from the Indian practice of annually burning the lands in order to encourage new growth and to keep down underbrush. The early sprigs of grass and other vegetation that were the earth's response to these fires attracted deer and other creatures that provided protein in the native diet, in addition to materials for manufacturing. The native herds of horses thrived on the new growth that appeared after the prairies were fired, in addition to bison that loved the young, tender blades of grass.[29]

Sometimes this annual rite of burning the prairies produced hardships for hunters and others who crossed the land. The Gaines exploration party in 1830 found that the Delawares living in two towns on the Canadian River had fired the prairie when they were returning from their fall hunt, leaving a scorched earth devoid of grass. The Gaines party could find no food for their horses.[30]

Fire had a deep spiritual meaning to Choctaw people. Sun and fire formed a belief complex, a major organizing principle for the worldview of southeastern native people. Choctaws regarded the sun as a deity, the eye of the governor of the world, and the possessor of the powers of life and death. One of the four Choctaw words for "God" was *Hushtahli,* a compound of *hashi,* "sun," and *tahli,* "to complete an action." Warriors gave thanks to the sun when they returned victorious from a fight, for the sun led them to find the bright path, the road to victory. In the war ceremony, one song commanded all warriors to trust their success to the sun and the fire, his mate—*Hushtahli, micha Luak Hushtahli itichapa.* Fire was referred to as the "sun's mate." Fire was the "representation of the sun," possessing intelligence, acting "in concert with the sun." Sun and Fire had "constant intercourse" with each other, according to Choctaw beliefs. One ancient Choctaw tradition held that if one did anything wrong in the presence of Fire, he would tell Sun of it, "before the offender could go *ashtapa*" (the length of his extended arms). Fire provided a conduit through which the Choctaw people enjoyed contact with the powers of the sun.[31]

The sacred fire, which among southeastern native people formed the ritual center of each town, or *talwa*, marked the center of the most important annual ritual observance, the Green Corn Ceremony. At this time, the Choctaws extinguished all the old fires in each town, and after several days of purifying themselves they ritually lit a new sacred fire, from which all others in the town were kindled. Each lodge relit its fires from this new one to signify unity, renewal, harmony, and the continuity of life. Fire was central to this ceremonial purification and renewal of life. The Choctaws set aside old grievances, beginning life literally anew.[32]

To the Choctaws, fire was important in relationships other than the one they had with the sun. The Choctaw name for Fire—*hushi itichapa*—means the sun's mate, "matched together." The oldest son in a family was called the *itichapa*, "father's mate." The Choctaw language also possesses a war and fire particle—*ito*, before a consonant, *it*, before a vowel. It implies "mutuality of action between the fire and what is put on it, or between those who kindle fires in a hostile manner against each other." Examples are *oti*, to kindle a fire; *itotia*, to go to war; and *ititaya*, to wage war by fire. Cyrus Byington, a Presbyterian missionary who spent much of his life among the Choctaws, suggested that this particle "may help us to understand how wars were formerly waged by fire rather than by weapon, these being very imperfect in construction, while fire was always on hand." Fire was perhaps used as a tool of warfare back to antiquity, suggesting an ancient, intimate relationship between the spiritual and physical dimensions of war and man.[33]

Fire had many uses—it could be used as a tool of war, to ease human access to game, to facilitate travel, for cooking, and for warmth. Yet it was also a significant part of the Choctaw worldview, in which it was seen as the messenger of a deity, embodying an external conscience that demanded proper behavior, and as an expression of human relations—between father and eldest son, between friendly, related peoples (clans) and towns, and between friend and enemy. Fire demarcated and regulated human bonds of kinship. Importantly, it formed the central symbol of a town's unity, renewal, and continuity. As southeastern scholar George E. Lankford has remarked, "each person owed his allegiance to his or her town, which was defined by the sacred fire. Even as towns grew large and split, the offspring 'towns' continued to regard their parent's fire as theirs also. Thus, close relationships between towns were expressed in terms of fire."[34] To be "of one fire" expressed a close, permanent relationship. When Tecumseh visited the Creeks of Tukabachee in 1811, the town's council asserted it was "of one fire" with the Shawnee.[35] Choctaws and other native people thus viewed fire as both a physical and a spiritual part of their world. It was, in fact, the "spiritual merged with the environmental."[36]

Just as fire was important in the Choctaw cosmology, water played a prominent and central role in their lives and belief system. Choctaws, like other Southeastern peoples, believed that they lived in This World, a world that existed between two others—the Upper World and the Lower World. The Upper World epitomized order and "expectableness," and was peopled with larger-than-life creatures, "that were not subject to all of the rules that limited ordinary people in their behavior."[37] The creatures who lived in the Upper World could do remarkable things that ordinary people could not, and could even change forms when necessary. The Lower World represented chaos, disorder, and change, and "was peopled by cannibals, ghosts, man-killer witches, monsters, and various thunder spirits."[38] The life of the Choctaws, in this cosmology, was to maintain balance between the Upper and Lower World, thus creating a world in which complete chaos was held off by perfect order.

Choctaws and other Southeastern native people believed that fire was opposed to water, "especially water in springs and rivers, which represented the Under [Lower] World, and it was up to man to see that these two substances were always kept apart."[39] Monster and ghosts could enter This World through rivers, lakes, and streams, which were thought to be entrances from the Lower World, doing harm to humans and other creatures in This World. All Choctaws knew how the tie-snake could sneak up on a person who was alone in an isolated spot near a river, wrapping itself around the unsuspecting victim and pulling him back into the river to drown and be heard from no more.[40] Countless southeastern native children must have recalled these stories and stayed back from rivers while they played.

In addition, the Under World and its spirits could be offended if humans did not pay proper respect. Each morning and evening Choctaw children plunged into the rivers along which they lived, even in midwinter. They then gathered on the riverbank to hear the stories and instructions of the elders.[41]

Choctaw people traditionally lived on or near rivers. Proximity of water was essential for survival and comfort. It also provided transportation and linked the Choctaw people to the outside world. The waterways of the new lands were, therefore, of primary importance to all the people of the Indian Territory. Rivers and streams were the primary method of transportation, providing conduits for communication, commerce, and travel. The exploring parties of Choctaws who went to survey the new lands prior to their eviction from the East carefully noted and commented on the rivers and streams and their viability as avenues of transportation. Of particular concern was a water route to the Mississippi, the main artery of commerce and most important link to the world market system. Although most Choctaws and other Indians of this region had little interface with the distant market, a small number of more acculturated Choctaws exported cotton and imported manufactured American goods and supplies. The north bank of the Red River, in particular, was lined with the cotton plantations of rich Choctaws and intermarried whites.[42]

As agriculturists, the Choctaws used the rivers and streams as sources of water for crops, livestock, and of course humans. Rivers attracted wild game, yielded fish and other aquatic products, served as bathing and watering places, and provided water for cooking and for the manufacture of material goods. Streams and rivers in the West differed significantly from those in the East. In the East, the riverbeds lay upon rock foundations. However, western rivers were lined with shifting, loamy soil, with little or no rock near the surface of the bed. For example, the Red River carried huge loads of silt over a broad bed of light and shifting sands from its source on the Staked Plain all the way to the Mississippi. The Red River passed through a "country covered with forest-trees of gigantic dimensions," where the surrounding alluvial soil was extremely fertile. As the bed of the Red River deepened, the river washed loose soil from its banks from one side to another, in a way that produced constant change in the channel. Flash floods caused the Red River to change course often. The river created new bayous and streams as it sought new routes around accumulated debris. These flash floods were awesome to behold; one missionary related an instance when the river was quite low as they began to set up to build a new mission school one day. They had laid lumber upon the beach, since there was absolutely no indication of a rise. Suddenly, a "torrent of water" came crashing down the stream, endangering the building materials for the new school. "All hands and teams fell to, and by great effort, their material was saved." Rivers in this region were "given to such freaks, especially at the time of its annual overflow called the 'June rise.'" The weather might be dry, the sky clear, the great channel almost bare in the evening, and by morning a "perfect torrent" could be rolling by.[43]

The Arkansas and the Red Rivers formed the two primary river systems of the new Choctaw Nation. Originating in the Rocky Mountains, the Illinois, Cimarron, Verdigris, Grand, Salt Fork, and Chikaskia Rivers fed the Arkansas River from the North. The Canadian River flows from its source in New Mexico across the High Staked Plains of Texas and into the Panhandle of present-day Oklahoma, eventually joining forces with the abundant waters of the Arkansas as it traverses the land on its way to the mighty Mississippi. Originating in West Texas, the Red River enters Oklahoma from the southwest, fed by the North Fork, Washita, Boggy, Blue, and Kiamichi Rivers. It follows a zigzag path for 250 miles as it makes its way to the Great Mississippi River. The Arkansas and Red River systems formed traveling companions for man, tracing out routes from east to west, and west to east, serving as water supplies to travelers, as a source of water for the crops of farmers, and as the waterholes for herds of bison, cattle, horses, and all other creatures.[44]

The navigability of rivers in the new Choctaw lands was of paramount importance. Overland travel was dangerous, slow, and fraught with difficulties from the natural elements and hostile forces. Few roads existed in the 1830s, and those that did were often impassable due to inclement weather. Manufactured goods that had been integrated into Choctaw culture were harder to obtain in this distant western locale than they had been in the East, with its extensive networks of rivers and roads. Shipments could be delayed for years in some instances. For example, many supplies and tools promised to the Choctaws by the U.S. government in the Treaty of Dancing Rabbit Creek took years to arrive. Rifles were ordered and delivered, but the gunpowder that arrived independently was of such inferior quality that the Choctaws could not use it. The American agent found that it took a year for delivery of the replacement powder, rendering the new rifles useless in the interim.[45]

Transportation costs could be enormous, and goods could never be counted on until they had arrived. Many residents of the Choctaw Nation complained that they could not obtain needed goods at any price. Mishaps en route occurred frequently, disappointing waiting customers sometimes for months. Many items that Choctaws viewed as necessities were unavailable or so costly that only the wealthiest cotton planters could buy them, so ordinary people had to make do without them. In 1841, for example, one young Choctaw mother wrote to her husband, who was living temporarily in Washington, D.C., that she could obtain no sugar or coffee, had no flannel for her children (for winter clothing), and could get no shoes for their black slaves.[46]

Transportation up and down the Red River was impeded by a huge obstruction formed from natural debris. Many of the early traders and explorers reported the blockage. In 1806, the expedition of Captain Sparks, Mr. Freeman, Lt. Humphrey, and Dr. Custin left Natchez to explore the Red River to its sources. On 19 May 1806 they left Natchitoches and traveled up the Red River. On 2 June they found a monstrous logjam stretching over one hundred miles, entirely blocking the flow of the river and diverting it into dozens of lakes, bayous, and streams. The "Great Raft" was approximately two hundred miles from Fort Towson, six hundred miles below the mouth of the Kiamichi.[47] Native peoples had long known of the Great Raft; according to their oral traditions, it existed for generations back into the distant past. Europeans and white Americans speculated that it had formed as a result of a great flood of the Mississippi River that could have caused the Red River to reverse its course, thereby accumulating driftwood logjams that grew over the years.[48]

Others conjectured that the Red River had accumulated pockets of driftwood because in many places (and in some seasons) it not only was shallow but also wended snakelike beneath banks of loamy soil that crumbled into the piles of driftwood below. Hardwood trees growing on the banks of the Red River would fall into the stream as the banks crumbled, often with their root systems intact. This heavy debris was almost impossible to displace.[49]

The Great Raft was a living, growing entity, harboring plants and trees in its debris and enlarging itself annually. According to historian Dan Flores, the Great Raft grew up the Red River at the rate of four-fifths of a mile of timber every year. By blocking tributaries as it moved steadily upriver, it created new lakes and swamps. When it reached the Great Raft, the Red River released its load of sediment, thus contributing to the "rapid development of floodplain prairies above it, as well."[50] Explorer Thomas Freeman reported in 1806 that the raft rose "nearly three feet above the water" and was "covered with bushes and trees." Freeman noted that the raft was so solid that his men could walk over it without danger. It was "composed in large part of cottonwood, cypress, red cedar and other trees."[51] Freeman's party continued up the Red River past the Great Raft, and presciently foretold that if these rafts were removed so that the Red River above the Great Raft could be navigated, "this country in a very short time would become the Paradise of America, growing corn and cotton in amazing abundance."[52]

In 1820, Timothy Flint explored the Red River and found the Great Raft an "insuperable barrier for all craft larger than the pirogues that went on to the military garrison at Kiamesha [Kiamichi]." The raft was so sturdy and thick that his men could easily cross it on horseback. Captain Henry M. Shreve was put in charge of improvement of navigation on the Mississippi River. He invented a machine called "Uncle Sam's Tooth-puller" to extract trees, logs, and other plant debris from the river. By freeing the river of at least part of the raft, Shreve inspired the gratitude of local citizens, who named their most westerly settlement "Shreveport" in his honor. This settlement later became a major shipping hub in river traffic en route to the Mississippi.[53] Unfortunately, in the spring following this first clearing operation, the debris simply reformed.

In 1825, the Arkansas legislature asked Congress to remove the Great Raft in order to facilitate trade with the newly established Fort Towson. General Winfield Scott of the United States Army thereupon ordered Captain Birch of Fort Jessup to take twenty-five men from the garrison and remove the raft. Birch reported that they found the Raft to be nearly ninety-six miles long, composed of logs of all sizes so thickly massed as to prevent removal.

From 1832 through 1839, the U.S. government made a serious attempt to remove the raft. Captain Shreve headed the work under the auspices of the War Department. The work continued for six years, until 1838, when the U.S. Army engineers announced the completion of the huge project. However, this was not the end of the raft, which continually reformed, requiring constant dredging to keep the river navigable.[54] After the removal of the Great Raft, at least for part of the year steamboats could ascend the river to the Kiamichi, enabling cotton plantations along the Red River and some of its tributaries to become profitable.[55] The Red River's Great Raft outlasted all attempts to completely remove it until after the invention of nitroglycerin. By 1873, however, after $633,000 had been spent to clear it, the Raft finally succumbed to human technology.[56]

Navigation was possible intermittently between 1840 and 1873. The Red River became a major artery facilitating the exportation of cotton and the importation of market goods. Steamboats plied up and down the Mississippi River by the mid-1830s, connecting its suppliers and consumers along the Red River and points inland. One prominent Choctaw merchant and farmer, Robert M. Jones, owned five steamboats and a like number of plantations, enslaving several hundred African Americans who worked the land and made him wealthy.[57] Jones and others exported cotton to world markets through Shreveport and New Orleans, and he and other wealthy, enterprising Choctaws were able to bring in supplies that they sold in stores they owned in the small towns in Indian Territory.

With the difficulties of overland travel, the Red River and other waterways forged important links between the Choctaw Nation and the outside world. Settlements, plantations, and farms dotted both banks of the Red River, connecting Choctaws with Texans, the old French and Spanish settlements of Louisiana, the towns and cities of the Mississippi, and all points beyond.[58] The river allowed easier transportation of trade goods from the East and formed and expanded markets in the new West.

In the "removal" treaties, the U.S. government had promised protection to the emigrant Indians. In order to provide this protection, the United States built Forts Towson and Washita to ward off attacks by the southern plains people. The Red River was the conduit for transportation of troops and supplies to these forts, and therefore the United States had a treaty obligation to keep the Red River navigable in order to supply these forts and honor the protection clauses of the treaties. The Red River continued to be the chief means of transportation in the southern Choctaw Nation until the railroad came after the American Civil War.[59]

Water travel gradually improved. Barges, keelboats, and pirogues regularly wended their way up the Red River and other waterways of the Choctaw Nation. In the 1820s and 1830s, when steamboats began plying the rivers of the West, ten thousand flat boats and keelboats were thrown out of work. Even so, these boats continued to provide essential connections between the people of the Choctaw Nation and the outside world.[60]

Quite apart from the practical aspects of river transportation and future commerce, the rivers of the Choctaw Nation attracted settlers because of their beauty and aesthetic value. The beautiful Blue River, one of the tributaries of the Red, was described in 1825 as abounding in fish, with water "so clear that small pebble stones may be seen where it is many feet deep."[61] Immediately after the Treaty of Dancing Rabbit Creek was signed, several Choctaw warriors left to go to the new Choctaw Nation to survey likely spots for settlement. They reported much information concerning the rivers and streams, indicative of the importance they assigned to bodies of water. Clear Creek was "beautiful" and had the best-quality water; Gates Creek, near Fort Towson, snaked through good agricultural lands; there were "a great many fine springs"; and the Kiamichi River was eighty yards or so wide and would allow for "fine navigation."[62] J. D. Hunter, another Choctaw explorer, reported to a friend back in the old Choctaw Nation that the Poteau was a "fine stream and navigable for more than 60 miles up." The lands bordering the San Bois River, the Canadian River, and Beaver Creek were rich and "lie well for cultivation." In the upper country, the land was not so flat and therefore collected fewer ponds, which were the breeding grounds for mosquitoes and the fevers that plagued those who lived in the low country along the waterways.[63]

Aside from rivers and waterways, the new Choctaw lands contained plants both similar to those they had known in the east and different. A large crescent-shaped area from the southeastern corner of the new Choctaw Nation, bulging out along the region of the Ouachita Mountains and its immediate surrounds, abounded with trees—oak-pine, oak-hickory forests, and a small area of loblolly pines. Mixed savanna and woodlands, in addition to tall-grass prairies, composed the remaining eastern half of the Choctaw lands. Missionary Cyrus Byington mentions that on a trip of about one hundred miles through part of the southeastern portion of the Choctaw Nation (near Hugo, Oklahoma, today), he and his companions crossed the Kiamichi River going west and entered "an immense prairie where the land was rich, the grass having grown very high—six feet—where they "rolled along as though . . . in a meadow."[64] Although in late spring it must have been pleasant to travel through the tall-grass prairies, in late winter and early spring they posed a severe hazard to the traveler. The grass was excessively dry at that time of the year, and if it caught fire, the flames would roar rapidly along, sometimes overtaking man and beast, destroying every living thing in their path.[65]

Cane had always been significant to the Choctaws. The rivers throughout their eastern territories abounded with cane and reeds, providing rich forage for Choctaw cattle and horses. Two varieties of cane, *Arundinaria tecta,* a small variety, and *Gigantea,* the large or great cane, grew in the old lands. Wild seeds from the latter provided an additional food source for the Choctaw diet. In the old Choctaw Nation in the East, Choctaw women wove baskets, mats, and even clothing from cane, and constructed sleeping cots from it. Cane provided roofing and housing materials. Large cane posts became the supports for frames of buildings and houses. Sharpened cane shafts produced arrows and spears, and hollowed out pieces of cane became the blowguns used by children whose job it was to guard the fields against small animals and birds. Choctaw men used cane and reeds to make fishing weirs and traps, in addition to fishing spears and spits for cooking or roasting. Cane breaks attracted all kinds of game, in addition to being nesting grounds for a variety of species.[66]

Cane brakes could be found in the new Choctaw Nation as well, but they were of a much smaller variety than that found in the East, and were not nearly as common as in the more humid East. The Gaines exploring party of 1830 (as mentioned above, composed of Choctaw and Chickasaw leaders who came to evaluate the new lands in the West) found no cane at all above the South Fork of the Canadian River, a disappointing development for people whose material culture and economy made extensive use of this plant.[67] In the West there were fewer streams and fewer cane breaks. Significantly lower moisture levels precluded the formation of swamps and marshes that favored the development of large cane breaks. The diminished availability of cane constituted an important loss and required significant adaptation by the Choctaw people.

Choctaws adapted for many differences in the plants and herbs available in West from those that had been used in the East in their subsistence, ritual, and medical practices. It took time for the Choctaw *alikchi,* or healers, to learn the locations of herbs and other plants in the new lands. Some were simply unavailable or scarce, and so others were substituted. The *alikchi* continued to be called upon throughout the nineteenth century. In the period from 1830 to 1860, they constituted the only medical help available to most Choctaw people, and certainly the only traditional help. The Choctaws believed that their *alikchi,* unlike white physicians, possessed "insight into the hidden laws of nature and a power over the elements, fish, and other animals." The *alikchi* was a spiritual leader who could give bravery, skill, or strength to the warrior and defeat and expel the evil spirits of a disease. Choctaw people believed that their healers had supernatural powers. *Alikchi* used plants, animals, dances, songs, chants, formulas, and supernatural practices in healing. They could identify witches and illnesses caused by evil spirits. Choctaws continued to use *alikchi* in addition to Western college-trained medical doctors well into the twentieth century.[68]

As with many other areas of Choctaw belief, healing involved both physical and spiritual elements. It was impossible to extricate one from the other. Healers generally visited the prospective patient first to determine whether they would attempt to heal him or her. After a preliminary diagnosis, the *alikchi* would go into the woods to gather plants, herbs, bark, and other natural substances with which to heal the patient. Choctaw herbalists often prepared plant and herb material using a mortar and pestle made of gum-tree wood, since this wood did not rot or split. Some of the most frequently used herbal remedies included blackroot tea, which was used as a purgative; tea made from the leaves and stalks of "burn-weed," which would cause profuse sweating and was used to break fevers; sun-dried persimmons mixed with corn bread, which were used to stop diarrhea; and a salve made from equal parts of honey, butter, the juice of green vines, and the leaves of pole beans, which was believed to cure external cancers.[69]

The new land of the Choctaw people varied in many ways from that of their old homelands. The climate and topography were different. The western stretches of the new lands consisted in great part of treeless plains. Aridity and high winds sculpted the surface of the earth in this region, rendering it alien and foreboding to Choctaws. The central and eastern portions of their new lands, however, had a similar climate and topography to their old homelands. In this area, the Choctaws felt more comfortable; here they would make their homes and redefine themselves individually and as a people. They would build a new nation, not of a conquered people learning to become "white," but of a people secure in their identity, yet flexible and innovative enough to meet changing circumstances and future challenges.

We have seen how the Choctaw worldview affected their approach to the earth and its creatures. Instead of arriving in Indian Territory with the intention of subduing or conquering the land, Choctaw people arrived acknowledging their intimate, mutual dependence on plants, animals, the earth, and all within the ecosystem. Most of them did not aim to turn a profit or to exploit resources or minerals of the region for personal enrichment, but instead intended to live in peace and harmony with the land. While they would abide with the earth and her creatures, they would be *of* the earth and all within it.

After their exile to the West, Choctaw people continued to see the spiritual in the physical, and continued to acknowledge the spirits who lived in all things. In these years of reestablishing and redefining the People, a remarkable pattern of persistence and continuity became clear. The Choctaws nonetheless retained a profound appreciation for traditional ways of living and believing. Choctaw society had an inherent flexibility built into relationships that continued to offer support and strength to the maintenance of a unique Choctaw identity, even while adapting and modifying that identity to accommodate new stresses and new demands, both physical and spiritual.

The Choctaws began arriving in the western lands in the early 1830s. Some returned to their homelands in the East. Some traveled back and forth, unable to let go of the homelands and the Great Mother, Nanih Waiya, but finding their old lands overrun with Euro-Americans who had taken over the sacred spots, the sites in which generations of Choctaws had lived, worked, and played. Those left behind were driven from their farms and villages, forced into the swamps unwanted by whites. Many never made the transition to the western lands, either physically or spiritually.

The Western lands provided new space for the People to rebuild their shattered lives. Yet the spirits and bones of the dead remained behind, near the Mother Mound and the sacred places given to the Choctaw people by the Creator for all time.

4 After Doak's Stand: Indian Territory in the 1820s

THE INK WITH WHICH THE AMERICANS WROTE THE TREATY OF Doak's Stand was hardly dry before they asked the Choctaws to give some of the land back to the United States. Mingo Pushmataha was correct when he pointed out to Andrew Jackson during the treaty negotiations that hundreds and hundreds of Euro-Americans were already living within in the area the United States proposed that the Choctaws to take in exchange for their homelands in the East.

White intruders had moved into the area that became the new Choctaw Nation in the West during the first decades of the nineteenth century. They did not scruple about titles. There were no land offices for claims to be registered; there were no fences marking boundaries. The land appeared to them to be available for the taking, and take they did. By 1819 the white population in this general area was five thousand or more. The *Arkansas Gazette* described how in 1817–19, hundreds of families moved to the Red river and Arkansas country: "They cross the country from about Fort Osage and strike the Arkansas above Fort Smith, and we understand are flocking in, in great numbers between the Poto [Poteau River] and Canadian, as well as below Fort Smith. The roads in that neighborhood are said to be literally swarming with emigrants to that country."[1] The chief of the Caddo Indians who lived along the Red River complained to the United States that too many whites were moving in, and had made settlements, and were killing all the game and disrupting the crossing place for the Buffalo.[2]

White hunters and farmers delighted in this eastern portion of present-day Oklahoma, finding the game abundant, the soil fertile, and the climate mild. Most lived in rude log cabins and raised some corn and cotton. The mild winters produced ideal conditions for raising livestock. Many of these settlers traded pelts procured in hunts not far from their homes for necessary supplies such as sugar, salt, and coffee. A few went to the prairies west of mid-Oklahoma to trade with the Comanches and other native people for horses or mules, often stolen from the Mexicans. The area gained a reputation as a great place to settle, and white intruders kept coming.

Many of these people were refugees from the law, or outcasts of "proper" society back East. Some ran stills from their houses to make whiskey that they consumed, sold to other whites, and traded to Indians. Nuttall, a botanist traveling in the region in 1819, described them, saying that they "bear the worst character imaginable, being many of them renegades from justice."[3] One settler described their community as being a "motley crew, emigrants from all parts of the world," made up of people good and bad—mostly bad.[4]

By the terms of the Treaty of Doak's Stand, the United States had given the Choctaws

all the land between the Arkansas and Canadian rivers on the north and the Red River on the south, extending west as far as the source of the Canadian, and bounded on the east by a line running from the mouth of the Little River northeast to the site of Morrillton, Arkansas.[5]

These boundaries included many of the white settlements in eastern Oklahoma. Although the white squatters in this area had no title to the lands, they had before them the example of the white invasion and settlement of the public lands that became Indiana, Illinois, and Missouri. The whites there who had dispossessed the original Indian inhabitants were successful in attaining titles to the lands, so the inhabitants of the lands in Arkansas Territory assumed that their improvements would be confirmed to them in a similar manner.[6] However, most of them found themselves and their farms and improvements sitting squarely in the lands the

United States now said constituted the new Choctaw Nation of the West. Immediately they raged at the injustice of the U.S. government giving "their" land to the Choctaws. From their perspective, the U.S. government was perpetrating a gross injustice, giving in to the demands of whites in Mississippi to expel the native inhabitants of that state at the expense of the white citizens who were staking claims in Arkansas Territory. Why should they have to move to accommodate a "fierce and savage enemy," who could be expected to glut "his vengeance on a weak and defenceless [sic] people for unjuries [sic] which he has sustained in his native country?"[7]

Mississippians tried to placate the enraged squatters in Arkansas by suggesting that they should allow the Choctaws to move to their region until the area became a state, at which time they could then force the Indians out of their state, as had the whites wanting the Choctaw Mississippi homelands. The idea had become commonplace in America that whenever whites wanted Indian land, the native people had to yield it up. Yet the Arkansans were not placated by the suggestion that they should accept the Choctaws and then expel them in a few years. They lobbied fiercely for their cause and found a champion in Senator Thomas Benton of Missouri, who was also the chairman of the U.S. Senate Committee on Indian Affairs. He campaigned vigorously for the U.S. government to renegotiate the boundaries with the Choctaws rather than force the white squatters to give up their claims. Congress obliged by passing an act in May 1824 fixing the boundary of the Indian Territory west of the most populated areas of the white settlements, encroaching significantly into the area given to the Choctaws, including a large portion of the very best lands of the Choctaw allotment.

Secretary of War John C. Calhoun decided to have the U.S. surveyors run two lines—one according to the boundary set by the treaty and another that would accommodate the demands of the whites living in Arkansas Territory. Calhoun made clear his intentions to abrogate this treaty in 1821, when he instructed the U.S. agent in charge of settling the Choctaws who were moving west that he should see that they settled as far as possible away from the whites living there, so that a "future alteration of the existing line could be made without further dislocation of the inhabitants." Furthermore, the territorial governor of Arkansas wrote to the *Arkansas Gazette*, "I am happy to have it in my power to say to the good people of Arkansas, . . . that they will not be disturbed in their possessions . . . for a new arrangement will be made . . . so as to put the Indians west of the white settlements."[8]

While the whites of Mississippi and Arkansas raged against each other and the federal government, the Choctaws looked on with anger and disgust. They flatly refused to discuss giving back Arkansas lands to suit the convenience of the white squatters living there. They reiterated that they had told Jackson during the treaty negotiations that there were hundreds of whites living in that area, but he had insisted that if there indeed were whites living there, they would be forced to move off the lands promised to the Choctaws. From the Choctaw perspective, of course, it was evident that as soon as any whites protested the terms of any treaty, the United States reacted predictably with requests that the Indians accommodate the whites. They were weary of a thousand broken promises and leery of entering into any agreement with the United States, knowing with growing certainty that the terms of any agreement were subject to revision any time the white population demanded it.[9]

In 1824, the U.S. government asked the Choctaws to send a delegation to Washington to discuss "adjusting" the borders defined in the 1820 treaty. A distinguished Choctaw delegation left the Nation, traveling to Washington to meet with the president to discuss the exact boundaries of the new Choctaw lands. Members of this delegation included three great chiefs of legendary fame: Apuckshunnubbee, chief of the Okla Falaya or Upper Towns District; Mushulatubbee, head of the Okla Tannap or Lower Towns District; and Mingo Pushmataha, chief of the Sixtowns District.

These chiefs were famous and well known to some Americans. Chief Pushmataha was a strong ally of the United States, and his efforts to reduce conflicts with the whites intruding into the native lands of the Southeast were familiar reading in the national newspapers. He had saved the white settlers of Mississippi, Alabama, and Georgia from almost certain destruction when he kept the Choctaw warriors from joining Tecumseh in 1811. Tecumseh's plan had included expelling all whites from the South, with the Choctaws playing a primary role. When Tecumseh had come to recruit warriors from the southeastern nations in 1811, many had been persuaded, and had rushed to join him. Yet Pushmataha firmly had placed himself on the side of the Americans, and through his oratory, his strength of character, and because of the plain fear he inspired in those who opposed him, few Choctaw warriors had dared to join Tecumseh.

Pushmataha was also instrumental in the American defeat of the Muscogee (Creek) Red Sticks in 1814, and in the defeat of the British at New Orleans. Yet American history has forgotten the essential services he and his fellow Choctaws rendered, and his name is now legendary only among the Choctaw people. To this day, many oral traditions are handed down in Choctaw families about the legendary exploits of the great Mingo Pushmataha.[10]

Far less is known of Chief Apuckshunnubbee. He was of the Haiyi-patuklo (Two Lakes) clan, and was known to be a quiet, steadfast, honest, courageous man. The third great chief was Mushulatubbee, who is remembered because he was the only one of the three great traditional Choctaw mingos to live to go into exile with the Choctaw people. Mingo Mushulatubbee was a true Choctaw patriot. He was a man of stunningly strong character, facing down the enormous strength of the advocates of assimilation and leading his people in maintaining traditional ways. He died in 1838, cut down by a smallpox epidemic that killed hundreds of Choctaws who had been forced into exile in Oklahoma.

The Choctaw delegation left the Nation in late September, traveling by stage, and reached Maysville, Kentucky, on 13 October 1824. After supper that evening, Apuckshunnubbee, who was quite elderly, lost his balance and fell off an embankment as he tried to reach the nearby river. He died two days later of a broken neck. The Choctaw delegation was stunned and shocked by his death, and several of the party recognized the sad event as a portent of what was to come in Washington if they continued their jour-ney. The people of Maysville, Kentucky, made a major event of his death and had him interred with military honors, while the entire town turned out for the services. Apuckshunnubbee's nephew, Robert Cole, succeeded the old chief, and the delegation continued on to Washington.[11]

The Choctaw delegation reached Washington, D.C., in early November 1824, and was feted at a reception in its honor. Liquor flowed like water, both at the official functions and at the Choctaws' lodgings. In fact, the U.S. government allocated a $3 per day stipend for liquor sup-plied to the delegates, but, predictably, this sum fell far short of their requirements. Each delegate's liquor tab averaged somewhat over $8 per day, over the three-month period of their visit to Washington. Adjusted to

2001 dollars, the Choctaw delegation spent $125 per day per delegate on liquor alone! The legendary chief Pushmataha was apparently overcome by his refreshments and the deleterious effects on his aged body and he fell ill and died on Christmas Eve. He was given a hero's funeral cortege and burial in the National Cemetery. The news shocked and stunned the Choctaw Nation, where the news of the deaths of the two great chiefs was known a few weeks later.[12]

It appeared to the Choctaws that no matter what course of action they followed, their nation was doomed. After several years of resisting all American overtures to cede more land, two of their greatest leaders suddenly died. The remaining delegates succumbed once again to the ploys of the United States. The U.S. government used a systematic plan to weaken and corrupt the judgment and integrity of the Choctaw leaders. They were deliberately plied with enormous quantities of liquor and given promises of favoritism and blatant bribes.[13]

Their hotel bar bill was $2,149.50 ($33,725 in 2001 dollars), in addition to another $349.75 ($5,487 in 2001 dollars) for "oysters and liquor."[14] Many of the Choctaws back in the Nation were disgusted and dismayed by the behavior of the delegates and the complicity of the American government. Yet historians term the results of this debacle as "favorable" to the Choctaws. Certainly by contrast with the usual experience of native people in dealing with the United States, this particular treaty failed to rob the Choctaws to the degree hoped. The delegates somehow managed, through their drunken stupor, to secure a small pittance in exchange for ceding part of the territory they had been promised in 1820, which in the overall scheme of U.S.-native relations could be termed a "success." It seems a sad and sordid tale, in retrospect.[15]

The results of the Treaty of 1825 were received with relief by many in the Choctaw Nation, who had feared that the delegates to Washington would be induced to sell out the entire Nation. The actual damage was a cession of the eastern portion of the land the United States had traded them in Arkansas under the Treaty of Doak's Stand of 1820. This area began east of Fort Smith, at about the present-day boundary between Oklahoma and Arkansas. In exchange, the United States promised to pay six thousand dollars annually for sixteen years. The Choctaws insisted that the United States include a provision specifically stating that the U.S. government would "not exercise the power of apportioning the lands, for the

benefit of each family, or individual, of the Choctaw Nation, and of bringing them under the laws of the United States, but with the consent of the
Choctaw Nation."[16] The Choctaws insisted that their communal view of
property be formally recognized and affirmed in the treaty because they
knew that the future existence of the Nation depended upon the reten-
tion of the communal ownership of property. They also were keenly aware
that the United States planned as soon as possible to force the Choctaws
to convert to the individual ownership of specific plots of their public
lands so that these lands would be accessible to the market. The
Americans fully recognized the inability of most native people to effectively deal with market forces, and once individual allocation of the community lands of the Choctaws was accomplished, it would be only a matter of
time before all of these lands were in the hands of white Americans. In
this instance, Choctaw leaders managed to hold the line against American
intrigues. However, within four short years the United States and the
southern state governments had forced the Choctaws to give up all of
their eastern homelands and go into permanent exile in the West.

The lands of this region of the West were in flux as enormous changes
continued to sweep over the Nation. In the lands given to the Choctaws
under the 1820 and 1825 treaties, native people waged war against each
other and the white intruders, who were busy establishing the institutions
through which they could dispossess the Indians. Aside from the hundreds of white families who had moved in and were establishing farms
and communities, there were preexisting communities and villages of
native people throughout the area. Along the Red River lived the Caddos.
The Wichita peoples lived along the Canadian. To the west were the
Comanches, the Kiowas, and small bands of Apaches, Arapahos, Chey-
ennes, and other Plains tribes who moved across the lands in their
nomadic way of life. Just north of the Choctaw lands, the Osages fought
an intense and prolonged war against Indian and white intruders. The
Osages dominated this region and had been battling intruding southeastern hunting parties and emigrants since before the turn of the century.

The Osages moved at will throughout the region, at war with almost
everyone. They created a reign of terror in the region that lasted well into
the 1820s. The Osages claimed all the lands west of the Mississippi River
to the Rocky Mountains, and from the Missouri in the north to the Red
River. The Quapaws' rival claim to part of this region was recognized by

the United States but was not admitted by the Osages, and with their superior military power the land they claimed was effectively theirs. The
Osages were enemies to almost all the native peoples living in the present-
day states of Missouri, Arkansas, Kansas, and Oklahoma, but their enmity
did not confine itself to this region. They had long traditions of warfare
against the Potawatomis, Sauks, and Foxes in the north, who used
firearms, as did the Osages, unlike the southern and western native peoples, who used lances and bows and arrows. The Potawatomis sent
hunters and war parties into Osage territory and contributed greatly to
the turbulence of the region.[17]

Shawnees, Delawares, Choctaws, Chickasaws, Cherokees, Panis,
Wichitas, Caddos, Arkansas, Alibamas, Kousattas, Taovayas, and whites all
fought the Osages, in continual warfare from 1790 into the 1820s. The
Osages certainly had legitimate complaints against many of these people—they were intruding on Osage lands. The United States, France, and
Spain had long ignored the rightful claims of the Osages, and had traded
and dickered in their lands between themselves as though the Osages did
not exist. Finally, as a result of the Osages' guerilla warfare, the United
States attended to their claims and made every effort to extinguish them
within the system the Americans had set up to dispossess all native people. The United States used one of its most reliable strategies to obtain a
fraudulent treaty with the Osages—they met in 1808 with a small, unrepresentative group of Osages, used trickery and bribery to get the leaders
to sign a document that they did not understand and could not read, gave
them presents, and sent them on their way. The U.S. government then
announced that it had obtained Osage consent to give up almost all the
land of present-day Arkansas above the Arkansas River and the entire
state of Missouri.

The majority of the Osages immediately objected, stating that they
had not been party to these negotiations and that the treaty was not valid.
The following fall, the United States met with representatives of the
Great and Little Osages, and they supposedly gave their agreement to
this treaty. The Osages ostensibly agreed to give up approximately
100,000 square miles of land to the United States in exchange for the following: the establishment of a U.S. trading post; a blacksmith; a water
mill; an unspecified number of ploughs; a "strong block house" for each
of two chiefs; the cancellation of claims against the Osages by whites for

"depredations" committed by various Osages, the sum of which was not to exceed $5,000; $1,500 in trade goods; and another $1,200 in cash. Thus, the United States acquired sixty-four million acres of land for $7,700, two blockhouses, and a water mill. The Osages protested that they meant to give the United States only the hunting rights to this region, not to sell their lands, but William Clark, of the famous exploring team Lewis & Clark, insisted that the treaty had been fairly procured.[18]

The United States was but an annoyance, however, compared to the threat to the Osages from the emigrant Native Americans. The Cherokees had been moving into the region since the early nineteenth century, and by 1816 they numbered in excess of two thousand people. They were joined by thousands of other native people who had emigrated to the region, most to escape intruders in their homelands. The United States did everything short of eviction at bayonet point to get the southeastern Indians to leave their homelands and move west of the Mississippi. In order to make more progress in the acquisition of the rich agricultural lands occupied by the southeastern Indians, the U.S. government had to have a place for them to go in the West, and the marauding Osages were in the way of this great American plan. To rid the region of the indigenous peoples, the United States procured several dishonest treaties over the first three decades of the nineteenth century with the Osages and the Cherokees, in which the United States displayed little true concern for justice, integrity, or honesty in its dealings.[19]

For example, in 1817, Andrew Jackson procured a treaty with the Cherokees to get them to cede rich Tennessee lands by inducing Cherokee chiefs from Arkansas, in addition to only a handful from the eastern Cherokees, to sign a treaty in which the eastern Cherokees were to cede thousands of acres in Tennessee. In the papers of the commissioners, the last in the series relates how Jackson and his fellow American agents induced the unrepresentative Cherokees present to sign this treaty by including a "private article" that was not included in the published treaty. In this article the Americans promised a bribe of one thousand dollars to John D. Chisholm, an intermarried white man living with the Cherokees, "to stop his mouth and obtain his consent; likewise, they awarded another thousand-dollar bribe to be paid to Col. Meigs, the U.S. agent to the Cherokees in Tennessee; finally, to the Arkansas Cherokees they awarded one hundred dollars each, and to three other "influential" chiefs, one hundred dollars in "presents."[20] When the main body of Cherokees found out about the so-called treaty, they vigorously protested, informing Congress that this treaty had been signed by people who had no right to sign for the eastern Cherokees and angrily denouncing the methods used to obtain the treaty. Soon afterward, the U.S. Senate ratified the treaty.[21]

The Osages kept the Cherokees, Choctaws, and many other easterners from moving west of Fort Smith, until finally the United States decided to establish a fort on the Arkansas River at a point where it intersected the Osage boundary in an effort to establish order and peace among the Indians. The United States erected and staffed Fort Gibson at the end of 1818. Meanwhile, the emigrant Indians, led by the Cherokees, determined to put together an army of warriors capable of dealing a fatal blow to the Osages. Six hundred warriors marched on Clermont's town, a major Osage village lying on the west side of the Grand River. Clermont and his warriors were away on a hunting trip. The combined Indian forces, numbering 565 warriors, took the opportunity to fall upon the undefended village, full of women and children and a handful of old men, where they killed 69 women and children and 14 men. They took another 103 Osage women and children as prisoners, stole everything they wanted, and burned the rest. After the initial attack the allied warriors pursued women and children fleeing the village to the Verdigris River, where several drowned in their desperate attempt to elude their attackers.[22]

The Cherokee people who had emigrated to present-day Arkansas and eastern Oklahoma staked their claim with a ferocity that stunned many white observers, who typically characterized the Cherokees as one of the most "civilized" of Indian nations. After the preposterous "treaty" of 1817, several thousand more Cherokees emigrated to the Arkansas Territory. In 1819, their numbers in the West were estimated at about 3,500, and these were supplemented by an incredible assortment of other native people from east of the Mississippi, from Oneidas in the northeast, to Shawnees, Delawares, and Potawatomis, to Chickasaws, Choctaws, Creeks, Seminoles, and many others too numerous to list. In addition, when they wanted to make war upon the Osages, other native people from Texas (Mexico) and east and west of the Mississippi joined them in inflicting damage upon everyone's enemy, the Osages.[23]

After the massacre at Clermont's Town, the Cherokees followed up their "victory" by demanding that the United States force the Osages to cede what is now eastern Oklahoma to the Cherokees. On 25 September 1818, the Osages ceded a magnificent region known as Lovely's Purchase to the United States in exchange for the U.S. government taking care of debts that totaled four thousand dollars for damages and theft allegedly committed by the Osages. In 1828, the United States ceded this land to the Cherokees.[24]

In the early 1820s, the region exploded into round after round of violence and warfare. The Osages were in a desperate fight against the intruding southeastern native people who were being forced out of their homes by whites moving into the southern states. The Osages were truly a nomadic hunting people, and they had never learned to farm or engage in pastoralism. There had been plenty of game for their subsistence for centuries, until the intrusion of large numbers of Cherokees and other emigrants, who, in addition to farming, engaged in commercial hunting. They were armed and well equipped, and although outnumbered by the Osages, they won nearly any contest through superior arms. The Cherokees were hunting primarily to acquire pelts to trade, not so much for meat for subsistence. The Osages complained bitterly to the United States that the Cherokees were coming onto their lands to hunt and were stealing their horses, fighting their young men, and causing an enormous loss in their subsistence activities.[25]

Although the major antagonists were the Cherokees and the Osages, many other native people fought with one group or the other, and oftentimes the war parties included white men. When hostilities erupted, anyone caught in between or near these forces was attacked, or had livestock or other goods stolen. The antipathies had become so intense that the usual warfare descended to the vilest acts committed against innocents.

For example, in 1821, the Cherokees and their allies massacred a number of Osage women, children, and old men while their warriors were away on a hunt. The Osages had come in for treaty negotiations, and since the Cherokees had not yet arrived and they had the assurances of the U.S. military that they would prevent the Cherokees from attacking their camp, the Osage warriors left on their hunt. The Cherokees fell upon the defenseless camp unexpectedly. The few warriors and old men who were still at the camp held back the Cherokees until the women and children could flee, but there were only ten or twelve men trying to stop more than a hundred attackers. One hundred of the Osage were killed, and the rest were taken prisoner. When the Cherokees returned to their village with sixty captive women and children, their victory celebrations got out of hand and they slaughtered a number of their defenseless prisoners.[26]

The leader of this group was Tom Graves, a white man who had lived with the Cherokees since he was a child, who carried a burning hatred for the Osages. He personally killed an Osage woman and her baby during the celebration. Their bodies were then thrown to the hogs. A missionary at Dwight Mission who wrote an account of the attack added that, "this murder was perpetrated by one Graves, a white, who was taken when very young by the Cherokees and brought up by them and is now a Captain and commanded 100 of the party and is a farther evidence to me that there is more savage verocity [*sic*] in the whites brought in Indian life and the half-breeds than in the genuine Indian."[27]

The United States increased its forces at Fort Smith, and brought about an armistice between the Osages and the Cherokees, signed on 16 May 1822. The subsequent conference was held at Fort Smith and was attended by 150 Osages and more than 100 Cherokees. Unfortunately, however, the war resumed in 1823.[28]

In February 1824, the United States established Fort Towson to try to address the continual complaints of whites living in the area that Indians were committing "depredations." The commander of the fort tried to enforce the U.S. laws against hunting and trespassing on Indian lands, which infuriated the whites living in the region. In one incident in January 1825, several U.S. soldiers were at a still a few miles from Fort Towson. A force of white civilians took them captive and force-marched them to the home of one of their leaders, who was an Arkansas Territory justice of the peace. Major Alexander Cummings, the commander of the fort, sent a party to rescue the soldiers. After their successful rescue, two hundred angry white civilians gathered at a nearby home and planned to attack and destroy Fort Towson. In the meantime, Major Cummings sent a list of the leaders of the vigilante group and the men trespassing illegally in Indian Territory to the U.S. district attorney for Arkansas Territory, Sam B. Roane. Roane at once informed Cummings that he would not prosecute the men on this list, and that, indeed, they were going to Little Rock to have Cummings and some of his men indicted. The civil authorities ordered men to take Cummings and the soldiers into custody and deliver them for trial. At this point Major Cummings was relieved of his command.[29]

The United States continued to pretend to acquire "legal" title to the lands of the region so that they could give them to the southeastern tribes in exchange for their homelands. In 1818 the United States forced the Quapaw Indians to cede their lands between the Red River and the Arkansas and Canadian Rivers, for which they received four thousand dollars' worth of goods and an annuity of one thousand dollars. Six years later this same tribe allegedly agreed to give up all the rest of its land lying in the central part of Arkansas Territory for a mere six thousand dollars and an annuity of one thousand dollars for eleven years, to move to a bit of land on Bayou Treache, which was a parcel of land below the floodplain that regularly flooded. In addition, they agreed to become a part of the Caddo nation.[30]

The Caddos refused to allow them to enter their lands and wanted nothing to do with the agreement made by the United States with the Quapaws. The Quapaws occupied and planted crops on the banks of Bayou Treache and lost their entire crop year after year. Finally, in 1827, Governor Izard of Arkansas Territory visited the Quapaw in response to complaints he had received about their condition from white settlers who had witnessed their predicament. Governor Izard found most of them ill and near starvation, and discovered that some of them had actually starved to death. The governor had corn distributed to the Quapaws and reported their condition to the federal authorities, who did little. The United States had succeeded in depriving the Quapaws of all their homelands, lands that were rich in game on which they had subsisted for generations, and within a few years the Quapaws were homeless and starving. Many of them tried to return to their homelands in Arkansas and to coexist with the whites who now lived there. This was impossible, so they finally obtained some land in western Missouri to which they retired.[31]

The emigrant tribes, led by the Cherokees, attempted to formalize the alliance of native peoples in the region, and to draw more emigrants into their ranks. Their goals were twofold: first and foremost, they hoped that by uniting they could form an alliance strong enough to be able to force the whites to concede sovereignty and they thus could attain insulation from white encroachment and aggression. Second, they planned to wrest the remainder of what is now eastern Oklahoma from the Osages and make it safe for the emigrant Indians. This movement was begun by Tahlonteskee, a legendary Cherokee chief who died in 1818. Takatoka and a chief of the Shawnees, Captain Lewis, led the movement in the 1820s. In 1823, representatives from the Cherokee, Shawnee, Delaware, Wea, Kickapoo, Piankashaw, and Peoria tribes met and extended a formal invitation to the native people east of the Mississippi to move to the western lands and join with them in a vast Indian alliance. Most particularly, the Shawnees, Wyandots, Tuscaroras, Ottowas, Potawatomis, Senecas, and Miamis were known to be interested in moving west to join them. Other native people in Indiana, Ohio, and New York had received wampum belts from the council and were considering joining them in this movement.[32]

In October 1824, Takatoka was given a formal commission by the Cherokee Nation in Arkansas to go to Kaskaskia to meet with native people from the Ohio tribes to discuss a future course of action. Most unfortunately, when Takatoka arrived at Kaskaskia, he became ill and died. He asked his fellow delegates to carry on without him, but his force of personality and natural leadership abilities were not readily replaceable. The other delegates did go on to St. Louis, as Takatoka had wished, and met with General Clark. They showed him the wampum received by Takatoka from nineteen eastern tribes to signify their interest in joining the alliance.

Captain Sandusky and others joined the delegates at St. Louis and persuaded Clark to send them on to Washington, D.C., where they wanted to meet with U.S. government officials to solicit the support of the president for their plans. The seventeen delegates arrived in Washington on 19 February and received approval of the plan from the president, whereupon they returned to Wapakoneta on 11 May. There the beleaguered native people of the East were not enthusiastic about their proposals. They had been told that the entire plan had been drawn up by the Americans to trick them into removing west. The delegation then went to St. Louis and met again with General Clark on 10 November.

After this meeting the alliance faded away, and the actions of the United States in forcing huge numbers of eastern native people off of their homelands in the East wrecked the plans of the native people of the West. With the mass in-migrations, the organization of a united movement became impossible in the face of the extreme struggle necessary to survive the Trails of Tears and the early years in Indian Territory. The

United States forced into exile hundreds of thousands of native people, in most cases over a very brief span of time, relegating them to destitution and starvation and destroying many, many lives.

Nevertheless, history must make note of the valiant efforts of the native people to unite in a Pan-Indian alliance reminiscent of those of Tecumseh and the Prophet. This continued a loosely connected movement to repel the invading whites and was a prominent feature of the native struggle for sovereignty and freedom. That the United States overwhelmed the native peoples in no way diminishes the extraordinary measures attempted by dozens of Indian patriots.[33]

The failure of the Pan-Indian Movement of the 1820s did not spell the end of the attempts to unite the native peoples of the Indian Territory in a movement to stop the white invasion and conquest of Native America. Indeed, the native peoples of the region tried and succeeded, to a degree, to rebuff repeated attempts over the nineteenth century by whites to take this last homeland away from them. They were not defeated until 1907, when the United States finally used its hegemony to dispossess native people not only of their last homeland but also of their very identity.

During the last years of the 1820s, violence and uncertainty reigned. Warfare continued on an unprecedented scale between the Cherokees and their allies and the Osages. By 1826, game was becoming scarce in the lands of western Arkansas and southwestern Missouri, where many immigrant Indians were living. The Delawares, Kickapoos, Shawnees, and Cherokees sent hunting parties west into the Osage lands to look for game. They crossed the eastern portion of Oklahoma, all the way down to the Red River, and traveled to the western prairies. When the Osages discovered one of these parties, they attacked them. The cycle of violence and mayhem escalated until no one was safe in the region. For example, in March 1826, a hunting party of Delawares and Kickapoos killed five Osage warriors south of the Canadian River. The party of Osages was returning from a war expedition against the Pawnees, and had invited the hunting party of Delawares and Kickapoos to camp with them. Just before daylight, the Delawares and Kickapoos suddenly attacked the Osages, killing five and wounding others before fleeing. The Osages retaliated a few months later, attacking an undefended Piankashaw and Delaware settlement, killing and scalping one Delaware. Then the Osages killed a

Delaware woman, two men, and a boy; destroyed their cache of six hundred pelts; and stole eight horses. Almost simultaneously, another war party of Osages attacked a Delaware hunting camp, killing and mutilating two adults. They threw a child whom they had captured into the fire.[34]

The Delawares were so enraged over these killings that they solicited warriors from the Cherokee, Kickapoo, Sauk, and other tribes to join with them in a war of extermination against the Osages. The United States feared that if the Osages were destroyed, the united warriors would then turn on the whites and rebel against their subjugation. U.S. agents worked feverishly to put together a cease-fire between the warring parties. The United States knew that the Delawares and Cherokees alone could field at least one thousand warriors, and the Osages had a like number of defenders. The U.S. presence in the region was weak, consisting of fewer than three hundred soldiers at Fort Gibson. General Gaines, the commander of the Western Military Department, ordered eight mounted companies to make ready to take the field in the event of further hostilities.[35]

The Osages became alarmed at the escalating number of potential combatants and asked the Delawares to meet with them in St. Louis in September to discuss peace. A peace treaty was signed between the Delawares and Osages in October 1826, but hostilities continued between the Osages and the Cherokees. Hostilities against other Plains people rose as a result of attacks made on other immigrant Indians' hunting parties to the western prairies of present-day Oklahoma. In 1829, a party of 279 Cherokees, Choctaws, Shawnees, and Delawares, primarily from the Red River, fought a battle against a force of Tawakonis, Wacos, and Comanches. The immigrants lost 5 warriors, but supposedly killed 60 of their enemy. Upon their return to the Red River, they began to plan a large war party to assail their foes in the fall.[36]

In early autumn, the Tawakonis attacked a group of Cherokee and Creek hunters. Victorious, they dragged the bodies of the slain back to their village. They drove stakes into the ground, fastened the bodies of the dead Indians in a standing position facing the dance ground, and mocked and derided the bodies of the dead in an all-night celebration of their victory. A group of visiting native people from another tribe witnessed the victory dance, and on their way home they told the Texas Cherokees who were living on the Sabine about the treatment of the dead Cherokee and Creek hunters. Enraged at the Tawakonis, the Cherokees and their allies plotted a retaliatory attack for the following spring. Early one morning in March 1830, sixty-three warriors began their journey west and surprised the Tawakoni village at dawn. They slaughtered men, women, and children, burning many in their huts as they fired the town, killing others with guns or tomahawks. They returned to their homes on the Red River, holding high a painted sapling from which many Tawakoni scalps hung, to a wild victory celebration, thus concluding one more round of the cycle of killing.[37]

The invading white settlers and U.S. soldiers of the region enjoyed no immunity from the attacks of the prairie Indians. On 31 August 1828, a small group of soldiers from Cantonment Towson were fishing in the Kiamichi River in the region where the Choctaw Nation would relocate in the early 1830s. A band of Pawnees attacked and killed two of them, while the rest fled back to the fort, sounding the alarm. A detachment of soldiers rode out to chase off the Pawnees and returned with the corpses of the two slain soldiers. The next day citizens from the area assembled to assist the outnumbered U.S. soldiers in pursuit of the killers. They came upon the Pawnees celebrating their victory, dancing around the scalps of the slain soldiers, ninety miles away on the banks of the Blue River. The white attackers fell upon the Indians and killed most of them, returning later to the fort with the scalps of the dead soldiers and of three of the Pawnees they had slain.[38]

Whites in Miller and Hempstead Counties on both banks of the Red River in southwestern Arkansas Territory were greatly alarmed at the incursions by the prairie Indians. In June 1829, the United States abandoned Fort Towson, which incensed the white inhabitants of the region, who complained bitterly to the president that "the citizens are almost daily subject to every species of outrage by the numberous [sic] tribes of Cumanchie and Pawnee Indians [sic], who reside for half the year within the limits of the United States, as well as from the revenged Cherokees, Shawnees, Delawares, and Kickapoos. That they are constrained at their own expense to keep scouts continually employed to repel minor aggressions and give notice of the approach of more formidable parties; that many of our citizens, hopeless as to the future, are abandoning their property and seeking places of more security."[39] As soon as the federal troops abandoned Fort Towson, the prairie Indians again invaded the region. They attacked and killed Isaac Murphy, who was working in his field only three miles from Miller Courthouse. Forty white civilians pursued the Pawnee attackers for miles, all the way to the Blue River. The white settlers sent word to the acting governor of the territory, calling upon the government for authorization to raise a voluntary militia to protect the Red River settlements from Indian attacks. Governor Fulton forwarded their request to Colonel Clark, who ordered all his soldiers to a state of readiness to repel any attack.

The Osages, discouraged by the military strength of the whites and the immigrant Indians, turned their attacks on the Pawnees to their west, where they hunted buffalo. Three hundred Osage warriors attacked the Pawnees in February 1830, chasing villagers into a lake, where they massacred dozens of them. Nearly one hundred were killed, with the Osages losing no men. The Osages were so happy over their victory that they decided to attack the Choctaws living on the Red River. Thus the cycle of violence in the region continued unabated.[40]

The prairie tribes continued their fight against intruders of all stripes—Osages, immigrant southeastern Native Americans, and whites. The Osages continued to war upon the southeastern Indians and the whites, as well as upon native groups to their north, west, and south. The actions of Cherokees and other southeasterners, as well as the invading whites, were no less "savage" than the atrocities perpetrated by the prairie tribes; the whites merely had better "press." American historians have colored and tweaked accounts of the battle for this region so as to make the Indians appear "savage" and the whites "civilized." Yet, cast in a more objective light, it is clear that the Osages, Pawnees, and other Southern Plains people were desperately defending their homelands against Indian and white invaders. The immigrant Indians were being forced into this region by the white conquest of their homelands. White individuals were caught up in a process of conquest in which, in many cases, they were unwilling participants, forced into certain behaviors through instincts of self-preservation. The U.S. government aided and abetted its constituents in the never-ending quest for native lands, lending military and political might, part of the American public wealth, and much of the ideological justification for the obliteration of hundreds of native cultures and hundreds of thousands of native people.

Back in the East, Andrew Jackson ran for president in 1828. He and the state legislators of Georgia and Mississippi finally struck upon a device that ended the struggle of the great southeastern nations to avert dispossession. Since the great majority of the southern tribes refused to cede the remaining portions of their homelands through the sham process of "treaty-making," which had been perfected by Americans over the preceding decades but which had now gotten nowhere with the big southern tribes, Jackson and his allies in state government decided to act out a version of the "good cop, bad cop" routine, on a governmental level. The state legislatures were to extend their laws over the Indians—depriving them of the basic civil rights guaranteed to American citizens and denying them the rights to free speech, free assembly, due process, the separation of powers, and the sole jurisdiction of the federal government in carrying on relations with native nations. The Jackson administration, knowing that this charade would abrogate all the American government treaty obligations incurred since the nation's founding, then announced piteously to the world that it did not have the power to stop the states from so doing, nor would it even try to do so. Even when the Supreme Court ruled that the United States had a sacred obligation to keep the states from these actions, ruling them unconstitutional, Jackson stayed the course. Jackson simply refused to enforce the Supreme Court decision, and declared that the native people of the South must either submit to losing their freedom or go into permanent exile in the West. The legal niceties were taken care of in sham "removal" treaties, and the American people turned their backs on justice and fair play for native people. The large southeastern Indian nations were forced into the cauldron of chaos of the West, where many of the prophecies of death and destruction came true.

5 A Perfect Picture of Chaos

DURING THE LATE 1820S, THE CHOCTAWS SCRAMBLED TO AVOID dispossession from their homelands. Various factions formed, each strategizing ways in which to deal with the U.S. government. All of these Choctaw factions knew that southern and western Americans would settle for nothing less than the confiscation of the Indian nation's lands, but still they fought to rouse the conscience of Americans through active alliance with the whites, living primarily on the East Coast, who seemed to side with them in their struggle. Each of the Choctaw factions was desperate in its attempts to stave off dispossession, and, unfortunately, the U.S. government used its usual tactics to disrupt and render incoherent the native peoples' efforts to save themselves and their homeland. The United States fanned the flames of factionalism and encouraged fears of betrayal and corruption, all the while posturing as an advocate of the welfare of the Indian.

Andrew Jackson and his agents worked to breed suspicion between the so-called mixed-bloods and intermarried whites and the full-bloods. They constantly repeated the charge that the mixed-bloods were acting solely out of self-interest and would lead the full-bloods down the path to destruction. The Americans also used the Choctaw fears that the United States would make an illegal treaty with the Choctaws who lived in the West, who were not recognized as legitimate representatives of the huge majority of Choctaws who lived in the traditional homelands in the East.

When facing Choctaw resistance, the Americans threatened to make a "treaty" with the few Choctaws in the West that would cede the homelands of the East, without the consent or knowledge of the eastern Choctaws. Jackson thus made it clear to the Choctaws that he would stop at nothing to obtain their dispossession and exile. Jackson and the American agents painted a picture in the press and Congress of a Choctaw majority who *wanted* to move west but were restrained from doing so by the efforts of the intermarried whites and "mixed-bloods," who wanted to remain where they were because of their financial interests, of which, of course, the average Choctaw had none. An examination of the coalitions that developed and their leadership, along with the on-the-spot reports of Indian agents and others, clearly demonstrates that this argument was entirely false. "Full-bloods," "mixed-bloods," and intermarried whites among the Choctaws all wanted the same thing—to retain their homelands. They knew, however, that they would not be left in peace unless the U.S. government enforced its treaty obligations and forced the intruding white hordes out of the Choctaw national boundaries. The U.S. government under Jackson made it quite clear that it had absolutely no intention of even making a show of living up to its solemn treaty responsibilities. Jackson knew that as the whites overran the Choctaw Nation and were free to commit every imaginable crime and depredation upon the them without fear of law or justice, the Choctaws would finally "see reason" and realize that they were simply going to be forced out or killed, either by unofficial, lawless elements of the white population or by the acts of the U.S. government.

The United States also actively pursued the corruption and bribery of any Choctaw that could plausibly be termed a leader. The strange Greenwood LeFlore, an extremely wealthy, corrupted leader of the most unacculturated of the three districts of the Choctaw Nation, was routinely plied with bribes and promises of special treatment by the U.S. government. He surreptitiously traveled outside the Nation to Tennessee to meet with agents of the American government to make a deal to sell out the Choctaws in 1829. Jackson, of course, knew the native peoples, especially the Choctaws, well and he exploited their weaknesses with impunity.

Aside from the direct issue of dispossession and exile, the Choctaws also were forced to deal with an economy in shambles, thousands of white intruders, the corruption of influential men in the Nation, and threats from the U.S. national and state governments. The State of Mississippi passed laws to force the Choctaw Nation to dissolve and individual Choctaws to accept a second-class state citizenship in which they would be deprived of due process of law. The abuse of alcohol was epidemic, crops went unplanted, and ritual and ceremony fell apart. Within this mess, American agents, sent by the U.S. government, worked to undermine unity, to corrupt every leader, and to cause endemic paranoia and distrust, followed by threats and rumors of impending state militia and federal military action against the Choctaw people.

During these turbulent years, factions formed and dissolved, gained strength and died away. These factions fractured Choctaw unity, turning individuals and kinship groups against one another. Since each person simultaneously belonged to an assortment of interlocking relationships (for example, clan, church, town, moiety, and various societies), loyalties seemed to shift daily; positions were never firm.

Loyalties during this period were extremely complex and dynamic. Persons of mixed white and Choctaw heritage both favored and opposed "removal," as did "full-bloods." Their positions frequently changed. Traditionalists versus progressives, assimilationists versus conservatives, rich against poor—none of these factors correlate accurately or consistently with political positions or loyalties. There were far too many complex variables. Clan membership and kinship certainly influenced one's political position, but traditionally, Choctaw society allowed for a variety of individual choices, none of which would be viewed pejoratively. This democratic individualism was responsible in great part for the inability of the Nation to act in concert. Yet it was also a great strength, acting as the locus for the gestation of new ideas and adaptations, while simultaneously encompassing inherent conservative impulses that acted against change. Unfortunately, change and direct and indirect threats came at the Choctaws too rapidly for a coherent, unified position to be agreed upon. Another traditional behavior—deliberation—was under assault, and fell by the wayside in the wake of the changes forced upon the Nation in these years.

The Treaty of Dancing Rabbit Creek was procured with the rankest sort of dishonesty and foul play on the part of the U.S. government negotiators. It stands as a memorial to the everlasting disgrace of the United States. Many of the Americans involved—negotiators, Indian agents, interpreters, vendors, and others duplicitous and out to make money off the native peoples in their extreme distress—were officially enjoined to be dishonest and double dealing. They were congratulated when they procured the results wanted by the president, Andrew Jackson, and generally took glee in using deception and fraud to line their own pockets and fool the honest Indians out of their rightful land and property. It is so disgraceful a record that American historians have spent the last century and a half ignoring and concealing the truth. The actions of the U.S. government were so riddled with fraud, deception, and every possible chicanery that decent men who witnessed the affairs were horrified and disgusted at what they saw. One such man was George Strother Gaines, an honest man from a prominent family who moved in 1805 to what became the state of Alabama. He became an important merchant in Alabama, served as a state senator in 1825 and 1827, and was known as an honorable man. He also happened to be a friend of the Choctaw people. In 1830, he was present at the treaty grounds while the U.S. commissioners, John H. Eaton, who was also the secretary of war, and General John Coffee, negotiated with the Choctaws for what they called a "removal" treaty.

The commissioners expressly forbade any missionaries to be present on the treaty grounds, with the exception of one who was an active advocate of removal. Cyrus Byington and Cyrus Kingsbury were expressly forbidden from attending, since they were well-known friends of the Choctaws and actively sought justice for the Indian people. They vigorously protested their exclusion and begged the commissioners to allow them to be present to assist the Choctaws if the commissioners intended for the negotiations to be honest. The commissioners flatly refused their appeals. They did allow and even invited several whiskey vendors to be present, and used U.S. government funds to buy liquor that these men were to give "free" to every Choctaw. They then delayed the start of the negotiations, evidently to make sure that the Choctaws had several hours to kill in hopes that they would drink up.

Secretary of War Eaton began the negotiations by announcing to the assembled Choctaws and their chiefs that this conference was to obtain a removal treaty for the sale and cession of all Choctaw lands east of the Mississippi, and for the Choctaws' agreement to their own dispossession and exile. General Gaines reported that this announcement "acted as a bomb thrown among them. It filled them with surprise, astonishment, excitement, grief, and resentment. Not a single Choctaw favored the sale and cession of the lands of the tribe. It had not a solitary advocate among them."[1] The Choctaw chiefs engaged then in what they called a "'Round Robin,' denouncing and threatening death to any chief who should sign a treaty for the sale and cession of the lands of the tribe and for the removal of the tribe across the Mississippi River."[2] The Choctaw Nation was, in reality, a confederation. It was made up of three separate and distinct districts, each with a *mingo,* or chief, and a separate council of elders. The chief and councils governed the local affairs of only their district, and had no say in the governance of the other districts. There was no supreme chief over the three independent district chiefs. In times of war or other national threat, the three district chiefs met as a council, and jointly decided the course of the Nation.

Each of the three Choctaw chiefs spoke at length at the negotiations, firmly reiterating his and his warriors' complete opposition to any cession whatsoever and to removal in general. The chiefs also reminded the American negotiators of the fact that the Choctaws had never taken up arms against the Americans when the Choctaws had been stronger than they, and now that they were weakened and in need of their ally, the Americans, they called upon the United States to honor its treaty promises and allow the Choctaws to remain on their homelands in peace.

Secretary of War John H. Eaton rose and replied to the eloquent appeals to American fair play by saying that "the Choctaws had no choice in the matter, but were bound to sell their lands and remove to the other side of the Mississippi River. If they refused to enter into a treaty to this tenor and effect, the president, in twenty days, would march an army into their country—build forts in all parts of their hunting grounds, extend the authority and laws of the United States over the Choctaw territory, and appoint United States judges to try the Choctaws by the laws of the United States. Sheriffs and constables would also be appointed and sent among them . . . their lands would be seized on as the property of the enemy and the Choctaws would be forcibly removed across the Mississippi."[3]

In great dudgeon, the Choctaw chiefs and headmen refused to continue the negotiations, and Eaton told them all to go home. Eaton persuaded Greenwood LeFlore and a handful of his followers, and a few other Choctaws who had been bought by the U.S., and from these few he procured the "treaty." In the absence of the great majority of the Nation, who had been told the treaty negotiations were over, John H. Eaton, secretary of war of the United States, fraudulently obtained a few signatures of Choctaws who were not empowered or authorized to negotiate by the Choctaw National Council, declared the negotiations finished, and left the Choctaw Nation in a rush to deliver this document to Washington, D.C., for ratification by the U.S. Senate. A few weeks later in Washington, D.C., Eaton swore to the U.S. Senate that this treaty was fairly, honestly, and legally obtained, with the full knowledge and consent of all the leaders of the Choctaw Nation.[4]

In 1830, when U.S. agents procured the fraudulent Treaty of Dancing Rabbit Creek, the Choctaws were divided as never before. As the date for the exile drew near, many individuals were completely unable to determine their course of action. The United States had abrogated all of its solemn treaty obligations in its recent actions to dispossess the Choctaws, and now the People were called upon to believe that, in the future, after the penultimate land cession, the United States would abide by its promises and treaty obligations and honor its pledges.

As the dispossession began, groups formed under leaders who had opposed one another during the crisis years. Often kinship groups traveled together. It appears that most Choctaw kinship groups and families maintained their clan loyalties, but broader duties of the clan seemed to diminish. Many groups were incomplete because not everyone went West. Some were delayed in leaving or undecided as to whether they would leave the old Choctaw Nation at all. The sick and frail elderly were told to wait for special accommodations, which never materialized. Some three to four thousand Choctaw people refused to leave their homes.

Many of these tried to take advantage of Article 14 of the treaty, which supposedly gave each Choctaw "head of a family" the right to 640 acres of land and 320 acres additional for each unmarried child of his over ten years of age, and 160 acres for each child under ten. Each Choctaw had to register within six months of the ratification of the treaty with the U.S. Indian agent to the Choctaws, William Ward. The Choctaws who elected to stay had to become citizens of the state of Mississippi, and subject to the level of citizenship the state decided to assign them. Under the laws of Mississippi in 1830, that meant they would live with only a subset of rights—they could not testify in court against a white man, could not serve on a jury, could not vote, and could not sue in court. This, in essence, stripped the Choctaw of fundamental property rights. If a white man sued him, claiming he owed him money, or that the Choctaw had sold him his land, when the case went to court, the Choctaw could not testify. This left the Choctaws subject to the false claims of any white person. Even so, many Choctaws wanted to remain on their homeland. Historian Arthur DeRosier relates that William Ward was vehemently opposed to this article, and did everything in his power, which was considerable, to prevent any Choctaws from registering, even "pretending at times to be ill, and occasionally going into hiding."[5] One of the Choctaws gave this account of his efforts to prevent them from being able to register within the allotted time frame:

> In the month of January, 1831, being within six months after the ratification of said treaty, a large body of Choctaw Indians attended at a council house to have their names registered for the purpose of obtaining citizenship, and acquiring reservations according to the customs of the Indians. Unacquainted with the English language, they presented to the agent a number of sticks of various lengths, indicating how many were present, and the quantities of land to which they were severally entitled, but the agent threw down the sticks. Then they selected two or three head men to speak for them, and these head men by means of an interpreter, told the agent their number, ages, and names, and demanded registration; but the agent would not register them and told them that there were too many—that they must or should go beyond the Mississippi. Many of the Indians ignorantly despairing of the justice of the United States, have reluctantly removed beyond the Mississippi.[6]

Although Ward was later condemned by the several U.S. commissions that investigated the allegations of fraud and dishonesty in the implementation of the treaty, nothing was ever done to restore the lost rights of these Choctaw people. Ward was removed from his post in 1833, because too few Choctaws remained to necessitate the continuing presence of an Indian agent.[7] Around four thousand Choctaws did remain in Mississippi, but they were forced off their lands, were never given their allotted reserved acreages, and lived in dire poverty in the swampland and backwoods unwanted by white Americans.

Many of the Choctaws who left to go West died en route, and the kinship system of clans was severely disrupted. Many of the elders did not reach the West; they were the Nation's important leaders, recognized through clan responsibilities. With their absence, some of the clan functions went unobserved, and the chaos in which the Nation found itself rendered the social and cultural systems almost inoperative.

Settlement patterns in the West further undermined Choctaw social organization. In the old Nation in Mississippi, there were three districts, each with its own autonomous government headed by a district chief. Mushulatubbee was Mingo of the Six Towns (*Okla Hannali*). Apukshunnubbee was chief of *Hatak-holata*, which had as many as forty clans who lived around the Mother Mound, *Nanih Waiya*. The renowned Mingo Apushamatahahubbee (Pushmataha) headed the third district, which included four clans. In 1834, the Choctaw people gathered in the new western land near the present-day town of Tuskahoma, *Tushka Humma*, which they designated as the central location of the new Nation in the West. Under a large water oak tree, on the banks of the Kiamichi River, the Choctaws selected a site for the new Council House and named it *Nanih Waiya* in memory of the Mother Mound of their homelands. They attempted to organize their government by continuing the old tradition of three divisions, naming them after the three great leaders mentioned above. Mushulatubbee was elected chief of his namesake division, which comprised the area along the Arkansas and Canadian Rivers; Thomas LeFlore became chief of Apukshenubbee, or Red River District [Oklafalaya], which was bounded by Arkansas on the east, by the Kiamichi River on the west, and by the Red River on the South; and Nitakechi, nephew of Pushmataha, was selected as chief of the district named after his uncle, which was the southwestern district.[8]

The kinship groups did not make the transition to the West intact. Many people stopped when they arrived at government depots just inside the boundaries of the Choctaw Nation, too ill, tired, and disheartened to continue. They stayed near the depots to obtain the supplies and rations promised them under the Treaty of Dancing Rabbit Creek. The larger loyalties of clan members to certain towns were in disarray, since those towns no longer existed and could not be replicated. Therefore, the kinship system seems to have continued the tendency begun in the East. It contracted to cover smaller local units rather than governing the entire town.

Extended family groups continued to act together, but the authority of the elders and the coercive powers of the clans diminished and were gradually replaced in the West by new institutions. Thus, loyalties and factions formed on the bases of religion, class, and culture, weakening traditional clan loyalties.[9]

In the constitution of 1834, the Choctaws began to differentiate between their polity and kinship system. Where formerly the national council was made up of clan leaders from each of the three districts, the new constitution provided for the election of delegates from each district to form the national council. In many communities, despite the new forms, however, the clan leaders continued to be influential, and they often were elected as delegates. In many respects, therefore, these changes were not strongly felt by the people, and Choctaw political differentiation did not lead to any abrupt or dramatic changes. More than fifteen years later, in 1849, the three clans—*Ahepotukla, Olilefeia,* and *Oklahannali*—nominated girls for admission to Wheelock Academy, evidence of their continuing viability.[10]

Matrilineality continued to be a prominent feature of Choctaw life throughout the nineteenth century. Women enjoyed many rights and an autonomy unlike anything experienced by Euro-American women in the United States. Husbands and wives usually kept their property separate, and until late in the century, a strong tradition of matrilineal property continued. Since most traditional, unacculturated Choctaws lived quietly in their homes on small clearings, they had almost no contact with the market. They did not buy or sell houses or other improvements, so women's traditional ownership of the home continued until the 1900s. Matrilineal inheritance and lifeways persisted. Women also retained the right to live on their husband's property after divorce or desertion. In cases of abandonment of the wife by the husband, "his property was liable to be seized by the Lighthorsemen and appropriated to the benefit of the divorced wife." A wife never took her husband's name upon marriage. The children were "called by their mother's name" and "received all their national rights and privileges through her."[11]

Missionary John Edwards, lecturing about the Choctaws of the mid–nineteenth century, said that although the traditional law of exogamy was weakened since the young did not always know to which clan they belonged, "the nomenclature was still intact and in use among the majority of the Choctaw people" late in the nineteenth century. In keeping with his Euro-American ethnocentricity, he identified a "serious difficulty" in this matrilineal system: the father was "denied his proper place at the head of his family." Edwards noted that much of the matrilineal kinship organization still existed in 1880, despite all "Christian" efforts to suppress it. In fact, many aspects of matrilineality still held strong among the Choctaw people into the twentieth century. Women today among many Choctaw families occupy a position different from that of their white counterparts. It is quite common, for example, for families to have a decided matrilineal cast, with the activities and decisions of many families heavily influenced by their elder women. Many families display deference to the eldest female, who participates fully in making decisions for the extended family and whose advice and counsel carries decided weight. Gatherings and events are shaped and guided by the head women of the extended family.[12]

The duality basic to the Choctaw worldview provides a glimpse of why women of this Nation enjoyed greater esteem than those in other societies. Women's female power was a mysterious, fertile, ancient power going back into antiquity, beyond the consciousness of human beings. The feminine power of women balanced the power of men. In the Green Corn Ceremony, the most important ceremony of the year, the Choctaw people ritually purified themselves. The Green Corn Ceremony cleansed the fundamental categories in the Choctaw worldview, the most important of which was gender roles. The ball play and dances conducted in this ceremony laid emphasis on the sexual dichotomy between men and women, and the balance of powers.[13]

Horticulture provided one illustration of female power, but did not limit or contain that power. The mysterious power of women imbued all of nature. It was the power of life itself, including the creative powers of making life. The position of women and things feminine within the Choctaw worldview cannot be understood without an appreciation of the spiritual dimension upon which it was based. As long as a distinct Choctaw worldview remains, the mysterious life power of women and their place in the balance and harmony of this world will continue.

Most important Choctaw ceremonies centered on an agricultural motif, often emphasizing corn. The earth was fertile and feminine, as was the Bringer of the gift of corn from the Great Spirit—*Ohoyo Osh Chisba*. *Nanih Waiya,* the birthplace of the Choctaws, was the Mother Mound.[14]

Interwoven with matrilineality and kinship, the Choctaw language continued to reflect the relationships and social bonds of the Nation. Matrilineal kinship was not only reflected in the language but was inherent in the conceptual foundation from which the language derived.[15] Matrilineal kinship relations ordered and defined Choctaw society and identity. These relationships, woven into the very foundation of the language, were the essence of Choctaw being. For example, in Choctaw there are two forms of the first person personal possessive pronoun: *am-* and *sa-*. The *sa-* form is used to express possession of parts of the body, such as "my hand": *sabak;* "my hair": *sapansi.* The *am-* form expresses ownership of an object or property, such as "my dog,": *amofi;* "my house,": *akoka.* Aside from designating the parts of the body, the *sa-* form is also used in a manner that reflects the matrilineal kinship system. Look again at the use of the possessive pronoun *am-*, used when describing ownership of property:

/*amofi*/ = "my dog"
/*acoka*/ = "my house"

Am- is also used when indicating possession or nonmaternal kinship:

/*ahatak*/ = "my husband"
/*amani*/ = "my older brother"

In contrast, *sa-* indicates an intimate relationship—expressing possession of body parts:

/*sabak*/ = "my hand"
/*sapansi*/ = "my hair"

Sa- is also used to indicate *maternal* kinship:

/*sashki*/ = "my mother"
/*sapokni*/ = "my grandmother"[16]

Other evidence of the persistence of matrilineality in the Nation is plentiful. Much of this evidence simultaneously demonstrates that the independence and autonomy of Choctaw women continued throughout the nineteenth century. In fact, it appears that other than the gender inequality imposed whenever possible by the American government, Choctaw women remained freer and materially better off, and enjoyed much greater autonomy, than Euro-American women in the United States.

Women in traditional Choctaw society considered the home and field their domain. Men assisted with heavy labor in the fields, but did not regularly participate in the day-to-day cultivation of crops. In the traditional matrilineal, matrilocal Choctaw society, women "owned" the land, inheritance was through the mother, and children belonged to the mother's clan. Women thus retained their children, homes, and fields in the absence of or during separation from their husbands. Matrilocality dictated that extended female lineages live in close proximity to one another. Often sisters and their mother would live in the same house or cluster of houses in a compound. Women had access to power, not only through their traditional roles at the center of Choctaw society, but also in a number of other forums: they could choose to be warriors, they could engage in sports, and they could choose to become healers. Women of the same lineage pooled labor in fields and in the home. Maternal aunts were also called "mother" and fulfilled the nurturing and sustenance roles with their own children and their sisters' children alike. As noted, children derived their clan membership, and thus their basic Choctaw identity, through their mother's lineage. In the event of the death of a woman, her maternal kin—her clan—would assume care of the children, claiming them for the clan. This claim took precedence over that of the children's father, who belonged to a different clan from his biological children.

For example, in 1877, one of Peter Pitchlynn's daughters, Rhoda, died in childbirth. When her husband, a white man, married Rhoda, she had charge of the family farm. He lived on the farm with her and was supposed to pay a portion of the profits from the farm as rent to Pitchlynn (who resided in Washington, D.C., as the representative of the Choctaw Nation to the U.S. government.) Immediately after the birth of their second child, Rhoda bled to death. Another of Pitchlynn's daughters, Malvina, who lived many miles away, immediately left home upon hearing of the death of her sister and traveled to claim her sister's children. She eventually obtained the children and reared them as her own, and retrieved the farm from her sister's widower. Traditionally, the sisters of a woman who died would rear her children. Her clan would also claim all of her material possessions, including the land and any improvements. Since Malvina's mother was deceased, as the eldest sister she had a duty to act to claim the children and property from the widower. This she did. Malvina acted as a traditional Choctaw woman in discharging her responsibilities to her kin.[17]

Choctaw women figured prominently in exacting revenge for a death in the clan. The women most directly affected called for revenge. Choctaw women continued to assert this function in the West, calling for retribution and a death for a death. The clan-based kinship system appears to have contracted in kinship reckoning, but extended families still played a major role when a death or similar crisis arose. In 1857, when a black slave murdered one Pitchlynn daughter's husband, all the males of the extended family rushed to her assistance. According to some sources, the widow directed the men to apprehend Prince, the slave whom she suspected. Upon Prince's confession and implication of others, she insisted that they burn the offenders to death, which they did.[18] The widow, a woman of mixed Choctaw and white heritage, continued the traditional role of the aggrieved in deciding the punishment or retribution extracted from the perpetrator of the death. Despite the fact that this woman had been educated by whites and was a member of a Christian church, she was evidently not deterred in her demands for justice, Choctaw style.

Matrilineal ties remained strong even as the clan-based kinship system decreased as the central feature of Choctaw society. Mothers, a mother's eldest brother, siblings, maternal aunts, and grandmothers formed one's closest relations. In the transition from the old lands to the new, however, kinship also underwent transition. Fathers became more responsible for the upbringing of their children, and maternal uncles became less of an authority figure. Households became geographically dispersed and separated from extended kinship groups. Maternal uncles continued to wield important influence with their nieces and nephews, however. They continued to be responsible for their education and were instrumental in deciding where they would attend school and making the arrangements for them to do so. For example, even the bicultural Peter Pitchlynn continued to be responsible for his maternal nieces and nephews throughout his life. He selected schools for them and was consulted whenever major decisions arose regarding their prospects. Over the period from 1830 through 1881, Pitchlynn's maternal kin made demands of him that reflected his role as mother's eldest brother to the younger generations.[19]

Choctaws began to consider generational differences relative to reckoning the degree of kinship sometime during the middle of the nineteenth century. Yet even as some characteristics of the kinship system changed, others remained fairly constant. The clans did not vanish overnight, and evidence of matrilineality persisted.[20]

A special relationship existed between maternal kin. In 1859, when two of the Pitchlynn sons were standing trial for the murder of a white man, their maternal uncles, their sisters, and their maternal aunts, not their father, came to their aid and comfort.[21] Likewise, Pitchlynn's maternal nephews and nieces enjoyed his special attentions and influence, and called on him for assistance with impunity. When Pitchlynn's maternal kin moved West, they settled in a compound with Pitchlynn and interacted with the Pitchlynns on a daily basis. Peter Pitchlynn treated his mother with far more tenderness and concern in his letters than he did his children. Because she was the eldest woman of his clan, not only did Peter owe her a son's devotion, as was common in white society, but it was also his duty to care for her before the needs of his children, as was traditional in the Choctaw culture.[22]

Relationships to other Choctaws; to other native people; to whites; to animals, plants, and inanimate objects; and to spirits and unseen beings, were all defined and regulated by relationships reflected by the language. Relationships both defined and were defined by kinship terms. Entire distinct sets of social regulations and behavior were readily summoned by the kinship terms. Where there was choice, anticipated relationships were forecast. For example, if one met a stranger, a Choctaw whom one did not know, one usually used the term *itibapishbi* (sibling, brother, sister) until one could determine a more precise kinship.[23]

The Choctaw language indicates that social relationships are central to Choctaw culture. Kinship terms are employed to show both relationship and degree of relationship. Choctaw kinship terms clearly reflect the matrilineal kinship system and the special, close bonds of maternal kin. Close relationships were with those who belonged to one's clan. For example, special terms denoted the eldest maternal uncle and maternal niece and nephew. "Mother" was *ishki,* as were all of her sisters. These close relationships included socially proscribed patterns of behavior. The people of the father's clan (which, of course, was not that of the mother or children) were treated with careful respect and with formality. They were careful not to offend the clan of the father, since the clan kinship system regulated behavior through these carefully devised kinship relations. With members of one's own clan, one could not only be more familiar but also informal. One could "joke" with one's brothers and sisters, but this behavior was proscribed with one's paternal uncles, for example. One could ask special favors of one's maternal uncle and other maternal relatives, because the nature of these relationships was close. Paternal relatives were not close. One did not impose on relationships with members of another clan.[24]

After the exile, the clans slowly began to fade as the locus of power in Choctaw society, primarily because the social organization had been physically and materially disrupted by the move from the East. In its stead, the extended family rose in importance. However, maternal relations continued to be very strong, important, and emphasized. Maternal kin made their residences close by one another, sometimes in clusters on one piece of land. The practice of living in a compound with other close kin originated in the East and was transplanted to the new Choctaw Nation in the West. Kinship reckoning through the maternal line, although weakened, remained a viable and recognizable distinction of Choctaw society.[25]

Gradually, Protestant churches began to take over some functions formerly provided by the clans. As their membership increased, churches easily assumed the societal function of group regulation of social and moral behavior. In addition, all Protestant denominations provided the recognition of "elders" in positions of prominence, similar to the place elders occupied in traditional Choctaw society. Church "camp meetings" began to replace some of the traditional gatherings for ceremonies, providing continuity in the gathering together of the people, with a prescribed, loose format. Singing and feasting formed central elements of these meetings, which took place out of doors, usually in wooded areas, where hundreds of Choctaws camped for several days. Traditional stories were told over the campfire; young people flirted and eyed one another; women cooked together, sharing childcare and laughter. Men discussed crops, hunting, and recent weather, and shared information about kin and neighbors. In many respects, the Choctaws molded their Christian churches in ways that gave the people a sense of continuity with the past. Hymns were sung in Choctaw, frequently the religious leader was Choctaw, and the forms of the institution paralleled or closely resembled traditional Choctaw social institutions, especially those of the clans and towns. Thus, even within new forms, important elements of Choctaw culture persisted. Although Choctaw society evolved, it still carried on as distinctly Choctaw.[26]

The vast majority of Choctaw people, however, did not belong to Christian churches. For these people, the clans continued and functioned into mid-century and beyond. Exogamy (marriage outside one's kinship group or clan) continued to be practiced. Maternal uncles and mothers continued to be consulted about marriages, although fathers exerted far more interest than in pre-dispossession days. The separation of households contributed enormously to the evolution of the role of fathers. Yet, although fathers began to assert more interest in their children after the move West, the children continued to be reared primarily by the mother, and in the case of her death almost always were reared by the mother's sisters or other maternal female relatives. Men's roles as authority figures to their sisters' children gradually diminished, but neither did they occupy the same functions as white fathers in a paternal society. Particularly in the 1850s, the wild, undisciplined young Choctaw men caused enormous problems, resulting in near anarchy and almost uncontrolled violence. Murders and deaths occurred with great frequency, confirming the diminution of the roles of maternal uncles, while simultaneously demonstrating the lack of control by fathers. It appears that Choctaw men did not assume the mantle of disciplinarian and authoritarian figure with their own children, as in Euro-American society, but rather their role in this function simply diminished in relation to their sisters' children because of the new patterns of more isolated homesteads and fewer large, extended groupings of matrilocal kinship.[27]

Many Choctaws attended schools like this one, which was built in 1877 in Skullyville, Choctaw Nation. Courtesy of the Research Division of the Oklahoma Historical Society, 241.1.

Samuel Garland, chief of the Choctaw Nation, 1862–64. Photo taken in 1865 in Washington, D.C. Courtesy of the Research Division of the Oklahoma Historical Society, 767.

Colonel George Harkins, circa 1870, was
the nephew of Greenwood LeFlore. Photo
taken by C. M. Bell of Washington, D.C.
Courtesy of the Research Division of the
Oklahoma Historical Society, 811.

Judge James Thompson, a
wealthy white man, with his
Choctaw wife and child.
Courtesy of the Research
Division of the Oklahoma
Historical Society, 915.

Sampson Folsom, the son of
David Folsom. Courtesy of the
Research Division of the Oklahoma
Historical Society, 1429.

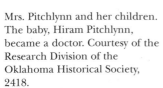

Mrs. Pitchlynn and her children.
The baby, Hiram Pitchlynn,
became a doctor. Courtesy of the
Research Division of the
Oklahoma Historical Society,
2418.

A Choctaw mother and child, circa 1870. Courtesy of the Research Division of the Oklahoma Historical Society, 2431.109.

Choctaw Lighthorsemen, the law enforcement of the Choctaw Nation. Courtesy of the Research Division of the Oklahoma Historical society, 2641.

A Choctaw grave house. Courtesy of the Research Division of the Oklahoma Historical Society, Barde Collection, 4961.

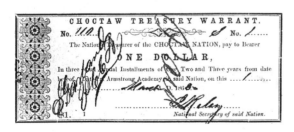

A Choctaw treasury warrant issued soon after the end of the Civil War. Courtesy of the Research Division of the Oklahoma Historical Society, 9249B.

A black Choctaw family and their home. Courtesy of the Research Division of the Oklahoma Historical Society, 8062.

Robert M. Jones and his wife, Susan Colbert, circa 1860. Jones was the wealthiest man in the Choctaw Nation and had thousands of acres of cotton planted along the Red River. Courtesy of the Research Division of the Oklahoma Historical Society, 11397.

The home of Thomas LeFlore, twice chief of the Choctaw Nation, was built in 1831. Courtesy of the Research Division of the Oklahoma Historical Society, 11553.

Peter P. Pitchlynn, chief from 1864–66. Courtesy of the Research Division of the Oklahoma Historical Society, 14223.

Typical Choctaw boy on a pony, circa 1875. Courtesy of the Research Division of the Oklahoma Historical Society, 15896.

Courthouse grounds in Eagle County, Choctaw Nation. At the base of the huge tree, Choctaw justice was meted out. Courtesy of the Research Division of the Oklahoma Historical Society, 19479.2.

6 A New Life in the Land of Death: Decade of Despair

ARRIVING IN THEIR NEW LANDS, THE CHOCTAW PEOPLE BEGAN TO build a new life. They had little choice but to put the horrors of their dispossession behind them. Despite the misfortunes and trauma of the past decade, the children still got hungry, crops and animals still had to be tended, water still had to be drawn—life had to go on. For some, anger and bitterness persisted. Others were in shock; their lives, their families, their loved ones—everything had been disrupted. As the Choctaw people began to build a new life, they re-examined their responses and adaptations to the crushing external forces that had forced them out of their eastern homelands. Even though they faced incredible losses—the land of Nanih Waiya, the deaths of thousands of kinsmen—still the Choctaw people survived. The unique Choctaw culture persisted. Despite all the chaos of the years of betrayal and injustice, the Choctaws did not vanish. Instead, they recovered and fought to survive, building meaningful lives in the new land. Supported by a remarkably resilient culture, Choctaw people adjusted to their new circumstances, reshaped identity, and reformulated kinship while maintaining language, values, and beliefs that set them apart as a distinct people.

The Choctaws' survival centered upon their ability to reform their society to accommodate necessary change, while simultaneously maintaining a cultural framework that set them apart, gave them comfort, and provided a permanent foundation on which to build. In the face of so much change, people needed an anchor to give them comfort and a sense of continuity in an era of intense instability. Choctaw people looked inward to traditional sources of power and understanding. They found succor and comfort in using the Choctaw language, in tradition, in spiritual beliefs, and in relationships with kinfolk and friends.

In the 1830s, many of the Choctaw people rejected all things that they perceived to be of white origin. This blanket rejection replaced the pre-dispossession impetus to appear to accommodate white demands for their assimilation ("progress"). Now that they had lost the battle to remain in their homelands, many Choctaws not only rejected white culture, they consciously returned to ancient traditions.

As they arrived in the new Choctaw Nation in Indian Territory, the Choctaws formed three districts that replicated those in the East. Each district had a Head Chief, or *mingo,* and subordinate *mingos* and captains. The districts traditionally acted in unison, and this centralization continued gradually over the nineteenth century until the nation adopted a new constitution in the 1850s in which the people elected a Principle Chief over all. After the dispossession, the three districts formed around the three Head Chiefs: Nitakechi, *mingo* of the Pushmataha District, Thomas LeFlore of the Apukshunnubbee District, and Mushulatubbee of the Moshulatubbee District. The latter district was headed by the old chief was the most conservative and traditional, flatly rejecting any overtures from the Christian mission activists who wanted to proseletyze among the Indians. Sadly, Mushulatubbee died during the horrendous smallpox pandemic that struck the Native peoples west of the Mississippi in 1838.

Before they were exiled from their homelands in 1830, Choctaw leaders petitioned the U.S. Government, asking them to keep the Christian missionaries from going with them to the new lands in the West. Mushulatubbee was especially bitter against the agents of white religion, and blamed many of them for their role in the dispossession. Mushulatubbee wrote that "we were promised [during negotiations for the Treaty of Dancing Rabbit Creek] . . . that the missionaries should not receive any more of our money. Neither do we wish for any of the present missionaries to go with us beyond the Mississippi; and Doctor Talley, who has already settled on our land, may be ordered out."[1]

Many Choctaws resented the condescending attitudes of all whites, but particularly the missionaries. Choctaw leaders complained to

President Andrew Jackson and Congress that money paid to the mission-ary groups who ran the schools in the east was "thrown away." Mushulatubbee and others charged that in return for the money taken out of Choctaw funds to pay for these schools, the Choctaw Nation had "never Recd. a Scholar out of their Schools that was able to keep a grog shop Book."[2]

Reverend John M. Steele, a Presbyterian missionary who tried to open a school in Mushulatubbee District, was completely rebuffed by the Choctaws. He complained to his superiors in Boston that in the entire Mushulatubbe District, "there were no Christians." He tried to start a school, but no one came. Those people who came to his church, he described as "mixed and mongrel." These attitudes were shared by other missionaries. One related that the Indians learned "what Sunday means; they now wash and comb themselves and put on clean clothes once a week."[3]

Choctaw historian Clara Sue Kidwell notes that the Christian mission-aries failed throughout the nation to convert many Choctaws. Instead, their churches were attended and supported by the black slaves of the more acculturated Choctaws. By and large, most Choctaws retained their traditional beliefs and resisted Christianity although they embraced liter-acy. The latter they recognized as empowering, and they were anxious for future generations of Choctaws to be better able to deal with the world market and other intrusions of the dominant white culture.

After their arrival in the West, the Choctaws continued to reassert Choctaw traditional ways, rejecting not only Christianity, but working to replace the mission schools with schools run by the Nation, taught in Choctaw, with a curriculum determined by the Tribal Council. Missionary Cyrus Kingsbury reported in 1839 that the removal had had a very harm-ful effect on their efforts to convert the Choctaws to Christianity. "Prejudice against white people was so bad that many could not even be approached on the subject of religion or education. A number of former converts were "totally adverse to instruction of any kind." They wanted control of their schools, and sought to have the Choctaw Academy in Kentucky closed and instruction brought into the Choctaw Nation, where the curriculum could be controlled by the Nation.[4]

In the Mushulatubbee District, there were no Christian churches because of lack of support from the Choctaws, and only one small mission

school. One missionary, the Reverend John M. Steele, who tried to pros-
elytize and open a church and school, was completely rebuffed. He
reported that in the entire Mushulatubbee District there were no
Christians. He tried to start a school, and no pupils came. He wrote that
the people who came to his church were "mixed and mongrel." [5] With
such sentiments informing his perspective, perhaps it is no wonder that
the Choctaws soundly rejected him and his message. These condescending attitudes were shared by many of the missionaries. One celebrated
that the Indians had learned "what Sunday means; they now wash and
comb themselves and put on clean clothes once a week."[6]

The Choctaws sought control over their education system almost
from its beginnings in the 1820s. By the mid-1830s, Choctaws began to
demand control over the curriculum and procedures at their schools,
turning away from the missionaries who were empowered by the United
States to "educate" the natives. The Choctaw people resented many
aspects of the missionaries' educational system. Choctaw parents thought
the students spent too much time working in the fields and performing
other labor for the missionaries, to the neglect of academic studies. They
also resented the condescending attitude displayed toward their culture
and belief systems. In many instances, the missionaries took every opportunity to humble and humiliate the Choctaws as the price of "education."
Nevertheless, Choctaws stubbornly refused to see the white culture as
"superior," and thus continued in their traditional way of life.[7]

By the winter of 1836, the Choctaw Council had built and opened
five schools, in which more than one hundred Choctaw children were
housed. Money for schools was promised by the United States in the
Treaty of Dancing Rabbit Creek, and the Choctaws quickly put the money
to good use. The National Council built an additional school in each governmental district with the annuity money from the treaty. The Choctaws
were determined to take over their children's education, and many of the
National schools thrived. The National Council contracted missionaries
to run the schools, but retained control over the tenure of the missionaries. In 1842, the Choctaws established a comprehensive system of schools
for the entire nation. Many Choctaw parents casually and frequently visited the schools, encouraging the young people to learn. Choctaws valued
the ability to read and write in the hope that their children would be better able to deal with the whites.

Differences in cultural traditions continued to cause problems between the Choctaws and their white instructors. The gender bias of the U.S. culture rankled the Choctaw people. The Choctaw Academy only accepted males, whose education was paid for by Choctaw Nation general funds. On several occasions, Choctaw leaders demanded that girls not be excluded from receiving an education, despite the proclivities and directions of the missionaries. The Choctaws were anxious that their girls should receive their fair share of education, apparently continuing to recognize the equal and complementary gender roles of traditional Choctaw culture. Within the first decade of residence in the West, the Choctaw General Council established schools for girls. Girls' academies, as well as those for boys, flourished in the new Nation. One National Council member expressed the sentiments of the majority of Choctaw people when he asserted that the school fund "belongs to the girls just as much as the boys."[8] For most Choctaws, it took years of exposure to Euro-American culture for them to assimilate the profound gender bias that typified white society. The predominant belief among Choctaws continued to emphasize gender relations that viewed males and females as different but equal. The Choctaws to this day traditionally view women as powerful life-givers, independent and self-reliant.[9]

Before their dispossession, Choctaw women were in charge of cultivating plants and controlling the communal fields and many individually worked fields, seen as part of the nurturing power demonstrated in their ability to 'create' life. Choctaw gender roles were severely disrupted by the Armstrong Roll, a census taken by the U.S. Government to organize Choctaw dispossession. In this roll, the U.S. agents listed each household as headed by a male. Women were listed as dependents, as was the norm among Americans of European descent. However, the traditional Choctaw matrilineal kinship collided fully with the patriarchal assumptions of the whites. Choctaw clans, organized matrilineally, controlled the communal lands. The senior woman of an extended family took her authority from the Choctaw matrilineal kinship system, and in effect, was the "owner" of her house and fields. In imposing a completely different order that ignored the tribal power and authority of women, the Americans dealt the traditional Choctaw matrilineal kinship system a terrible blow. "Improvement" claims were thus listed as belonging to the senior male of each family, who had no responsibility under the traditional system, and little or no experience in asserting power or control over the house and other material wealth of the kinship group. Not only were Choctaw men, then, inexperienced and uncertain in dealing with the U.S. representatives and individual whites who were trying to divest them of all they had, now the Americans imposed another level of confusion and chaos among Choctaw families. Men did not welcome or understand their role, but were forced by the Americans to assume it. Payment for improvements, and all other forms of annuities, including supplies for the exile to the west, were ordered around the patriarchal system imposed by the U.S. Government. The more traditional Choctaws were thus rendered even more susceptible to fraudulent activities and outright theft by avaricious whites, who took advantage of the many naïve men who were suddenly empowered to make decisions about land, improvements, and other "property" by the foreign American system.

Despite numerous protests by the Choctaws (and later, the other matrilineal nations of the southeast), the Americans insisted on imposing their alien kinship system on the Choctaws. From the Armstrong Roll, the United States listed the claims of each man and the land and improvements he "owned" in order to figure compensation in terms of land allowed in the West. Only men were allowed to make these claims, with the exception of widows who had no grown men within their household.

The women had always controlled the land and improvements in the Choctaw Nation and other matrilineal nations. This kinship system formed the bedrock of Choctaw identity and culture. By deliberately imposing an alien form of kinship with which the Choctaws and others were forced to comply in order to secure any claim to the communal land holdings, the Americans succeeded in dealing a deathblow to the traditional organization of Choctaw society and culture. Removing this most important aspect of power from their control destroyed the clans and led to severe cultural dislocations in the decades following dispossession. Later, in the West, rations were dispensed according to male heads of households. The Choctaws again were forced to comply with the American imposition of gender inequity and its attendant long-term cultural disruption.

Over the following decades, from the 1830s until the U.S. Civil War, the power and presence of the clans slowly but surely declined, and this had enormous negative consequences. By subjugating women, Euro-Americans and their market system marginalized females, making them subject to all manner of suffering and economic dependence. Americans saw their system as "civilized." Yet, instead of suffering women and children to starve when their male providers died or deserted them, native women in the matrilineal kinship system rarely had such disasters. The clans took care of their needs. Women controlled their areas of power—the growing of crops and the attendant fields, farming, and trading that accompanied this. When the matrilineal clans lessened in importance, the power of women declined, although many Choctaw women continued (and continue still) to assert themselves as equals and powerful human beings.

With the imposition of patriarchal norms on southeastern peoples, the unwritten laws of behavior, the mechanisms triggering imposition of punishment for breaking societal mores, and the clarity and recognition of gender roles and distinctions were increasingly undermined. This led to a whole host of problems assailing the Choctaws while they were trying to rebuild their Nation. As women lost control of the communal lands, more women and children became dependent on men who had to at least appear to the Americans who doled out rations to be the acknowledged leader of the family. Young people respected women less as their traditional arenas of power contracted. One of the most serious problems resulting from this phenomenon was the unbelievable increase in violence in the Nation. As the traditional clan powers waned, the societal ability to regulate behavior plunged. Through cultural imperialism, the U.S. actions destroyed distinct yet complimentary Choctaw gender roles, and with their demise the very foundation of Choctaw culture was severely weakened. The U.S. imposition of alien beliefs and values on the Choctaws threw their society into disharmony and imbalance, creating a chaos that resulted in tremendous violence, criminality, and death among the Choctaw people in the late 1840s and 1850s.

In an effort to save their traditional culture, Choctaw leaders acted decisively to take over the education of their young. They allocated a portion of the proceeds from land cessions to the United States to establishing and maintaining neighborhood schools for Choctaw children. The U.S. government and the president's appointees controlled these resources, however. After 1830, many Choctaws felt that the school funds were being used to enrich the white men who controlled the money, rather than to provide an education for the Choctaw youth.

The school established by Richard Johnson in Kentucky in the fall of 1825 under the patronage of the Baptist general convention was a particular target. Founded as a boarding school for Choctaw children and other primarily southeastern native children, the school was named the Choctaw Academy.[10] Children were nominated by white missionaries teaching in the Choctaw Nation and were sent to the academy for a few months or years. Many of the traditionalists refused to send their children off to board at such a distance. The majority of participants in these schools were the offspring and matrilineal kin of Choctaw leaders. During the 1830s, the Kentucky academy came under increasing criticism partly as a result of the resurgence of anti-white, anti-Christian sentiments among the Choctaw people.[11]

The Choctaw Council sent Peter Pitchlynn, the nephew of traditionalist chief Mushulatubbee, to Kentucky to investigate the complaints of Choctaw students at the Academy in 1840. The Choctaw students complained to him that they had too little "meat on the table" and they did without "anything that is necessary about the table such as cups, knives, forks, and coffee pot."[12] Many of these students were the children of intermarried whites or their descendents, accustomed to the social niceties of white society. They were humiliated and indignant at being deprived of what they saw as the basic equipment for polite society.

During this time frame, many Choctaws, especially those with some education, became acutely aware of the racial bigotry of Euro-Americans and became defensive and angry that despite their ability to conduct themselves as "civilized" persons, they continued to be scorned by whites and treated as innately inferior. This shift in their response to Euro-American expectations and results reflects the increasing influence and prominence of a system of racial hierarchy rapidly gaining sway among white Americans. Later in 1841, the Choctaw General Council decided to close the Kentucky school and to relocate it within the lands of the Choctaw Nation.[13] During these years many of the so-called mixed-bloods began to change their attitudes about trying to be a part of the white society that rejected them and their offspring. Choctaws and Cherokees, especially, were appalled at the bigotry encountered by their young when they attended white schools outside the Nation. John Ross, chief of the Cherokee Nation, was so disgusted that he withdrew his son from his stateside school and enrolled him in a school in the Choctaw Nation.

Many others withdrew their children from stateside boarding schools and brought them home to attend native-run schools in the Indian nations.

In the late 1830s and 1840s the Choctaw Nation established new institutions that began to differentiate the clan system from the Choctaw polity. Yet clearly these changes were molded to conform to Choctaw traditions. The Choctaw people adopted a new constitution in 1834, a document that was forced upon them by the threat that if they did not so act, the U.S. government would "assume management of Choctaw national business." Under the new constitution, legitimate coercive force was centralized in a national government, and the Choctaws accepted a minimum of political and social (kinship) differentiation. However, the traditional organization of three autonomous districts, each presided over by a chief, persisted and was minimally affected by this formal change.[14] In addition, sociologist Duane Champagne informs us, "Choctaw court procedures and legal norms . . . continued to conform to the rules that governed kinship groups." Although they appeared to U.S. government leaders to conform and "progress" in assimilating white Christian practices, in effect, the Choctaws retained their traditional forms while appeasing white demands through the appearance of "progress."[15]

In 1838, necessitated by their decision to allow the Chickasaw people to settle on land ceded to the Choctaw Nation, the Choctaws adopted another new constitution. This document established a fourth district for the Chickasaw people and established a supreme court. Although the institutionalization of a court system divested the kinship system of some traditional functions, other traditions were reaffirmed within the new constitution. For example, the new legal code reaffirmed the system of communal ownership of land, resoundingly rejecting once again the demand of the American government for the allocation of land in severalty, a demand that would continue to be almost unanimously rejected throughout the nineteenth century. The fundamental framework of the traditional Choctaw community was thus preserved and strengthened. Despite the efforts of the U.S. government to force the Choctaw Nation to alter its traditional form of government, the Choctaws consistently resisted centralization of legal authority and differentiation between the polity and kinship system.[16] Despite further changes to the constitution in 1842 and 1850, strong autonomous local and district governments continued to be retained.[17]

The 1830s were tremendously difficult for the Choctaw people. The Choctaw Nation tried to recover from the disaster of its dispossession, but this was merely the first in a series of disasters that struck the Choctaws in the West. At first, some appeared to be recovering reasonably quickly from the dispossession. By 1833, several hundred families had settled on the banks of the Arkansas River and had planted crops in order to supply corn for the emigrants who were en route to the Nation. The U.S. government had located two of the three provisioning depots on the Arkansas River—one at Pheasant Bluff, five miles below the mouth of the Canadian River on the Arkansas, and one near the Choctaw Agency on the Arkansas. Many Choctaws settled at least temporarily within reach of the provisioning depots, from which they were to draw their first year's rations, as agreed in the Treaty of Dancing Rabbit Creek.

However, all of their hard work went for naught. The first week in June 1833, the Arkansas River overflowed its banks in one of the greatest floods in its history. The flood washed away the government corncribs and all buildings and houses built near the river, according to the U.S. agent. The storehouses would also have been lost, but instead stood "in water to the eaves and would have been swept away but for 6,000 pounds of iron and a quantity of arms that weighted it down." The gent reported that the "high water mark would be visible for years," and that the Indians "would have to hunt for the places where their houses had stood." He continued, "Nearly all the people who lived upon the river have been ruined. . . . On the bottoms near several of the creeks every house has been washed away. . . . All the Fork of the Canadian was inundated." [18] Elsewhere, the almost incessant spring rain caused excessively high waters on almost all of the rivers of the Choctaw Nation. The U.S. agent could not reach these places for many days, and many families went hungry and almost starved, waiting for relief from the U.S. government. Refugees wandered the area in shock, searching for sustenance and shelter.

Terrible sickness followed the floods. Carcasses of dead animals killed in the floods lined the riverbanks and floated in the waters. Many Choctaws sickened and died. Agent Armstrong reported that "within the hearing of a gun from this spot," [the Choctaw Agency] one hundred Choctaws had died within five weeks. "The mortality among these people since the beginning of fall as far as ascertained, amounts to one-fifth of the whole number." The remaining Choctaws began to starve. The government rations had expired, and their newly planted crops had been destroyed.[19] They begged for food from the U.S. agent, who referred them to Lieutenant Rains of the United States Army, the provisioning officer for Fort Gibson. He was "happy to inform General Gibson" in April 1833 that the Choctaws "had been obliged to accept fifty barrels of his bad pork," which had putrefied and spoiled. Although the Choctaws had refused to accept these provisions prior to the flood, Lt. Rains noted correctly that since they were now reduced to starvation, "they would doubtless be glad to get it."[20] Agent Armstrong wrote in February 1834, asking the military to lend the Choctaws five hundred bushels of corn, because "The situation of these people is worse than I really thought when I saw you. . . . The women and children . . . have been from 4 to 6 days without anything to eat; *anything*."[21]

On 13 November 1833, an extraordinary celestial phenomenon occurred that profoundly frightened the Choctaws and the other native people living in Indian Territory. Shooting stars lit up the sky in an incredible meteoric display unlike any in memory. Called "the Winter that the stars fell," by the Kiowa people, it lighted the night sky as bright as day, "with myriads of meteors darting about in the sky." The Choctaws, as did all native people, watched the night sky and were accustomed to the regular rhythms and movements of the stars and constellations. Traditional peoples took great comfort in the regular and predictable nature of the celestial bodies. Many stories and oral traditions centered on stars and planets, providing all Choctaws with knowledge of their society's cultural and spiritual beliefs. They believed that the Great Spirit "communicated his will to man in dreams, in thunder and lightning, eclipses, meteors, comets, in all the prodigies of nature, and the thousands of unexpected incidents that occur to man."[22] This meteor shower was considered an omen of disaster. Added to the trauma of dispossession, the exile, the deaths of so many kin, and the floods that had wiped out all of their labor, the meteor shower was seen as a message from the Great Spirit and was regarded with great fear and dread. Since the world and all within it were intimately connected, this great and unusual event portended a message of doom. Many Choctaws believed that these events had resulted from their abandonment of their sacred obligations to the spirits of their dead in leaving the ancestral homelands. From the moment they left the old Choctaw Nation, death had dogged their footsteps. Thousands died on the road to the West, hundreds more died monthly in the new Nation. Clearly, the Choctaw world was out of balance, and for this, many believed the old prophecy that the Nation, and all of its people, would die.[23]

Hundreds of Choctaws returned to the old Nation in the East that year, calling the western lands the "Land of Death." Disease, famine, floods, the nighttime turned to day, and death, death everywhere—were these the beginnings of the disasters promised by the prophets if the Choctaws ever left *Nanih Waiya?* Was this the death of the Nation?[24]

In addition to disease resulting from contaminated water after the great flood of 1833, other illnesses plagued the people, causing a great many deaths and widespread illness. Malaria, assorted fevers, cholera, measles, and whooping cough repeatedly struck the population, killing many Choctaws in the decade after their move to the West. Those who had settled on the Red River plains suffered almost continuously from fevers and ague; chills and "bilious remittent fevers" and "intermittent fevers" killed hundreds. One missionary estimated that one in five died; another estimated one in fifteen.[25] More than four hundred Choctaws who had made their homes on the banks of the Red River died. Many called it the "stream of death."[26] The settlements along the rivers throughout the Nation quickly earned a reputation for being very unhealthy.[27] One of the missionaries at Bethabara mission reported that, "In this country of four or five hundred souls not one child under a year old is left."[28]

Whooping cough was a disease that afflicted and killed children disproportionately. In one densely settled area, a woman reported that, "in this neighborhood most all the small children has died with the hooping [*sic*] cough." When the whooping cough came, it raced through the unprotected population, killing many of its youngest victims. Mothers watched helplessly as the fever and cough attacked their babies. Days would pass, with the child slowly dying. Toward the end, babies became so weak they were unable to suckle, and would lie there, waiting to die. Friends, neighbors, and kin avoided the victims, afraid they would carry whooping cough home.[29]

The ultimate disaster struck between 1836 and 1840: a massive smallpox pandemic afflicting native peoples throughout the West. It killed over ten thousand native people in the Northern Plains alone. Entire Nations were wiped out in a matter of weeks.[30] News of the epidemic reached the Choctaw Nation when French traders came south, reporting the horror and devastation of the Mandan Nation, among others. A prominent Missouri River people, the Mandans, who at one time numbered eight thousand, were reduced to a few dozen survivors. Terror spread throughout the Choctaw Nation, as people hunkered down, awaiting the end. The horror finally passed, taking more than seven hundred Choctaw, including the renowned Mingo Mushulatubbee, who, as district chief, was one of the most important people in the Nation.[31]

Many Choctaws believed the prophecies were coming true. Disaster followed disaster. Death and disease swept the Nation. The people were starving; the hunters could find no food. Just as the Bookbearer had admonished them at *Nanih Waiya* in the old Nation, "I give you these hunting grounds for your home. When you leave them you die."[32] Historian Grant Foreman recorded how the "unhappiness and discontent over their removal, bitter factional and political feuds and jealousies growing out of the treaty" and their "inability so soon to readjust themselves to their new environment" had resulted in no "provision for the future when the year's allowance of rations had expired." The physical and material plight of the Choctaws was apparent to Agent Armstrong, but the despair occasioned by knowledge of the Choctaw traditions—and their conviction that they would be punished for abandoning the dead and leaving their homeland—apparently eluded him. To avoid starvation, the Choctaws begged food and parted with every material item of any value to procure sustenance. White traders and merchants took advantage of their plight by inflating the cost of provisions to six times their normal cost. In order to survive some Choctaw people ate the carcasses of animals killed in the floods.[33]

In many respects, the decade of the 1830s was the nadir for the Choctaw people. Their dispossession and permanent exile accomplished, with disaster upon disaster following in their new lands, many Choctaws saw little hope for the future. In addition to the tremendous number of deaths, the Choctaws' social institutions were in disarray and were thus unable to provide the structure and foundation upon which the comfort and security of the Nation relied. Nevertheless, the Choctaw people found the strength to go on. The cultural and spiritual turmoil that resulted from their dispossession waned as the Choctaws began to build a new life in their new lands.

7 Making Death Literal

DURING THE PERIOD BEFORE THE CIVIL WAR, THE CHOCTAW PEO-
ple were assailed by new forms of old, familiar problems. Three
major issues emerged to threaten their future existence. These
issues were interrelated, and derived from their subjugation by the
United States, and the Americans' efforts to increase their hegemony.
First, the whole nation seemed to be erupting into a state of anarchy.
Serious crimes occurred daily, and "who was killed this week" became an
almost daily topic of conversation.[1]

Second, conflict escalated with American encroachments on Choctaw
legal jurisdiction. This concern was, in actuality, a gradual, but constant,
erosion of Choctaw sovereignty, one that produced stark echoes of the
years leading up to their so-called removal in the 1830s. The U.S. government claimed jurisdiction over all crimes that involved a white person, no
matter whether they occurred on U.S. or Choctaw soil. The Americans
continually expanded their jurisdiction. Defining who was "white" and
who was "Indian" made the difference between a trial in the U.S. federal
court in Fort Smith or answering to the tribal system of justice. Disputes
also arose over the differing criminal codes of the Choctaws, as opposed
to the Americans. Crimes and punishments varied markedly, depending
on which legal system applied. As the United States asserted increasingly
broad jurisdiction, the Choctaws worried that they did so as a prelude to
forcing the Choctaw national lands into the U.S. market, by breaking up

the communal landholdings into small plots of land owned by individuals. No one could sell the Choctaw lands in their communal, undivided state. Yet, as soon as they were individually allotted, the Choctaws knew most of the land would be gone in a generation. The Choctaws and other Indian nations of the Territory fought "allotment" tooth and nail. They recognized it to be a thinly disguised device that the U.S. government would use to destroy the Indian nations. Once their land was owned by individuals within the tribes, the Indians knew that fraud, violence, and sharp dealing would hound them until all the Indian lands were in the hands of the whites.

The third major problem facing the Choctaws and other Indians of Indian Territory was the growing conflict over slavery. In each of the "Five Civilized Tribes" the Choctaws, Cherokees, Chickasaws, Creeks (Muscogees), and Seminoles—slavery was legal. The nature of slavery among the Indians varied in several respects from white southern plantation slavery, but it nonetheless constituted a labor system of forced lifetime servitude. Most Indians owned no slaves at all, but the richest Indians usually had dozens of them. The growing national debate ensnared the native people of Indian Territory. In addition, significant acts of violence associated with slavery occurred in Indian Territory with increasing frequency. Efforts to retain control of their future were compromised by this insidious institution. It restricted their room to maneuver in the coming cataclysm in the States, and presaged their involvement with the South, despite significant sentiment favoring the North or neutrality.

Violence in the new Choctaw Nation became more and more of a problem in the 1840s and 1850s. Many Choctaws complained that the young men drank too much whiskey and then got into drunken brawls in which someone was killed. Almost all the men carried handguns. They were ready to take offense, and ready to use their guns. Drinking of alcohol was a daily affair with many, and with the decline of the traditional social controls that had once held violence in check, very little stood between men and sudden death. The old male gender roles—those of warrior and hunter—became increasingly irrelevant as the years passed. Young men now had no way to mark their passage into manhood and no distinct, socially sanctioned and sustained role into which they passed. As one of the missionaries stated, "Still there is manifested much of recklessness and desperate depravity, especially by a portion of the young men."[2] Traditionally, Choctaw men had always had warfare, preparations for warfare, and hunting as activities that occupied the bulk of their time. Not only did rituals mark their passage into manhood, but also their progress over their lives was publicly recognized by their membership in age-graded societies comprised entirely of men. Women had their societies, too, but many women's activities in the new Choctaw Nation substituted effortlessly for the older ways, so they had far less of a transition to make than did the men.

Modern Choctaw society supplied the young men with very few social restraints after the decline of the clans. In the new land, Choctaw homes were more spread out than back in the East, so older men, even close kin, were less often present when young men got together. The older men had traditionally enforced the clan law, the most important of which was the law of revenge. This law held that if anyone died, the person who caused the death had to be surrendered to the clan of the victim for execution. Even if the death was accidental, the offender would pay with his life. In large part this tradition served the purpose of holding in check the passions of men. Men were careful with those outside their clan, and they always knew that a serious fight would probably end in their death, along with that of their opponent. In the new lands in the West, the clans were in rapid decline, and their social-regulating responsibilities likewise diminished. The boys becoming men in this era often ignored the old customs, which were enforced less and less frequently. Unfortunately, the decline of traditional adult male gender roles left a vacuum exacerbated by the progressive weakening of clan law, the abuse of alcohol, and the ready accessibility of guns. These combined to wreak havoc in the new Choctaw Nation.[3]

The leaders of the Nation tried to combat the scourge of alcohol with stricter enforcement by the Lighthorse. The problem, however, was in many cases beyond the control of the Choctaw people. Whites imported alcohol for sale to native people, as did some Indians. One Choctaw even complained that the white missionaries were involved in the importation of liquor in great quantities, relating that they brought in whiskey packaged in tenths, and "labeled expressly for the Indian Trade!"[4] Choctaws resented the fact that whites could legally import liquor, as long as it was for their private use. "What right," one Choctaw asked, "has Missionaries [sic] to use Wine at their Sacrament and would put me in the Penitentiary if I was caught with only a Gill for a sick child?"[5]

Abuse of alcohol certainly contributed greatly to the violence that was rampant in the Nation, but there were other factors that many Choctaws felt also contributed to this scourge. One father blamed much of the delinquency of young men on overindulgence. "We Choctaw half-breeds don't raise up our children aright [*sic*]—we show them to much indulgences [*sic*]—if we would make them work in the corn field from the time they are able to do any thing and at the same time give them the hickory every time they transgressed they would be some account when they grew up."[6] However, traditionally, the Choctaws were judged by most whites to be indulgent with their young. Many white observers remarked that the boys were especially indulged by Choctaws. Their boyhood often consisted of a remarkable freedom, and the Choctaws never punished their children by striking them. Only the most recalcitrant was ever "disciplined" among the Choctaws, and then it was through the use of shaming the child, which evidently worked wonders to curb aberrant behavior. In fact, shaming was so effective that by the time Choctaws reached about the ages of five or six, one could not imagine having to undergo the humiliation associated with shaming. It was an extremely powerful deterrent, but one that was more effective if done before one's social peers and the rest of the village, as in the old days. In the new Choctaw Nation, people had less social interaction and thus shaming was not nearly as effective.

As the Choctaw Nation moved away from traditional mechanisms of social control, it found new institutions, such as the Lighthorse and other forms of external control, inadequate to the task.

Social control gradually became the purview not of kin, family, and clan, but of the impersonal, remote institutions of the state, which remained very weak throughout much of the nineteenth century. Therefore, young men had few consistent, local social constraints. Maternal uncles were not as intimately connected to their maternal nephews as they had been in the old Nation, and Choctaw fathers did not exert the kind of authoritarian familial discipline and control typical of the Euro-American family.[7] One missionary who was resident for years in the Choctaw Nation remarked that there was "little order or discipline in the family. Each does what is pleasing to himself."[8]

For many years, the Lighthorse constituted the only law enforcement agency in the Choctaw nation. Although the Choctaw Nation had a judiciary, it relied primarily on the social constraints that had prevailed in earlier times. Jails were almost unknown. A prisoner was usually kept in a guarded room, or even simply chained to a tree. Punishment for crimes was never a jail sentence, which many Choctaws thought was an unbearable and inhumane punishment. Instead, criminals were whipped, fined, or executed by shooting. Execution by hanging was considered barbaric, and was never practiced among the Choctaws. They had sheriffs and deputies, and in later years, the chiefs would call out a militia if needed. One of the major problems with curbing the rate of crime in the Indian Territory was not so much that the nations could not control their own people, but that the fast expanding number of white intruders included all kinds of refugees from U.S. law who fled to Indian Territory to try to elude U.S. authorities. A handful of U.S. marshals operated out of Fort Smith. Their jurisdiction in the Indian Territory was limited to crimes committed by whites, and all cases involving a U.S. citizen. The U.S. federal court was located in Fort Smith and this fact worked as a real hardship on the Choctaws, since witnesses had to travel long distances to appear in court. Even preliminary hearings took place in Fort Smith. Many witnesses were simply too old, too poor, or too lazy to make such an arduous and expensive trip. The location of the court encouraged people to avoid testifying, and wrought havoc with the American system of justice. The court docket was always backed up, causing delays of trials up to one year. In addition, many of the whites in the system were blatantly racist, hated the Indians, and did everything they could to convict them, even if they were innocent, and to make their lives as prisoners unbearable. The jails in Fort Smith were horrible. Filthy and crowded conditions could be avoided only through payment of huge bribes. People frequently died before their case came up for consideration. So in addition to the Choctaws' normal horror of being deprived of their liberty, they had to put up with nightmarish living conditions. Aside from these unpleasant aspects of involvement in the U.S. legal system, white people had merely to accuse an Indian of a crime, and the marshal would apprehend him or her. Many Choctaws and other Indians complained that if a white man had a grudge, he could simply accuse the Indian of committing a crime, and the Indian then would be locked up for nearly a year in Fort Smith, separated from family, friends, and business, simply on the say-so of a white man.[9]

Peter P. Pitchlynn, a prominent man in the Choctaw Nation, chief during two different periods of Choctaw history, had two sons who were caught in just such a dilemma. Two white men came up to the Pitchlynn residence when only his two sons, aged twenty-four and twenty-seven, were at home. The white men came up to the house with whiskey in hand; they had been drinking and were drunk. They offered drinks to the Pitchlynn sons, who came out on the porch to imbibe. As they did, Leonidas Pitchlynn saw that one of the men had brought a sick horse, which appeared so ill that it was going to die. He told the man to take his horse away, because he "did not have time to hunt up oxen to haul away a dead horse. The white man replied—very insultingly, 'You are too saucy for a damned Indian—and I will do as I please about that,' whereupon Leonidas Pitchlynn struck the owner of the horse and a fight ensued in which the other white man took part. Seeing this, Pushmataha Pitchlynn seized a gun and rushed out to the reserve and support of his Brother Leonidas, with a view to intimidate the whitemen [sic], at the same time aiming the gun above the man's head, he without any intention to shoot him. The man threw up his hands suddenly and received the charge through the palm of one hand extended above his head."

Pushmataha Pitchlynn was known as a very good shot, and no doubt could have easily killed the man, had he desired to do so. Nevertheless, a grand jury in Van Buren indicted him, "based upon the ex-parte testimony of the white men, both of whom were engaged in the affray." Subsequently, the white man who was the principle witness against the Pitchlynns offered to "disappear" for a price. This offer was rejected by the Pitchlynns. There were no other witnesses to the affair, but the indictment was returned solely on the basis of the two white men who the Pitchlynns claimed were the aggressors. They were convicted by an all-white jury of assault with intent to kill and were sentenced to three years in the Arkansas Penitentiary.

Interestingly, because their father was a very prominent man in the Choctaw Nation, his friends appealed the conviction, petitioning the president, James Buchanan, for a pardon. The basis of the appeal stated that the Pitchlynn brothers did not engage in premeditation or malice, and that "The two young Pitchlynns are themselves almost whitemen [sic]—had no prejudices or ill feeling toward whitemen [sic]—and they as well as their Father, were always hospitable and kind to citizens of the United States and travelers through the Choctaw Nation—frequently extending the hospitality of their Father's house to strangers from the

United States and always without charge or remuneration." The appeal further stated that a presidential pardon would "result beneficially not only to the young men, but towards the people of the United States in cementing kind and fraternal feelings between them and our people."[10]

President Buchanan pardoned the young men, to the great relief of themselves and their people. The appeal to Buchanan highlights a number of assumptions made on behalf of the Pitchlynns that were obviously designed with the intent to favorably influence Buchanan. First, the statement that they were "almost whitemen" shows that the two Choctaw authors were very conscious of race, suggesting that the nearer a non-white could approach to being white, the better would be his or her character. Furthermore, the appeal implied that it logically followed that if a person were almost white then he or she would be just like Buchanan, not part of the Other. Second, the statement that they had "no prejudices" against whitemen, demonstrates that these authors assumed that Buchanan might expect Indians to harbor antipathy toward whites. Since these men were also of mixed heritage, like the Pitchlynns, perhaps asserting the Pitchlynn men's "near-whiteness" suggests the authors' racial anxieties about themselves. Perhaps the Pitchlynns felt no ill will toward whites at the time of the fight, but it would be surprising if they were not angry at their treatment in jail in Van Buren, and at the fact that the whole affair would not have taken place had they not been classified racially as Indians. As such, they were extended only a subset of the rights and guarantees granted to white, male American citizens, despite their protest that they were "almost white."

Their father, nonetheless, was extremely embittered by the experience. He complained about the "weak and unjust judge" who found them guilty, asking, "What can be more unjust than that we should be dragged to distant points for trial, far beyond the reach four [sic] witnesses and friends, for every alleged infraction of the white man's rights; and placed in the power of a Judge, as my children were, whose every prejudice is against us, and every sympathy in favor of the whites—let them be never so degraded." The senior Pitchlynn continued that he hoped that "the protecting shield of the law . . . will soon be thrown over us, and the whites, who came to dwell with us and to share our hospitality and property, be no longer left free to rob, despoil, and trample upon us and laugh in our faces."[11]

In the midst of all this cultural distress, one traditional means continued to provide an alternative to drunken brawls and gunfights. The favorite Choctaw pastime, the ball play, presented young men with the opportunity in practice and in games not only to display athletic ability, strength, and endurance, but also to demonstrate the characteristics applicable to battle and the hunt. Ball plays were called the "little brother of war" in Choctaw, and prowess on the field of play led to status and the presumption of excellence as a warrior, even after the period in which traditional warfare was practiced.[12]

In the West, ball plays continued to be an important form of entertainment for most Choctaw people. The games were so rough that many white spectators were surprised when few deaths occurred. One Choctaw man described playing ball for one of the "county" teams, saying that the games "were really rough, any kind of rough treatment as long as the hands alone were used was permissible. You were not allowed to use these Indian clubs as defensive weapons, but you were allowed to take your opponent with your empty hands, and, if you were the stronger of the two, throw him down against the ground as hard as you were able to do. . . . After many of these County Indian ball games in my young days, you could see a great many skinned up young bucks as they called them in that time."[13]

Artist George Catlin, accompanying a military expedition to the West, observed many ball plays, reporting that while he was visiting the Choctaw Agency in Indian Territory in 1838, he witnessed several games played. The "whole tribe" assembled to see the games in what seemed to Catlin to be a "national holiday." "Six or eight thousand young men would play in one game, with five or six times that as spectators." Generally, the games began about 9:00 A.M. and lasted until sundown, "without more than one minute of intermission at a time."

The teams were made up three or four months in advance, with two champions choosing sides. Runners were sent throughout the Nation with ball-sticks ornamented with ribbons and red paint, "to be touched by each one of the chosen players." The night before the game, the people held the ball play dance, "where they rattle their ball sticks together violently and sing as loud as they can. Women also dance, all praying to the Great Spirit for favor." Four old medicine men, who were to start the game, sat at the point where the ball was to be started, "busily smoking" to the Great Spirit for their success "in judging rightly, and impartially, between the parties." They repeated the dance every half hour throughout the night. All the players stayed awake all night.[14]

Ball plays were historically very rough and dangerous, and provided the occasion for gambling, which sometimes led to violence. They were frequently taken very seriously and were sometimes used to settle disagreements. About 1790, the Choctaws challenged the Muscogees to a ball play that would settle a dispute over the ownership of a pond where beavers were found. Each tribe chose fifty champion players. Five thousand people came to see the game.

The advantage in the game tipped back and forth from one team to the other. The excitement was tremendous, and rival parties even stripped themselves of their clothing, blankets, and jewelry to stake upon the outcome. The Creeks were the eventual victors and their triumphant yells resounded over the field. They called out insults, naming the Choctaw champions "squaws," and flung a petticoat at the Choctaw team. A Choctaw warrior immediately took up his tomahawk and attacked the Creek warriors, joined by hundreds of his teammates. The fight began at sundown and lasted all night and until eight the next morning. Finally, the fight stopped due to the sheer exhaustion of the warriors, and the chiefs were then able for the first time to intervene. Three hundred warriors, the "flower of the two tribes," lay dead on the field, and many more were mortally wounded. Many women had been slain. After the fight, the Creeks, though they had won the pond, relinquished it to the Choctaws, who refused to use it ever again, saying that the beavers had deserted it directly after the fight, due to the anger of the Great Spirit.[15]

Roughness and violence inhered in ball plays, which served as a legitimate social outlet for aggression. In 1835, the Creeks and Choctaws met near the Choctaw Agency for a game. One spectator reported that the Creeks ganged up with more than half a dozen men on one Choctaw player at a time, which "break down [sic] the Choctaw. So as it was Creek got 5 balls while Choctaw got none—And all broke up in confusion and great many of the Choctaws lost their property as well as horses—and some got their horses and property back but they had to fight for it like Bull Dogs—no one was killed."[16] Ball plays remained important in Choctaw society well into the twentieth century, but these games were no substitute for actual combat against an enemy as an outlet for male aggression.

Another factor that exacerbated the violence that afflicted the new Choctaw Nation was the tremendous rise in the number of whites who illegally entered the Choctaw Nation during the 1840s and 1850s. The problems with white intruders, especially Texans and occasionally Arkansans, increased greatly from 1840 until the Civil War. As the national debate on abolition, states' rights, and slavery intensified, whites from bordering slave states crossed into the Indian nations, sometimes looking for "runaways," other times with the intent of kidnapping free blacks and subsequently selling them into slavery. One Texas newspaper carried ads seeking the capture of runaway slaves, thought to be in the Choctaw Nation. Bounty hunters, drifters, criminals, and others crossed over into the Choctaw Nation, terrorizing both African American and native families. As the outbreak of the Civil War drew near and the national debate over abolition intensified, white slaveholders in neighboring states regularly invaded Indian Territory in attempts to demonstrate what would occur if the native nations did not continue to support pro-slavery forces.[17]

Other white intruders were fugitives from the law in the United States who were trying to avoid capture. Notorious criminals operated out of Indian Territory, drawing U.S. marshals onto native lands in pursuit of them. Belle Starr, the James Gang, and many other famous white outlaws hid in the rugged back country to elude capture. Other whites entered the Choctaw and other native nations and remained, squatting on land that clearly was native soil. These people erected buildings and cleared fields, sometimes also running herds of cattle. The Choctaws constantly protested their presence to the U.S. government, requesting that the United States expel intruders, as they had pledged to do in the treaties. Despite a few halfhearted attempts, the United States did little to enforce this extremely important treaty provision. As the years passed, therefore, the number of white intruders rose, as did the number of resident outlaws and fugitives from justice. This criminal element contributed to the lawlessness and violence that plagued the Nation. The interlude of the U.S. Civil War introduced even more undesirables from Union and Confederate forces, in addition to war refugees from other native nations.[18]

The Choctaw adherence to traditional values continued through the institution of slavery as practiced by all but a handful of Choctaws who were full participants in the market economy of the U.S. Many Choctaws had no slaves, a few had dozens or hundreds, and some had one or two.

The latter characteristically worked alongside their "slaves." It was evidently rare that a Choctaw in this position would discipline the person(s) enslaved. They generally coexisted in a traditional relationship of vassalage. The major distinction between this form of slavery and that of the American South was that the master-slave relationship was more equitable.

Choctaws who owned dozens or hundreds of slaves grew crops for the world market. These few people were generally far more assimilated to white culture than were other Choctaws. They generally kept to themselves, fitting neither in Choctaw nor in white culture, but forming instead a small group of similarly minded, privileged people in the middle of an ocean of traditional subsistence dwellers. This group of intermarried whites and Choctaws of mixed heritage has been disproportionately represented in the historical literature. Because their interaction with white American society was far more frequent and substantive, and because they conformed to the American ideals of success, these prominent individuals have formed the exemplar from which many white historians have extrapolated what they thought were Choctaw "norms." In reality, the effect of these few men on the Nation was minimal, and their issues, interests, and aspirations were atypical of the Choctaws.

By far the most numerous and politically important group of people in the Choctaw Nation was the traditionalists. They generally lived their lives much the same way their ancestors had, but in a new physical space. They were somewhat more dispersed than people had been in the old eastern homelands, but most still retained very close ties—physical and spiritual—with kin groups. Many lived in compounds, consisting of a group of houses within calling distance of each other, which were extended family groups—much the same living arrangement as in the old Choctaw Nation.

These folks continued to exist in a barter-subsistence economy, getting along without many material possessions and continuing to practice the old ways of life. Most spoke nothing but the Choctaw language, although many knew a smattering of English. Few had any formal education, and most continued the old ways. As the years passed and more whites intruded into the Nation, the latter were occasionally invited to witness or participate in gatherings among the Choctaws. One white person interviewed in the 1930s about her childhood among the Choctaws recalled taking part in the funeral rites of a Choctaw neighbor and calling on a Choctaw medicine man for treatment.[19]

As the Civil War years drew near, three major issues emerged to threaten the Choctaw Nation—violence and the decline of legitimate roles for young men, conflict over U.S. claims of jurisdiction and escalating white intrusion, and the external pressure on the Choctaws to choose sides between what became the Confederacy and the Union. Kansas was in chaos, with pro- and anti-slavery forces battling one another and contending for the support of Cherokees, Creeks, and other native peoples. The violence spilled over into Indian Territory and eventually engulfed the native peoples in a sea of war.

Confusion and conflict over legal jurisdictions exacerbated the problems experienced by the Choctaws. The United States used its superior power to impose a random, unilaterally defined scenario of jurisdiction on the Choctaws. Whites who broke the law in the Choctaw Nation were under the jurisdiction of the U.S. federal court in Arkansas. Choctaws who were involved in criminal activity with whites were also subject to U.S. jurisdiction.

There were two major problems with this system. First, Choctaws who committed crimes against whites had to stand trial in Fort Smith, Arkansas, and were tried before white juries, who were grossly prejudiced against Indians. Choctaws continually complained that they were unfairly charged, based on the mere word of a white man, and that they were grossly mistreated once they were in the custody of the U.S. criminal system. They were almost always convicted and usually had poor or no legal counsel. In addition, getting native people to travel to Arkansas to testify on one's behalf was very difficult. Most witnesses could not afford the trip; many also could not travel such a long distance because of logistical or health problems. Therefore, many Choctaws and other native people similarly situated were convicted without the testimony of friendly witnesses. Choctaws also charged that white criminals falsely accused them of wrongdoing, knowing that the native person would often pay them off so that they would not press false charges. This became a regular racket with some white outlaws, who frequently preyed on Choctaws of mixed heritage whose family might be capable of making a significant payment in lieu of the threatened charges.

The second problem caused by jurisdictional ambiguity was that white outlaws who came into the Nation were technically subject to removal only by the U.S. marshal or his deputies. U.S. lawmen violated the Nation's sovereignty with impunity under the guise of searching for white refugees in the Choctaw Nation. One Choctaw judge complained that the U.S. lawmen came in and harassed Choctaw citizens, holding them up for payment under false threats of arrest, but that when the Choctaws asked the marshals to remove white intruders who had broken the law or committed crimes against Choctaws, they could get no cooperation or response.

These situations worsened over time, until many Choctaws despaired of any solution. A similar situation had preceded their expulsion from their eastern homelands. White intruders had overrun the Choctaw Nation with the connivance of the Mississippi and federal governments, as one of a set of tools used by the United States to force the Choctaws to sign a removal treaty. In the 1850s, numerous white intruders were again coming into the Nation, and the United States was once again failing to expel them, as it was obligated to do under the terms of the Treaty of Dancing Rabbit Creek.

Choctaw leaders knew that some U.S. congressmen were already voicing their constituents' desire to create a territory out of the Indian nations and their lands in Indian Territory as the prelude to statehood, just as they had done in the East. A territory bill was proposed almost yearly in the U.S. Capitol, and the Indian nations had little reason to expect that the American government would uphold the sanctity of the native lands in the West anymore than they had in the East. Lawlessness and confusion over jurisdiction, not to mention refusal to expel white intruders and outlaws from the Indian nations, led to a state of anarchy bitterly protested by Choctaw leaders.

In the late 1850s, pro- and anti-slavery forces began to campaign for the loyalty of the Indian nations. Many foresaw the coming war, and there were many subtle and obvious attempts to secure the loyalty of the native peoples in the coming conflict. White historians have had an incredible blind spot in reporting on the Civil War in the West. Other than discussing the maneuvers of white troops at battles in the United States, and occasionally the Far West, these scholars have failed to note the tremendous impact of the Civil War on the Indian Territory.

Within the Choctaw Nation, there were a handful of slave owners who practiced Southern-style chattel slavery, as mentioned earlier. This was a tiny group numerically, most living on the Red River, growing cotton for the market, many quite well-to-do. These were almost all either intermarried white men or assimilated Choctaws of mixed heritage who lived white. When the lines began to be drawn in the United States over slavery, these people, too, were directly concerned with their future economic well-being. These men loudly declaimed their support for slavery and tried to persuade their compatriots to support their position. The vast majority of Choctaws, however, did not favor slavery, and were generally committed to remaining neutral in the coming conflict in the United States.

The Choctaws were not allowed to remain neutral, however. They were surrounded by pro-slavery states. Texans formed into groups and rode into the Choctaw Nation, terrorizing innocent citizens, demanding that the Nation join the Confederacy. At the first sign of trouble, the United States pulled out all of the federal troops from the forts in Indian Territory and shipped them back East, leaving the Choctaws at the mercy of the marauding Texans. Almost all commodities coming into the Choctaw Nation entered through the river system from New Orleans up the Mississippi, to the Red River through Louisiana and along the northern border of Texas, and then overland to the handful of stores and traders in the Territory. The Texans strove to "persuade" the Choctaws to align themselves with the Southern cause, and they had plenty of leverage in doing so in the absence of a U.S. military presence. Principal Chief Peter Pitchlynn at first succeeded in taking a position of neutrality in the conflict, but he and other Choctaw leaders realized that this stand was unsustainable with the presence of Texan and Arkansan troops all around them.

The anarchy of lawlessness in the Nation was soon replaced with the anarchy occasioned by the Civil War. The Cherokees and Creeks split into two factions, one siding with the North while the other joined the South, causing an internal civil war in the Indian nations of the Territory. The Choctaws and Chickasaws, of course, joined with the Confederacy. Many Choctaws rushed to join up, and we see evidence of their great relief at reviving the traditional male role of warrior, especially among the young men. War dances, paint, song, and language were revived to celebrate and ritualize the state of war, and the men of the Choctaw Nation eagerly went to battle. Young men quit killing each other and turned their aggression against the outside enemy. War honors and stories came back, repeated around campfires and in Choctaw homes.

The increasing lawlessness of the 1850s, the fading of traditional male role of warrior and hunter, the invasion of white intruders, and the confusion and near-anarchy that resulted from unilateral American extensions of jurisdiction were exacerbated by the fear of a coming civil war between American states. However, the turmoil of the 1850s had an important political dimension yet to be explored. During this decade, the split between Choctaws who wanted to retain the old ways and those who believed change would be beneficial led the Nation perilously close to a civil war. The next chapter will look at the great struggle among the Choctaws among these two opposing forces, and will reveal the outlines of those who sought cultural continuity and those who chose change.

8   Cultural Continuity and Change

I N THE PREVIOUS CHAPTER, THE VIOLENCE THAT RESULTED FROM
the disintegration of traditional male gender roles, white intruders, confusion over jurisdiction between the U.S. and the
Choctaws, the importation of alcohol, and the growing anxiety over slavery and the coming Civil War in the U.S. was explored. The Choctaws had
another major crisis in their government and political system that exacerbated these conditions.

In the 1850s, two oppositional forces continued to wreak havoc within the Choctaw Nation. Intermarried white men and more acculturated
Choctaw men of mixed heritage tried to steer the Choctaw people toward
further adaptation of white culture, economics, and behavior. The large
majority of the Choctaw people, however, refused to submit to the leadership of this minority. Most Choctaws saw value in adopting some white values and behaviors. Yet only a few wanted to extirpate the traditional
Choctaw way of life, customs, and culture.

This cultural and societal clash is exemplified in the political
upheaval that occurred in the 1850s, when the minority advocates of
acculturation met the unstoppable determination of the majority to limit
the adoption of policies that would lead to assimilation with the American
people. This episode also illustrates the willingness of the United States to
interfere in the internal affairs of the Choctaw Nation.

In 1857, the Choctaws and the Chickasaws separated their governments from the unified government that had been the result of their dispossession in the 1830s. Under the constitution adopted in 1838, the Choctaws had allowed the Chickasaws to settle within the boundaries of the Choctaw Nation. The Chickasaws had formed a fourth district within the Choctaw Nation, agreed to abide by the Choctaws' laws and customs, and been incorporated into the Choctaw Nation body politic. Many Chickasaws had expressed opposition to this accommodation from its inception, but the untenable exigencies of the dispossession had necessitated this resolution. However, during the two decades of co-residence, friction had increased, resentments had smoldered, and finally, the two peoples had devised a method to separate. The Choctaw constitution therefore had to be changed to reflect the separation of the Chickasaw people from the Choctaw Nation.

On 5 January 1857, the minority faction who advocated assimilation into the American states met in a hastily arranged constitutional convention and adopted a new constitution. In this instrument, the power of the traditional three coequal district chiefs was consolidated in the person of a governor. The impetus for this change was the desire of this tiny minority faction to facilitate the creation of a U.S. territory that would encompass the Choctaw Nation. The vast majority vociferously repudiated this idea and accused the minority of usurping the democratic government of the Choctaw Nation, and, in effect, implementing a coup d'état. An immediate, vocal opposition movement sprung up to save the Nation from the designs of this minority faction, which was made up of many intermarried white men and their offspring, whom the majority of the Nation regarded as outsiders.

The Skullyville Constitution, as most termed it, was the culmination of years of debate and failure to reach a consensus. This method of resolving differences was traditional, stretching back into antiquity. The majority of the Choctaw people were well satisfied with this process of decision making, but the intermarried whites and advocates of assimilation were frustrated. Finally determined to have their way, they instituted a quick convention in which only part of the nation was represented, and produced a constitution that would lead to the incorporation of Indian Territory and the Indian Nations into the political forms of territory and then statehood.

Those in the minority stood to individually profit from the incorporation of the Choctaw Nation into the United States. Many of them were also adamant advocates of "progress," as they termed it. The belief that American society, values, and institutions were more advanced derived from the racist philosophy so dominant in American thought. They believed that the Choctaw people should abandon all of the traditional ways of life and incorporate themselves into the dominant American society. Of course, that process would be a simple one for the faction advocating this view. Most were white, and those of mixed heritage among them lived like whites, often were educated, and almost always were involved in the market economy of the United States, far more so than were the traditional Choctaws.

The Skullyville Constitution abolished the office of district chief and created a governor for the Nation. Traditionally, the Choctaw Nation had been governed by three district chiefs, coequals in every way. The clan-based kinship system supported and sustained these divisions, and provided a foundation for the ongoing relations between the districts, villages, clans, and individuals within the Nation. After dispossession, despite the decline of clan power and organization and the difficulties in re-forming villages and towns as they had been constituted in the East, the Choctaws still wanted to retain these traditional divisions, and most were adamantly opposed to amalgamation with the United States.

Many Choctaws of mixed heritage opposed the Skullyville Constitution, and they and the majority of the Choctaw people fought to nullify it. They protested that the Skullyville Constitution was illegal because it was not submitted to the People for a popular vote. The most important charge was that it, in effect, created a nation-state to replace tribal rule. The People demanded that the constitution be submitted for a national vote, but the faction that created it wanted to avoid that possibility at all costs. They refused to place it before the People for a vote.

One group of active opponents then called for a new constitutional convention to meet at Doaksville, where they created a constitution that embodied the majority view. A new legislature and district chiefs were elected at this convention and the People were promised that the Doaksville Constitution would be submitted for popular vote. Neither rival government would step down, resulting in a period of anarchy that could have led to civil war.

In August 1857, the Skullyville faction called an election to fill offices created by their constitution. Several counties on the Red River did not hold the election, refusing to participate in what they termed a sham government. In December they called another election, with much the same result. At this point, the U.S. government intervened. Americans who wanted to see the remaining Indian lands forced out of native hands and onto the American market motivated the U.S. government, which insisted that the Choctaw Nation adopt and abide by the Skullyville Constitution. U.S. interests were behind the creation of the Skullyville Constitution, which would have created a U.S. territory out of the Choctaw Nation, in direct violation of all the so-called removal treaties. The Choctaw advocates of Skullyville and their American co-conspirators then exerted pressure on the American government to insist that the majority of the Choctaws be ruled by the minority that had created the Skullyville Constitution. The opponents of the Skullyville Constitution received orders from the United States to cease opposition to it, or face American military action that would force them to comply.

The vast majority of Choctaws remained adamantly opposed to the Skullyville Constitution. With the U.S. throwing its support (and threats of military intervention) the two factions moved close to civil war. Finally, in October 1858, the Skullyville adherents compromised, narrowly averting violence. The office of chiefs of Apukshunnubbee and Pushmataha would be filled by opposition leaders, which restored order to the Nation and led to the adoption of yet another constitution, on 24 October 1859. This document provided for a principal chief and three district (but subordinate) chiefs. All were to be elected by the people by popular vote. This move derailed the coming strife, and the Choctaw Nation recovered to deal with issues pressing from outside the Nation. The new capital of the Nation would be located at Doaksville. Peace, of a sort, was restored for a brief while.

In 1856, a terrible incident was uncovered that turned many formerly supportive New Englanders against the Choctaw people. This incredible incident not only affected the well-being of the Choctaw Nation, it also had national ramifications in the fight over slavery and was a partial cause of the permanent schism of at least one major Protestant denomination.

The incident began with the murder of a man of mixed Choctaw/white heritage by one of his slaves, a man named Prince. Richard Harkins left his house one morning to hunt for a missing ox. The next day, his horse was found near the river with the saddle under its belly. Of course the family was greatly alarmed and sent for all the relatives to come and hunt for Richard. After five days of searching, Prince was "taken aside and questioned" and he "made a full confession of the crime." During his confession, he implicated his aunt, Lucy, as "the chief instigator of the whole affair." Harkins was married to another person of mixed heritage, Lavinia Pitchlynn (who was the daughter of the principal chief of the Choctaws from 1860 to 1865), and a man of great importance in the Choctaw Nation. According to the account of one of Lavinia's brothers, Prince was making rails for a fence some three hundred yards from the house on the morning that Richard left home. Richard rode on the road where Prince was working, and as he passed by, Prince was unsuccessfully trying to roll over a heavy log. Richard dismounted and walked over to help. As he bent over the log, Prince hit him on the back of the neck with the butt end of the axe, repeating the blows until Richard was dead.

Prince then hid the body in some tree branches that he had cut down to make rails. He rode Richard's horse down to the river to a spot called Ashley's Ford, where there was a very deep crossing, and turned the horse loose to make it appear that Richard had drowned in the river. That accomplished, the murderer returned to where he had concealed the body, and then dragged the corpse to a deep hole in the river. Tying a large rock to the body to weigh it down, he threw the corpse into the river. He then went back to work and pretended that nothing had happened.

Richard's wife, Lavinia, became alarmed when Richard did not return later that day, and she sent a message to her brothers and other kin to come to her house to help look for him. The men and women began arriving in the middle of the night, and at dawn they were out hunting for signs of Richard. They interrogated the slaves, including Prince, and continued to search for several days.

Meanwhile, Lavinia was overwrought and hysterical in the throes of fear. She told her kin that she suspected the slaves had killed her husband and hidden his body in retribution for Richard depriving them of the Christmas treats they usually had every year. Harkins was evidently a harsh slaveholder who practiced a form of chattel slavery similar to that of white southerners.

After searching for a day or two without success, Harkins's relatives seized the prime suspect, Prince, and took him out to be whipped.

Before that took place, he confessed that he had killed his master and thrown his body into Little River. He also implicated his aunt, Lucy, who, he said, created the entire scheme. Lucy planned Harkins's death for months, Prince asserted, and put her plan into action after Harkins refused to provide the Christmas treats and respite from work to which the slaves were accustomed.[1]

After his confession, Prince led the assembled Choctaws to the place on Little River where he had sunk the body. When he reached the spot, Prince went wild, seeing his master's ghost. He "howled" and screamed furiously, and ran around, screeching that Harkins's ghost was torment-ing him. At last he let loose a single bloodcurdling scream and plunged into the river. The Choctaws tried to retrieve Prince from the deep river crossing, but could not locate him. Finally, they pulled his lifeless body from the stream and then returned to the place where Prince had said he sank Harkins's corpse. The Choctaws found the body at the bottom of the river, tied to a heavy rock.

The party of Choctaws then returned to Harkins's home, where they seized Lucy and began to interrogate her. The Choctaws believed that there was another person involved in the murder, but they were unable to obtain any further information on this. They burned the body of Prince, and then tied Lucy, quite alive, on the top of the pyre. She maintained her innocence to her death. Many Choctaws witnessed the burning, hav-ing traveled from far and wide to assist in the search, some attracted, no doubt, by the excitement of an execution.[2]

Soon after, the Reverend Cyrus Byington was called to the scene to comfort Lavinia, the widow, who was a member of his Presbyterian con-gregation, as had been Lucy. Lavinia requested that she be brought before the Session so that the ruling elders could question her. Her appearance and answers evidently satisfied them that she had not acted with impropriety, and she continued to be received as a member of the congregation. Byington went back about his business, and all appeared to be forgotten.[3]

A year passed by. Then, a disgruntled former employee of the mis-sions released information about the incident in retribution for his per-ceived ill-treatment by the Presbyterians, who, he implicitly charged, had fired him in order to rid the Choctaw Nation of all vestiges of abolition-ism. This incident was printed in the Eastern papers, embarrassing the

Foreign Missionary Boards of the Presbyterians and the American Board of Commissioners for Foreign Missions, which was ostensibly interdenominational, although it was, in reality, dominated by Congregationalists. In 1859 the American Board withdrew its missionaries from Indian Territory and gave up its missions, supposedly in response to the continuing escalation of the debate over Christian missions conducted among slaveholders. The Presbyterian Board of Foreign Missions took over most of the American Board's missions. The missionaries who wanted to continue their work in Indian Territory were brought under the Presbyterian Board, and life continued much as it had in Indian Territory.[4]

The storm of controversy provoked by this incident in the Choctaw Nation in the American press centered on the position that Christians and their organizations should take in deciding whether slaveholders should be allowed to be church members. The practice of slavery among the southern Indian Nations was supposedly countenanced, and therefore tacitly approved, by the Presbyterians, since they admitted slaveholders as members of their congregation. This led, in part, to the characterization of the Presbyterian Church as the "Slave Church of America." Yet the revelation of the "awful secret" was only indirectly damaging to the Choctaw Nation. Northeastern abolitionists were often also interested in the fair treatment of the native peoples and were among those who protested and opposed "removal" and other methods the U.S. government employed to dispossess native people. Thus, in highlighting the horrible incidents that resulted from the emulation of southern-style slavery among the Choctaws, many of the Indians' historical sympathizers were alienated. It certainly added fuel to the American national debate on slavery, and added one more horror story to bolster the anti-slavery artillery.[5]

Certainly, this incident makes the racism of white Americans toward native people apparent. Laced throughout the writings protesting the continuation of Christian missions among the southern Indians was a thinly veiled charge that the Indians' barbarism found expression, in part, through their enslavement of others, thus joining the white American South with the savages of Indian Territory. In addition, in many instances in these writings, the white authors implied or stated outright their assumption that native people were to be taught by the superior culture of the whites how to be civilized. It was an embarrassment to some whites that native people, in emulating their superior white brothers, had the temerity to think of themselves as on the same level as whites, who historically had enslaved Indians along with blacks.

Indians thus were conceptualized historically as belonging to a category inferior to that of white people—a category shared by blacks and based on race. By the 1850s, of course, the racial hierarchy in America demanded the explicit rejection of people of color from parity with Americans of European heritage. Thus, the Choctaws were "uppity" Indians, assuming themselves equal to whites, manifested by their enslavement of blacks, in an attempt to distinguish themselves from African Americans, and arrogating the status that most Euro-Americans believed reserved strictly for whites.

Therefore the Choctaw practice of slavery was doubly offensive. Not only did they practice an odious institution that many northerners thought thoroughly barbaric, but they also usurped the exclusive prerogative of white America in erecting a racial hierarchy in Indian Territory in which they placed themselves at the pinnacle of privilege, reserved in American society for whites only. *That* was what rankled the American public, abolitionist and anti-abolitionist alike. Quite aside from the various political and moral positions on the institution of slavery, white America was indignant that one set of people of color had the audacity to view themselves as equal to whites, and that they had the cultural, social, and political freedom to set up a society that allowed them to do so. In this interesting dilemma, then, we see the exacerbation of the growing national debate on slavery by the practice of slavery among those who ought to be enslaved. In fact, the shrill cries of outrage over the Choctaw incident from Americans in the North suggests that racism overrode moral arguments against slavery in animating American public opinion. Slavery was bad; American Indians practicing slavery was intolerable.

Traditional Choctaws generally continued a much milder form of enslavement that would have been more accurately termed vassalage. It was slavery in a nonhereditary form that essentially expected a yearly tribute or portion of the crop from the slaves, a form that reached back into ancient times among the Choctaws. Slavery was traditionally a temporary phase in a process of adoption of captives into the tribe. Once adopted by a clan, the "slave" became a full, free citizen of the Nation and enjoyed all of the privileges and status of one who had been born into the Nation.

In the case of Prince and the other slaves owned by Harkins, however, their enslavement was a harsh, grinding form of slavery that was a life sentence with no hope of any other future. Some of the Choctaws of mixed heritage had rapidly "progressed" in assimilation of white ideals and values, and they had adopted this vicious southern American form of enslavement in their quest to become "civilized."

Lavinia's father, Peter P. Pitchlynn, was comfortable with the white world and spent many years as the formal representative of the Choctaw Nation in Washington, D.C. He was adept in both the white and the Choctaw culture, but his family retained their view of themselves as Choctaws, making a deliberate and carefully considered election of their Indian identity as their only one. The Pitchlynn family had slaves, but they were treated in the traditional Choctaw manner, rather than in that of southern chattel slavery. This incident occurred in the late 1850s, a time in which a vicious debate continued over the incipient conflict between abolitionists and pro-slavery factions in the Choctaw Nation.

Choctaws who grew crops for the market—especially the big cotton plantation owners along the Red River—were vigorous defenders of the harsh southern form of slavery that they practiced. In the meantime, of course, the growing debate over slavery and the hardening of positions and failure of compromise animated the American national scene. One important part of the national debate over slavery was the question among Christians as to what their position should be, based on their religious beliefs.

The Baptists and Methodists had split into two separate bodies, Northern and Southern, by 1844. The Presbyterians had avoided breaking into two branches by separating any moral or spiritual duty from what they saw as strictly a political debate. Opponents of slavery called them the "Slave Church of America" because the Presbyterians continued to sponsor missionaries in Indian Territory who were pro-slavery and whose churches included some Choctaws who enslaved Africans.

The debate at the national level over slavery was at its peak in 1859. The moral and spiritual ramifications of slavery naturally drew the various denominations into the great debate, causing several to split along pro- and anti-slavery lines. The publicity surrounding the Choctaw slave-burning incident was brief because the incident was rapidly succeeded by the ignition of the conflagration of the American Civil War.

Slaveholding in the Choctaw Nation in 1860 was not a widespread practice. It was almost exclusively practiced by Choctaws who grew cotton to sell on the world market, and there were fewer than one hundred families in the Nation that owned any number of slaves. The majority of Choctaw people tolerated the enslavement of Africans in part because it was an ancient tradition among the southern Indians to make slaves of captives, adopting them into the Nation to supplement population. When the Civil War broke out among the American states, as mentioned elsewhere, the Choctaws tried to maintain a neutral position, vigorously trying to avoid being drawn into the American conflict. Choctaws of mixed heritage, who constituted the majority of slaveholders in the Nation, formed the primary impetus to remain neutral, if possible, for they knew that if the Choctaw Nation was drawn into taking sides, and that side lost, the Americans would use their perfidy as yet one more opportunity to rob them of their land.[6]

Peter P. Pitchlynn, the father of Lavinia, widow of Richard Harkins, was the principal chief of the Choctaws during the Civil War, and he tried assiduously to keep the Choctaw Nation out of the conflict. As detailed elsewhere, however, the Choctaws found themselves unable to stay neutral when the United States withdrew all foreign troops from Indian Territory, leaving them at the mercy of marauding Texans, Arkansans, and Louisianans, who insisted that if the Choctaws failed to join their cause, they would be looked upon as enemies.

Another interesting aspect of the Choctaw slave burning was the fact that Lavinia called her male kin to find and punish her husband's murderers. She evidently decided that Lucy would be burned, continuing a traditional prerogative afforded women in the southern nations that went back into antiquity.

One other event in this period gives us insight into the inner workings of the Choctaw Nation and the remarkable changes that had taken place among the Choctaws. In 1856, two of Peter Pitchlynn's sons were arrested for assault and battery of a white man in the Choctaw Nation. This remarkable incident and trial, and the conviction and eventual pardon of the brothers, illustrates the problems occurring in the Nation, and the change over time of certain attitudes and aspirations of the Choctaw people. It also highlights the racism encountered by Choctaws in their dealings with the U.S. judicial system, and the violations of their rights that occurred as a result of the diminution of their civil rights at the hands of white Americans.

Lycurgus and Leonidas Pitchlynn were at their residence when two white men came to the door, asking for assistance. Their horse was ill, and they had no means of continuing their journey unless they could borrow a horse from the Pitchlynns. There was an exchange of words that resulted in a fight, and in the ensuing altercation a gun went off, shooting off the finger of one of the white men. They fled to Arkansas, where they pressed charges against the Pitchlynn brothers. The Pitchlynns were jailed in Van Buren, Arkansas, where they waited in prison for many months to stand trial. Sentiment ran strongly against the Pitchlynns, in a classic example of the treatment of people of color at the hands of a system created and implemented to serve whites. This trial highlights the many problems that pervaded the points at which the two societies met.

There were questions of jurisdiction and of an ever-evolving definition and redefinition of power, logistical problems that reflected the primitive systems of transportation and communication, and an obvious corruption of fundamental human rights. Ambiguous jurisdiction led to an increase in the number of white outlaws who fled from American states into the Choctaw Nation. These outlaws perpetrated crimes against native people and created a dangerous and growing problem for the Choctaw Nation. As discussed elsewhere, the Choctaws had no jurisdiction over these intruders, and so the U.S. marshals invaded the Nation in search of these refugees from the law, causing problems with the Choctaw citizenry. The U.S. government refused to commit the manpower needed to expel these white invaders, so they remained free to enter and exit the Choctaw Nation at will. The men who showed up one day at the Pitchlynn farm were intruders who were violating the law by being in the Choctaw Nation. They were able to commit violence against Choctaw people with impunity.

Once a crime involving whites within the Nation occurred, the United States entered the picture, and the resulting trial was conducted within the state of Arkansas, in this case at Van Buren. The latter town was located many miles from where the incident occurred, making it extremely difficult for witnesses to attend the proceedings. Often witnesses for the Choctaws involved in trial were unable to make the long trip, resulting in one-sided trials, which were heard by a jury and a judge made up of white men. Rarely was a Choctaw or other Native American acquitted, and the sentences were harsh.

The Pitchlynn brothers experienced majority rule in its worst form. They were taken to Van Buren, made to stand trial with several of their witnesses unable to show, and their fate was decided by grossly bigoted whites who hated "Indians." The letters the young men wrote from prison while awaiting trial described mistreatment by their white captors and expressed great fear of the local populous from whom their jurors would be selected. They remained in jail for months, under great duress. Their "crime" would have been classed as self-defense if it had occurred among a group of all whites or all Choctaws. Yet, they were convicted without a fair trial and sentenced to three years in prison. Finally, after months of intense lobbying, they were freed by a pardon signed by President Ulysses S. Grant, procured by their father, who was well known in influential circles in Washington, D.C.

The entire incident left Peter Pitchlynn, who became principal chief of the Choctaws in 1861, a bitter, despairing man. The depth of his bitterness seems to indicate that he was out of touch with the reality of life on the border areas of the backwoods, where whites hated native people and the niceties of Washington diplomacy were unknown. The case against his sons demonstrated the lengths to which the frontier white element would go to subjugate native people. Pitchlynn watched helplessly as his sons were railroaded in a process in which they had no presumption of innocence; inadequate legal representation; logistical problems that prevented them from presenting friendly testimony, thereby insuring an unfair trial; and a jury anxious to convict them in order to demonstrate solidarity with the white men who brought the complaint.

Despite the "progress" (read "acculturation") of the Choctaws, especially those of mixed heritage, despite their Herculean efforts to educate and enlighten their citizens, the Choctaws were forced to acknowledge that they were playing a short hand in a rigged game. As the outbreak of hostilities between the states drew near, Choctaw leaders saw clearly that the United States would one day move to entirely subdue all the native people of Indian Territory, and would confiscate their lands regardless of promises and treaties to the contrary.

Despite this realization, the Choctaws did not give up. They continued to struggle against all odds to create a reasonably prosperous Nation and to remain separate from the American union. Unfortunately, the U.S. Civil War, and the subsequent invasion of Indian Territory by the railroads and huge mining and lumber interests, gave rise to the critical mass required for the United States to abrogate its solemn word and end the existence of the sovereign native nations of Indian Territory.

By 1880, railroads had brought thousands of white intruders into Indian Territory. Cheap agricultural land was no longer available, and the clamor of the remaining land seekers and speculators overcame moral and ethical scruple. Once again the process of dispossession was set into motion. As they did in the dispossession and exile of the 1830s, U.S. leaders used their language and legal system, along with fraud, misinterpretation, and deliberate distortion of the facts, to deprive native people of their last land holdings and the very existence of their societies. The Dawes Act was passed in 1885, and by 1907 all the Indian nations had lost their remaining lands, many forced to move to reservations that contained only a tiny fraction of the land needed for their subsistence. The United States had run out of "excess" lands, so in this dispossession the Americans, in effect, deprived the native peoples of their last remaining acres. Despite years of vigorous protest and legal and political fights by the Choctaw Nation, in 1907 the U.S. government declared that all Choctaw institutions, their constitution, and their very existence were no more. All of the Choctaws were forced to give up their communal land holdings and to take a few dozen acres each under the American system of individual property. Within years, most of the nonacculturated Choctaws had been swindled or defrauded of even these few acres.

The officials and people of the United States had finally achieved the complete dispossession and subjugation of the Choctaw people. However, despite these disasters, the Choctaw people did not disappear. The Choctaw language continued, as did Choctaw traditions, stories, values, and beliefs. The Choctaw people refused to give up, and in the 1960s the American government once again acknowledged the existence of the Choctaw Nation of Oklahoma. Today there are roughly ten thousand native Choctaw speakers in Oklahoma and Mississippi, and the Oklahoma counties that comprised the old Choctaw Nation are enlivened by the presence of thousands of Choctaw people.

Conclusion

HE CHOCTAW PEOPLE HAVE A LONG TRADITION OF SURVIVAL AS A separate, identifiable people. The greatest challenge to their independent identity was the American onslaught of the nineteenth and early twentieth centuries. The most damaging aspect of this onslaught has been the American construction of natives as savages and Euro-Americans as civilized. Many generations of Choctaws were affected by these teachings, which engendered a sense of self-loathing. The internalization of the norms of white people and of their scorn for native cultures produced many Choctaw people who were ashamed of their heritage and who taught their children to be ashamed, living lives in which they denied the rich culture and heritage that was theirs to claim. Others were taught to hide being "Indian," as though they suffered from some hideous, disfiguring disease.

In recent times, the attitudes of whites and people of mixed heritage have begun to change. Now I am frequently asked by students and others how they can begin to make the connection with their native heritage. Native language programs have enjoyed a huge resurgence of interest, and native arts are admired and sought for the finest collections. Every third person I speak to, it sometimes seems, has a grandmother who was a "Cherokee princess." (I have yet to meet a person outside of the native community who claims to be the descendent of a "Cherokee nobody." Americans seem enamored of royalty.)

Most distressing to me and some of my native colleagues in academia is the current state of American history texts, and the way native people and relations are depicted in these texts. White scholars, especially those reared in upper-middle-class families, believe that they now can speak adequately for native people on native history and perspectives. Sometimes their liberal predispositions suggest to them that they can somehow equate speaking *for* a people with allowing those people to speak for themselves. It always astonishes me that white scholars apparently understand fully the necessity for cultural diversity, yet feel it is unnecessary to bring native people into the inner circles of the academy, because "we [whites] already cover all that."

Native voices are rarely allowed to speak. Usually white, liberal intellectuals take up all the places at the table of academia, allowing for no uninvited (or unauthorized) "guests." As a result, native people have little input into the writing of academic history, and the status quo continues, cloaking itself in the form, but not the substance, of diverse and representative voices.

The story of the Choctaw people has been distorted in the telling by non-native academics. For example, a fundamental problem with almost all of these accounts has been the authors' lack of knowledge of the Choctaw language. The arrogance and condescension of historians who would presume to explain the actions of Choctaws (or of any other people) without knowing even a word of their language is as stunning as it is widespread. Doctoral students in native history are rarely required to acquire a knowledge of the language(s) of the people they study. Yet an aspiring historian of the French people would get nowhere without a working knowledge of the French language. Written sources in Choctaw and other native languages are common. These sources often are the only contemporary accounts written by native people. How can a white historian, with no knowledge of the language, presume to exclude important documentary sources? Furthermore, those who have no knowledge of a language cannot benefit from the cultural knowledge conveyed through learning *about* that language. Without this knowledge, how can they consider their scholarship complete?

In this account of the Choctaw people I have attempted to give voice to the thousands and thousands of Choctaw people who lived before our modern times. Choctaws always preferred to remain separate from other cultures, even when amalgamation was in their best interest. Choctaws living in the nineteenth-century West asserted their Choctaw identity even when they appeared, through mixed heritage, to be white. The Choctaw language has been kept alive, and many traditional practices continue.

In the early years of the existence of the American Union, the Choctaw people tried to remain on friendly terms with the Americans, despite the constant and unrelenting American demands for Choctaw lands. When at last the Americans perceived that they had reached the end of voluntary Choctaw land cessions, American leaders devised a plan to dispossess the Choctaw Nation and steal the eastern homelands. After the forced move to the West, the Choctaw people attempted to build a new nation and recover from the terrible trauma of the era of dispossession. In the 1830s they made little progress and suffered from many setbacks not of their own making. Floods, disease, social anomie, and incredibly hard times followed the Choctaws on their Trail of Tears. By the early 1840s, some of the Choctaws had slowly begun to recover and prosper in their new lands. The Choctaw economy began to emerge, and aside from the vastly predominant barter and subsistence economy, some Choctaws even built thriving plantations along the northern bank of the Red River, on the border between Texas and Oklahoma.

The 1850s saw a sharp increase in violence that marked every single life in the Choctaw Nation. Murders, assaults, and robberies were common, and we find many poignant accounts of premature death and the emotional devastation resulting from these events. In the 1850s, a civil war was narrowly averted in a dramatic confrontation between a small faction of intermarried whites and a few Choctaws who sought to assimilate with the American white society, and the rest of the Choctaw Nation, which staunchly wanted to remain separate. The latter were by far the greater majority of Choctaws, and this crisis brought even the quiet, peace-seeking traditionalists nearly to the point of war in order to preserve the Choctaw way of life.

Their efforts were effective in saving the Nation from within, but there was little they could do to stop the United States from using its vastly superior power to invade and subjugate the Choctaw Nation of the West. When political and economic demands converged in the 1870s, a critical mass of people willing to use any and all dishonorable means to confiscate the last remaining acres under Indian sovereignty ramrodded through the institutional and legal means to do so—the Dawes Act of 1885. Despite all the protests of the Indian nations, despite the grossly unethical and clearly immoral acts required of the Americans in repudiating all of their solemn promises in treaties ratified and in effect for a generation, the twin juggernaut of capital expansionism and civilian occupation put the finishing touches on the final American solution to the Indian problem: if they wouldn't disappear through natural processes, the American government needed to make the Indians invisible, economically, politically, and culturally.

At the turn of the nineteenth century, the great southern Indian nations of Oklahoma were unilaterally made to disappear, their people supposedly absorbed into the greater white society. In reality, many of these people were instead merely deprived of their lands and the means to support themselves and their families, and were thrust into the depths of poverty and deprivation. Despised by generations of white Americans, the native people of Oklahoma nonetheless quietly maintained their communities as best they could. They hung on to their identities and tried to continue the traditional communal practices.

Much of this struggle was in vain, because the United States forced the Indian nations to dissolve their communal landholdings. They assigned each native family an individual piece of private property, then stood aside watching as the mad, unseemly scramble of white sharpsters separated the People from their last remaining pieces of land. The U.S. government was well aware that taking away the communal landholdings would effectively dispossess most Indians of the lands on which they lived and farmed. They initially made laws seeming to protect the less well assimilated Indians for a number of years. This they did to get the votes necessary to implement taking the Indian lands. Then they passed exception after exception to these laws to allow whites to deprive the native people of their holdings. Within twenty years, 90 percent of the lands owned by the Choctaws and other native nations in Oklahoma had been swept away into the world market and, of course, into the hands of white men. The U.S. government passed laws requiring the Indian governments to dissolve themselves, insisting all the while that these measures were passed only for the welfare of the Indian people. Indian children were forced to attend white schools or no schools at all. Many were forced to attend boarding schools, where all vestiges of their Indian-ness were mercilessly extirpated, at least outwardly.

The United States continued for many decades to take native children away from their parents and homes and force them to go to distant boarding schools, in which they were subjected to harsh, alien regimens; deprived of the love and support of their families, friends, and familiar environments; shorn of their hair; made to wear uncomfortable clothing; and forced to abandon their beloved language and songs. They were compelled to outwardly adopt white religion and to comply with white models of student behavior. They were inundated with Euro-American norms and taught to hate and despise everything about their own culture. In Oklahoma, these features of white imperialism wiped out the pride, dignity, and self-confidence of thousands of native people, substituting in their place self-loathing and mortification at being "Indian."

Subsequent generations were treated to rudderless communities, deprived of the teachings and beliefs developed over countless generations of native people. Many of the languages were lost, the old ways were rubbed out, and the security and peace of close, extended kinship were destroyed. In the face of this crisis, alcohol abuse soared, crime became common, and young men and women searching for meaning in their lives often found none. Suicide rates soared, poverty became endemic, and the only way to profit was to adopt a white way of life, to deny native culture and heritage, and to distance oneself from the old counties of the Choctaw Nation.

After World War II, returning Indian veterans from Oklahoma brought a new knowledge of the outside world to their lives. Some found a way to proceed through the maze of white-ness as Indian people who were bicultural. Sure of their identity, they prospered in the white world and moved their families into distant suburbs of out-of-state towns and cities. A large number of Choctaw people still reside in places as distant as Los Angeles, Dallas, and St. Louis. Relocation programs instigated by Congress in the 1950s led to more Choctaws and other native Oklahomans moving to slum areas of Dallas and other large cities. There they were generally unable to acculturate themselves, and many dysfunctional families produced children who grew up with none of the strength of the native ways of life to help them find a way through life.

In the 1960s, some native people began to take note of the national civil rights movements, finally hearing the message that non-white people had value and potential. Unaccustomed to success, they were nonetheless starved for positive values and sought a new route in the white world. In the 1960s and 1970s, it became fashionable to be "part" Indian. Most people of native heritage at least wondered where their culture had gone, and many began searching for the ways lost to them and their families.

The Choctaw Nation of Oklahoma was officially recognized again in the 1960s. In this and the following decades, many cultural traditions were brought out of hiding, and the Choctaw language and arts began to be taught in schools and other public places. The Choctaw people now number over 100,000 strong, spread across the nation, with a concentration in the old Choctaw Nation counties of Oklahoma. Despite every tool of conquest, military, political, and cultural, that the American government brought to bear, the Choctaws continue to this day to be a viable, unique Indian community, whose members can still be heard to proudly declare, *Chah-tah siah,* I am Choctaw!

Notes

INTRODUCTION

1. See Michael Paul Rogin, *Fathers and Children: Andrew Jackson and the Subjugation of the American Indian* (New York: Alfred Knopf, 1975; reprint, New Brunswick, N.J.: Transaction Publishers, 1991), 33–36, 114–16 (page citations are to the reprint edition); Arthur H. DeRosier Jr., *The Removal of the Choctaw Indians* (New York: Harper & Row, 1970), 2, 70.

2. See, for example, Geoffrey C. Ward, with Rick Burns and Ken Burns, *The Civil War: An Illustrated History* (New York: Alfred A. Knopf, 1990), in which the index has no listing at all under "Indian," "Indian Territory, "Battle of Honey Springs," "General Stand Watie," or "Native Americans." The map entitled "The Civil War, 1861–1865" (Charthouse, 1992), which accompanies the text, ends in the West with the states of Arkansas, Louisiana, and Missouri, omitting Indian Territory altogether. In his Pulitzer Prize–winning text on the Civil War, historian James M. McPherson describes Indian participation in the war in two sentences, omitting the entire western theater of Indian Territory, tens of thousands of soldier participants, and generals Tandy Walker and Stand Watie, among others, in his 905-page volume. James M. McPherson, *Battle Cry of Freedom: The Civil War Era* (New York: Oxford University Press, 1988).

3. See R. David Edmunds, "National Expansion from the Indian Perspective," in *Indians in American History: An Introduction*, ed. Frederick E. Hoxie (Arlington Heights, Ill.: Harlan Davidson, 1988), 159–177.

4. Cyrus Kingsbury to Jeremiah Evarts, January 1831, Box 6, File 19; Cyrus Kingsbury to Jeremiah Evarts, 17 November 1830, Box 6, File 25, Cyrus Kingsbury Collection, Western History Collection, University of Oklahoma, Norman, Oklahoma; and DeRosier, *Removal*, 59, 61, 123.

5. Angie Debo, *The Rise and Fall of the Choctaw Republic* (Norman: University of Oklahoma Press, 1934), 290.

6. Grant Foreman, *Indian Removal: The Emigration of the Five Civilized Tribes of Indians* (Norman: University of Oklahoma Press, 1932), preface. Also see Anders Stephanson,

Manifest Destiny: American Expansionism and the Empire of Right (New York: Hill and Wang, 1995). His discussion of the half-truths and outright lies used as the foundation of the philosophical "justification" for the confiscation of Native lands in the American Southeast in the 1820s and 1830s is especially informative. Unfortunately, most American history survey texts continue to echo these distortions as though they were factual; in effect, passing on the propaganda of the era to generations of students of American history.

7. Foreman, *Indian Removal,* 399.

8. Ibid., 399–404.

9. Ibid., preface.

10. Debo, *Rise and Fall,* 243–44.

11. Foreman, *Indian Removal,* 17–18.

12. W. David Baird. *Peter Pitchlynn: Chief of the Choctaws* (Norman: University of Oklahoma Press, 1972); Richard White, *The Roots of Dependency: Subsistence, Environment, and Social Change among the Choctaws, Pawnees, and Navajos* (Lincoln: University of Nebraska Press, 1983).

13. White, 116.

14. White, 116.

15. White, 117.

16. White, 119.

17. White, 121.

18. White, 125.

19. Immanuel M. Wallerstein, *The Modern World System* (New York: Academic Press, 1989); and White, *Roots of Dependency,* xvi, xvii, xix, and 146.

20. White, *Roots of Dependency,* 146.

21. Ibid., xix.

22. Ibid., 146.

23. Debo, *Rise and Fall,* 45.

24. In Richard White's conclusion to the Choctaw section in *The Roots of Dependency,* he asserts, "For the Choctaws as a whole, trade and market meant not wealth but impoverishment, not well-being but dependency, and not progress but exile and dispossession. They never fought the Americans; they were never conquered. Instead, through the market they were made dependent and dispossessed" (146).

25. Clifford E. Trafzer, *Death Stalks the Yakima: Epidemiological Transition and Mortality on the Yakima Indian Reservation, 1888–1964* (East Lansing: Michigan State University Press, 1997), 5.

26. Jack D. Forbes, "The Manipulation of Race, Caste, and Identity: Classifying Afro-americans, Native Americans and Red-Black People," *Journal of Ethnic Studies* 17 (winter 1990): 24.

27. See Frederick E. Hoxie, "Interpreting the Indian Past," in *Major Problems in American Indian History,* ed. Albert L. Hurtado and Peter Iverson (Lexington, Mass.: D. C. Heath and Company, 1994), 35–37, for a discussion of Bernard Bailyn's assertion that he had to omit Indians from his two prize-winning recent works on American history because "we know as yet relatively little about their histories." Bernard Bailyn, *The Peopling of North America: An Introduction* (New York: Knopf, 1986). See also Forbes, "Manipulation," 1–51, in which he argues that "the uncolored have for too long been able to possess a near monopoly over the interpretation and organization of our col-

lective experience in the Americas." Later in the same article see his discussion of "Making Americans (and Africans) Vanish," 27–30. See also the writings of Fernand Braudel, especially *The Mediterranean and the Mediterranean World in the Age of Philip II* (New York: Harper and Row), 1972.

28. Denise Lardner Carmody and John Tully Carmody, *Native American Religions: An Introduction* (New York: Paulist Press, 1993), 6–9.

29. Charles Kappler, ed., *Indian Affairs, Laws, and Treaties* (Washington, D.C.: Government Printing Office, 1929), 2:112. The United States negotiated a treaty with the Quapaws in 1818 for almost all the land lying between the Red River and the Arkansas and Canadian Rivers, extending west from the Mississippi River to Mexico, for $4,000 and an annuity of about $1,000 in goods. Ravaged by smallpox, this nation had dwindled to a number that could not defend its former lands. The United States further demanded that the Quapaws were to be confined to the lands of the Caddo Indians on the Red River, and were to become a part of that nation. After the Caddos refused to receive them, this once strong nation was reduced to starvation. Their plight was so appalling that the governor of Arkansas investigated, finding that a number of them had starved to death. Governor Izard reported that they had been shamefully mistreated by the United States government, their land and all means of subsistence taken for a pittance. Some private white citizens attempted to relieve the worst suffering by offering a supply of corn. The Quapaws wandered about their old hunting grounds for years, finally merging with the Osages. The U.S. secretary of war eventually required that a tiny strip of the land so shamefully taken from the Quapaws be restored. See George Gray, Indian Agent, to Secretary of War, 30 June 1828; Izard to Secretary of War, 6 June 1827; Willliam Clark to Thomas McKenney, 24 February 1828; Clark to McKenney, 3 July 1828; and John Pope to Secretary of War, 22 June 1829, Office of Indian Affairs, Retired Classified Files, "1828 Red River Agency."

Chapter 1

1. John R. Swanton, *Source Material for the Social and Ceremonial Life of the Choctaw Indians* (Washington, D.C.: Government Printing Office, 1931; reprint, Birmingham, Ala.: Birmingham Public Library Press, 1993), 17 (page citations are to the reprint edition).

2. Jackson to McKee, Choctaw Agent, 22 April 1819, *American State Papers: Indian Affairs* 2:229.

3. Patricia Galloway, *Choctaw Genesis: 1500–1700* (Lincoln: University of Nebraska Press, 1995), 358.

4. Charles M. Hudson, *The Southeastern Indians* (Knoxville: University of Tennessee Press, 1976), 438–39.

5. John Pitchlynn to Peter Pitchlynn, 5 April 1834, Box 2, File 47, Peter P. Pitchlynn Collection, Western History Collection, University of Oklahoma, Norman.

6. Horatio B. Cushman, *History of the Choctaw, Chickasaw, and Natchez Indians* (Greenville, Tex.: Headlight Printing House, 1899; reprint, New York: Russell and Russell, 1962), 331–32 (page citations are to the reprint edition).

7. Arthur H. DeRosier Jr., *The Removal of the Choctaw Indians* (New York: Harper & Row, 1970), 28.

8. Thomas Jefferson to Benjamin Hawkins, 18 February 1803, *The Writings of Thomas Jefferson, Memorial Edition Containing his Autobiography, Notes on Virginia, Parliamentary*

Manual, Official Papers, Messages and Addresses, and other Writings, Official and Private, now Collected and Published in their Entirety for the first time Including all of the Original Manuscripts, Deposited in the Department of State and Published in 1853 by order of the Joint Committee of Congress with Numerous Illustrations and A Comprehensive Analytical Index, ed. Andrew A. Lipscomb and Albert E. Bergh (Washington, D.C.: Thomas Jefferson Memorial Association of the United States, 1904), 10: 362–63.

9. DeRosier, Removal, 25–26.

10. Thomas Jefferson to John Breckenridge, 12 August 1803, Memoir, Correspondence, and Miscellanies, from the Papers of Thomas Jefferson, ed. Thomas Jefferson Randolph (Charlottesville, 1829), 3:512.

11. DeRosier, Removal, 28.

12. Treaty of Hopewell, on the Keowee, near Seneca Old Town with the Choctaw, http://www.councilfire.com/treaty/treaty4.html.

13. Treaty of Fort Adams with Choctaw, 17 December 1801, http://www.councilfire.com/treaty/treaty20.html; DeRosier, Removal, 30; Dunbar Rowland, ed., The Mississippi Territorial Archives, 1798–1803: Executive Journals of Governor Winthrop Sargent and Governor William Charles Cole Claiborne (Nashville: Press of Brandon Printing Company, 1905), 1:476–78.

14. www.flash.net/~kma/t19.htm.

15. Charles Kappler, ed., Indian Affairs, Laws, and Treaties (Washington, D.C.: Government Printing Office, 1929), 56–58, 63–64, 69–70, and 87–88; Forbes to Dearborn, 5 September 1806, American State Papers: Indian Affairs 1:750–51; James D. Richardson, ed., Message and Papers of the Presidents, 1789–1817 (Washington, D.C.: Government Printing Office, 1896–99), 1:434–35; DeRosier, Removal, 32; Richard White, The Roots of Dependency: Subsistence, Environment, and Social Change among the Choctaws, Pawnees, and Navajos, (Lincoln: University of Nebraska Press, 1983), 112–13; and Robert S. Cotterill, "A Chapter of Panton, Leslie and Company," Journal of Southern History 10 (February–November 1944): 287.

16. DeRosier, Removal, 30–31; www.flash.net/~kma/t19.htm.

17. Annie Haney, interview by author, Hugo, Choctaw Nation (Oklahoma), May 1992; notes in possession of author.

18. DeRosier, Removal, 36–37.

19. American State Papers: Indian Affairs 6:95, and DeRosier, Removal, 36–37.

CHAPTER 2

1. Thomas L. McKenney to Andrew Jackson, 23 April 1829, Records of the Office of Indian Affairs, Letters Sent, MSS, War Department, National Archives, p. 417.

2. Arthur H. DeRosier Jr., The Removal of the Choctaw Indians (New York: Harper & Row, 1970), 40–46; John C. Calhoun to United States House of Representatives, 8 December 1818, Reports and Public Letters of John C. Calhoun, ed. Richard K. Cralle (New York: D. Appleton & Co., 1888), 5:19.

3. Michael Paul Rogin, Fathers and Children: Andrew Jackson and the Subjugation of the American Indian (New York: Knopf, 1975), 174–75.

4. Andrew Jackson to James Monroe, 4 March 1815, Correspondence of Andrew Jackson, ed. John Spencer Bassett (Washington, D.C.: Carnegie Institution of Washington, 1928), 2:278–81; Rogin, Fathers and Children, 166–68.

5. DeRosier, 47.

6. On economic change, see Richard White, *The Roots of Dependency: Subsistence, Environ- ment, and Social Change among the Choctaws, Pawnees, and Navajos* (Lincoln: University of Nebraska Press, 1983), 146.

7. William E. Unrau, *White Man's Wicked Water: The Alcohol Trade and Prohibition in Indian Country, 1802–1892* (Lawrence: University Press of Kansas, 1996), 14; Bureau of Indian Affairs, Letters Received by the Office of Indian Affairs, Choctaw Agency, M 234, RG 75, National Archives.

8. Unrau, *Wicked Water*, 18.

9. *American State Papers: Indian Affairs* 2: 810–11.

10. White, *Roots*, 99–105; Horatio B. Cushman, *History of the Choctaw, Chickasaw, and Natchez Indians* (Greenville, Tex.: Headlight Printing House, 1899; reprint Stillwater, Okla.: Redlands Press, 1962), 105 (page citations are to the reprint edition); *Niles' Weekly Register*, 15 (1818): 186.

11. Dunbar Rowland, *History of Mississippi, Heart of the South* (Chicago: S. J. Clarke Publishing Co., 1925), 1:100.

12. Thomas Jefferson to Benjamin Hawkins, 18 February 1803, *The Works of Thomas Jefferson*, ed. Paul Leicester Ford, 12 vols. (New York: G. P. Putnam's Sons, 1904–5), 9:362.

13. Patricia Galloway, *Choctaw Genesis, 1500–1700* (Lincoln: University of Nebraska Press, 1995), 340, 360.

14. *Niles' Weekly Register*, 37 (1829): 181.

15. The Cherokees likewise devised a law that affirmed traditional beliefs but brought them within the form of American law. Their law allowed the killing of the animal into which the spirit of the witch had been projected, but did not allow for the death of the human being. See Grant Foreman, ed., *A Traveler in Indian Territory: The Journal of Ethan Allen Hitchcock, late Major-General in the United States Army* (Cedar Rapids, Iowa: Torch Press, 1930), 192–93.

16. John Pitchlynn to Peter P. Pitchlynn, 30 September 1834, Box 1, File 43; John Pitchlynn to Peter P. Pitchlynn, 10 January 1835, Box 1, File 45; Mary Rhoda Pitchlynn to Charles G. Lombardi, 27 October 1870, Box 4, File 49, Peter P. Pitchlynn Collection, Western History Collection, University of Oklahoma, Norman; and Nancy Fulsom Cox, Interview, 1935, no. 309, reel 1, vol. 2, *Indian-Pioneer History Collection*, Indian Archives, Oklahoma Historical Society, Oklahoma City.

17. DeRosier, 50.; Walter Lowrie and Walter S. Franklin, eds., American State Papers: Documents, Legislative and Executive, of the Congress of the United States, from the first session of the Fourteenth to the second session of the Nineteenth Congress, inclu- sive, commencing Dec. 4, 1815, and ending March 3, 1827. (Washington, D.C.: Government Printing Office, 1834), 6:230.

18. *Mississippi State Gazette*, 8 January 1820.

19. Lowrie and Franklin, *American State Papers: Indian Affairs* 6:230.

20. Lowrie and Fraknlin, *American State Papers: Indian Affaris* 6:238; "Treaty with the Choctaw, 1820" in *Indian Affairs, Laws, and Treaties*, ed. Charles J. Kappler (Washing- ton, D.C.: Government Printing Office, 1904–1929), 2:192.

21. Cushman, *History*, 64–67.

22. Ibid; *Arkansas Gazette*, 7 October 1820.

23. Lowrie and Franklin, *American State Papers: Indian Affairs* 2:230.

24. Cushman, *History*, 67.

25. "Treaty with the Choctaw, 1820," 2:191–95.

26. Lowrie and Franklin, *American State Papers: Indian Affairs* 2:394–95.

27. S. S. Hamilton to John Eaton, 16 December 1830, Bureau of Indian Affairs, Letters Sent by the Office of Indian Affairs, M21, RG 75, War Department, National Archives.

28. Duane Champagne, *American Indian Societies: Strategies and Conditions of Political and Cultural Survival* (Cambridge, Mass., Cultural Survival, Inc., 1989) 52–59.

29. Cushman, *History*, 88–89.

30. Chillaten, *Tushma ben* to Peter Pitchlynn, 15 May 1837, File 53, Peter P. Pitchlynn Collection, Western History Collection, University of Oklahoma, Norman; Henry C. Benson, "Life Among the Choctaw Indians," *Chronicles of Oklahoma* 9 (June, 1926): 156–61; and Angie Debo, *The Rise and Fall of the Choctaw Republic* (Norman: University of Oklahoma Press, 1934), 16.

31. Clara Sue Kidwell, *Choctaws and Missionaries in Mississippi, 1818–1918* (Norman: University of Oklahoma Press, 1995), 68, 72, 94, 144–46; U.S. Senate, 23d Cong., 1st sess. S. Doc. 512, 2:58–59.

32. Anna Lewis, "Oklahoma as a Part of the Spanish Domain," *Chronicles of Oklahoma*, 3 (1924): 48–49, translation of a letter in the Archives of the Indies at Seville.

33. White, *Roots*, 122.

34. Donna L. Akers, review of *White Man's Wicked Water: The Alcohol Trade and Prohibition in Indian Country, 1802–1892*, by William E. Unrau, *American Indian Culture and Research Journal* 21, no. 4 (winter 1998).

35. *Natchez* (Natchez, Miss.), 13 February 1830, 6; *Natchez* (Natchez, Miss.), 20 February 1830, 1.

36. "Article XIII, Treaty of 1825" in *Indian Affairs, Laws, and Treaties*, ed. Charles J. Kappler (Washington, D.C.: Government Printing Office, 1904), 2:193; Cushman, *History*, 88–89.

37. Mingo Mushulatubbee to Peter P. Pitchlynn, 25 September 1824, Box 1, File 3, Peter P. Pitchlynn Collection, Western History Collection, University of Oklahoma, Norman.

38. Cyrus Kingsbury to Jeremiah Evarts, 28 January 1829, Box 8, File 32, Cyrus Kingsbury Collection, Western History Collection, University of Oklahoma, Norman.

39. John Edwards, "The Choctaw Indians in the Middle of the Nineteenth Century," *Chronicles of Oklahoma* 10 (1932): 396; *Boston Missionary Herald* 26 (August 1830): 251–52; and George Harkins to Peter P. Pitchlynn, 20 December 1827, Peter P. Pitchlynn Collection, Thomas Gilcrease Institute of American History and Art, Tulsa, Oklahoma.

CHAPTER 3

1. Charles Hudson, *The Southeastern Indians* (Knoxville: University of Tennessee Press, 1976), 319.

2. Alfred Wright and Cyrus Byington, *Chahta holisso Ai isht la ummona* (Boston: American Board of Commissioners for Foreign Missions, 1835), 9–11.

3. Hudson, *Southeastern Indians*, 336–50.

4. Ibid., 184–99.

5. Jedediah Morse, *A Report to the Secretary of War of the United States, on Indian Affairs, Comprising a Narrative of a Tour Performed in the Summer of 1820, under a Commission from the President of the United States, for the Purpose of Ascertaining for the Use of the Government, the Actual State of the Indian Tribes in Our Country* (New Haven, Conn.: Davis and Force, 1822), 186–87.

6. Hudson, *Southeastern Indians,* 185.

7. J. F. H. Claiborne, *Mississippi As a Province, Territory and State, with Biographical Notes of Eminent Citizens* (Jackson, Miss.: Power and Barksdale,1880; reprint, Baton Rouge: Louisiana State University Press, 1964), 1:512–14 (page citations are to the reprint edition); Peter P. Pitchlynn to Thomas Pitchlynn, 23 September 1846, Columbus, Mississippi, Box 1, File 109, Peter P. Pitchlynn Collection, Western History Collection, University of Oklahoma, Norman.

8. J. S. McDonald to Peter P. Pitchlynn, 13 December 1830, Box 1, File 19, Peter P. Pitchlynn Collection, Western History Collection, University of Oklahoma, Norman; and John R. Swanton, *Source Material for the Social and Ceremonial Life of the Choctaw Indians* (Washington, D.C.: Government Printing Office, 1931; Birmingham, Ala.: Birmingham Public Library Press, 1993), 197 (page citations are to the reprint edition); Horatio B. Cushman, *History of the Choctaw, Chickasaw, and Natchez Indians* (Greenville, Tex.: Headlight Printing House, 1899; reprint, New York: Russell and Russell, 1962), 196 (page citations are to the reprint edition).

9. Cushman, *History,* 232–33; Charles Billy, interview by author, Tuskahoma, Okla., 5 August 1995.

10. Colonel Cobb to U.S. Commission, quoted in Clairborne, *Mississippi,* 512.

11. Cushman, *History,* 270.

12. Edwin James, *Account of an Expedition from Pittsburgh to the Rocky Mountains Performed in the Years 1819, 1820,* vol. 4 of *Early Western Travels, 1748–1846,* ed. Reuben Gold Thwaites (New York: AMS Press, 1966), 147; Zebulon Montgomery Pike, *The Expedition of Zebulon Montgomery Pike* (1896; reprint, Minneapolis: Ross and Haines, 1965), 525.

13. Cushman, *History,* 64; Grant Foreman, ed., *Marcy and the Gold Seekers: The Journal of Captain R. B. Marcy, with an Account of the Gold Rush Over the Southern Route* (Norman: University of Oklahoma Press, 1968), 33–34.

14. James, *Account,* 147; Pike, *Expedition,* 525.

15. John Wesley Powell, *Report on the Lands of the Arid Region* (Washington, D.C.: Government Printing Office, 1878), 46–56; Donald Worster, *Under Western Skies: Nature and History in the American West* (New York: Oxford University Press, 1992), 101–3

16. Walter Prescott Webb, *The Great Plains* (Lincoln: University of Nebraska Press, 1981), 23–24; Randolph Marcy and George B. McClellen, *Exploration of the Red River of Louisiana in the Year 1852,* Senate, 32d Cong., 2d sess., 54 (Washington, D.C.: Government Printing Office, 1853), 85.

17. Lizzie, Choctaw Nation, to Mother, 13 November 1859, Colonial Dames Collection, Western History Collection, University of Oklahoma, Norman.

18. Margaret Zehmer Searcy, "Choctaw Subsistence, 1540–1830: Hunting, Fishing, Farming, and Gathering," in *The Choctaw Before Removal,* ed. Carolyn Keller Reeves (Jackson: University Press of Mississippi, 1985), 33.

19. Webb, *Great Plains,* 13.

20. Lizzie, Choctaw Nation, to Mother, 13 November 1859, Colonial Dames Collection.

21. Isaac McCoy, *History of the Baptist Indian Missions* (1840; reprint, New York: Johnson Reprint Corporation, 1970), 6; Paul G. Risser et al., *The True Prairie Ecosystem* (Stroudsburg, Penn.: Hutchinson Ross Publishing Company, 1981), 14–15.

22. Reginald Aldridge, *Ranch Notes in Kansas, Colorado, The Indian Territory, and Northern Texas* (London: Longmans, Green and Company, 1884), 27–28; and Orlando, Choctaw Nation, to Mother, 27 August 1860, Colonial Dames Collection, Western History Collection, University of Oklahoma, Norman.

23. Aldridge, *Ranch Notes*, 10; and Henry A. Wright and Arthur W. Bailey, *Fire Ecology: United States and Southern Canada* (New York: John Wiley & Sons, 1982), 89–91.

24. Wright and Bailey, *Fire Ecology*, 1.

25. George Catlin, *Letters and Notes On the Manners, Customs, And Condition of the North American Indians, Written during Eight Year's Travel amongst the Wildes and Tribes of Indans in North America* (1841; reprint, Minneapolis: Ross and Haines, Inc., 1965), 16–18.

26. Lt. A. W. Whipple in Grant Foreman, ed., *A Pathfinder in the Southwest: The Itinerary of Lt. A. W. Whipple During His Explorations for a Railway Route from Fort Smith to Los Angeles in the Years 1853 and 1854* (Norman: University of Oklahoma Press, 1941), 68.

27. Catlin, *Letters and Notes*, 16, 18; Foreman, *Pathfinder*, 62.

28. Foreman, *Pathfinder*, 68.

29. Ibid., 62, 73; Aldridge, *Ranch Notes*, 79–81.

30. Grant Foreman, *Indian Removal: The Emigration of the Five Civilized Tribes of Indians* (Norman: University of Oklahoma Press, 1932), 33.

31. Alfred Wright, *Boston Missionary Herald*, 24, no. 6 (June 1828): 179–80.

32. George E. Lankford, ed., *Native American Legends: Southeastern Legends* (Little Rock, Ark.: August House, 1987), 55; and Claiborne, *Mississippi*, 492–93.

33. Wright and Bailey, *Fire Ecology*, 180; P. G. Brinton and Cyrus Byington, eds., *Grammar of the Choctaw Language by the Reverend Cyrus Byington. Edited from the Original Manuscript in the Library of the American Philosophical Society by P. B. D. Brinton.* (Philadelphia: McCalla & Stavely, 1870), 43; and Swanton, *Source Material*, 196–97.

34. Lankford, *Legends*, 54–55.

35. Ibid.

36. Ibid., 43.

37. Hudson, *Southeastern Indians*, 125, 127.

38. Ibid, 127.

39. Ibid, 128.

40. Ibid., 132; and John R. Swanton, "Social Organization and Social Usages of the Indians of the Creek Confederacy," *Bureau of American Ethnology Annual Report* 42 (1928): 492.

41. Adam Hodgson, *Remarks from North America, Written During a Tour in the United States and Canada* (London, 1824), 75.

42. Henry C. Benson, *Life Among the Choctaw Indians and Sketches of the South-West* (New York: Johnson Reprint Corporation, 1970), 70–77, 33–34; and *Report of the Commissioner of Indian Affairs* (Washington, D.C.: Government Printing Office): 1836, 391; 1837, 541–42, 545; 1843, 336; 1852, 412.

43. William H. Goode, *Outposts of Zion, With Limnings of Mission Life* (Cincinnati: Poe and Hitchcock, 1863), 47.

44. Edward B. Espenshade Jr. and Joel L. Morrison, eds., *Goode's World Atlas*, 14th ed. (Chicago: Rand McNally & Company, 1974), 117–18; and John W. Morris, Charles R. Goins, and Edwin C. McReynolds, *Historical Atlas of Oklahoma*, 3d ed. (Norman: University of Oklahoma Press, 1986), 3–7.

45. U.S. Senate. 23d Cong., 1st sess., S. Doc. 512, 3:662.

46. Rhoda Pitchlynn, Eagletown, Choctaw Nation, to Peter P. Pitchlynn, 26 October 1841, Box 1, File 70, and 5 January 1842, Box 1, File 74, Peter P. Pitchlynn Collection, Western History Collection, University of Oklahoma, Norman.

47. Muriel H. Wright, "Early Navigation and Commerce Along the Arkansas and Red Rivers in Oklahoma," *Chronicles of Oklahoma* 8 (March 1930): 74–76.

48. Dan L. Flores, ed., *Jefferson & Southwestern Exploration: The Freeman & Custis Accounts of the Red River Expedition of 1806* (Norman: University of Oklahoma Press, 1984), 127–28; H. N. Fisk, "Geology of Avoyelks and Rapides Parishes," *Louisiana Geological Bulletin no. 18* (New Orleans: Louisiana Department of Conservation, 1940), 40–42.

49. Flores, *Jefferson & Southwestern Exploration*, 129–30; John Sibley, "Historical Sketches of the Several Tribes in Louisiana South of the Arkansas and Between the Mississippi and the River Grand," in *Message from the President of the United States, Communicating Discoveries Made in Exploring the Mississippi, Red River, and Washita, by Captains Lewis and Clark, Doctor Sibley and Mr. Dunbar,* by Thomas Jefferson (New York: Hopkins and Seymour, 1806), 40.

50. Flores, *Jefferson & Southwestern Exploration*, 129–30.

51. Thomas Freeman, quoted in Flores, *Jefferson & Southwestern Exploration*, 131.

52. Peter Custis, quoted in Flores, *Jefferson & Southwestern Exploration*, 154.

53. Katharine Coman, *Economic Beginnings of the Far West* (New York: Augustus M. Kelley, 1912; reprint, New York: AMS Press, 1969), 2:61.

54. James D. Morrison, "Notes from the *Northern Standard*, 1842–1849," *Chronicles of Oklahoma* 19 (1941): 273.

55. Foreman, *Indian Removal*, 49, 50, and 71; Coman, *Economic Beginnings*, 2:25 and 61; James, *Account*, 71; Grant Foreman, "River Navigation in the Early Southwest," *Mississippi Valley Historical Review 15* (June 1928): 36–42; and Carl Newton Tyson, *The Red River in Southwestern History* (Norman: University of Oklahoma Press, 1981), 94–101, 150–53.

56. Carl Newton Tyson, *The Red River in Southwestern History* (Norman: University of Oklahoma Press, 1981), 94–101, 150–53.

57. Donna Akers Whitt, "Robert M. Jones and the Making of the Choctaw Red River Elite," manuscript in possession of author, 3–8.

58. Morrison, "Notes," 272, 283.

59. Ibid., 276.

60. Coman, *Economic Beginnings*, 2:60.

61. J. D. Hunter to John Pitchlynn, 28 September 1825, Box 1, File 9, Peter P. Pitchlynn Collection, Western History Collection, University of Oklahoma, Norman.

62. David and Robert Folsom, *Report of Exploring Party*, 23d Cong., 1st sess., 24 December 1830, S. Doc. 512, "Indian Removal," 2:197.

63. J. D. Hunter, Arkansas Territory, to John Pitchlynn, Choctaw Nation, 28 September 1825, Box 1, File 9, Peter P. Pitchlynn Collection, Western History Collection, University of Oklahoma, Norman; and *Report of the Commissioner of Indian Affairs* (Wahsington, D.C.: Government Printing Office, 1838), 1838: 73.

64. Cyrus Byington to Wife, 23 January 1840, Foreman Collection, Thomas Gilcrease Institute, Tulsa, Oklahoma.

65. Catlin, *Letters and Notes*, 18.

66. Hudson, *Southeastern Indians*, 272–73, 282, 300; Benson, *Life Among the Choctaw Indians*, 42–43; and Richard White, *The Roots of Dependency: Subsistence, Environment, and Social Change among the Choctaws, Pawnees, and Navajos* (Lincoln: University of Nebraska Press, 1983), 13, 103.

67. Foreman, *Indian Removal*, 34–35, 41.

68. Virginia R. Allen, "Medical Practices and Health in the Choctaw Nation, 1831–1885," *Chronicles of Oklahoma* 48 (spring 1970): 63, 65, 73; and Cyrus Kingsbury to General Secretary, 1852, "Changes in the Choctaw Nation," Cyrus Kingsbury Collection,

Western History Collection, University of Oklahoma, Norman.

69. Bafra Alice Dobbs, interview, 1936, *Indian-Pioneer History Collection,* 22:294, Indian Archives, Oklahoma Historical Society, Oklahoma City; Susan G. Maxey, interview, 1936, 6:460, Ibid.; Josephine Usray Lattimore, interview, 1936, 33:57, Ibid.; Alice Marie Cook, interview by author, Choctaw Nation, January 1993, transcript in possession of author.

CHAPTER 4

1. *Arkansas Gazette,* 3 February 1821, p. 3, cols. 1, 2, 3, and 4; and 20 November 1822, p. 3, col. 3.

2. Foreman, *Indians and Pioneers,* 138.

3. R. G. Thwaites, ed., *Early Western Travels, 1748–1846* (Cleveland, 1904), 222.

4. William B. DeWees and Clara Cardelle, comp., *Letters from an Early Settler of Texas* (Louisville, Ky.: Morton & Griswold, 1852).

5. Grant Foreman, *Indians and Pioneers: The Story of the American Southwest before 1830* (1936; reprint, Norman: University of Oklahoma Press, 1967), 148.

6. *Arkansas Gazette,* 3 February 1821, p. 3, cols. 1, 2, 3, and 4.

7. *Arkansas Gazette,* 7 October 1820.

8. *Mississippi State Gazette,* 25 November 1820; *Arkansas Gazette,* 6 January, 25 November 1820, in Arthur H. DeRosier Jr., *The Removal of the Choctaw Indians* (New York: Harper & Row, 1970), 74.

9. Horatio B. Cushman, *History of the Choctaw, Chickasaw, and Natchez Indians* (Greenville, Tex.: Headlight Printing House,1899; reprint, New York: Russell & Russell, 1962), 66; DeRosier, 74.

10. Interviews with Irwin T. Dodd, Oklahoma City, 1965–73, notes in possession of author; Annie Hanie, interview by author, Hugo, Okla., July 1992; Cushman, *History,* 234–73.

11. *Kentucky Gazette,* 28 October 1824, p. 3, col. 2, and Cushman, *History,* 274.

12. "Consumer Price Index (Estimate) 1800–2000," Federal Reserve Bank of Minneapolis, www.woodrow.mpls.frb.fed.us//economy/calc/hist1800.html.

13. U.S. leaders apparently had no qualms about the means they used to procure so-called treaties. Furthermore, once a treaty was signed, U.S. agents and political leaders knowingly and deliberately misrepresented the process. Unfortunately, successive generations of American historians have simply repeated these deliberate misrepresentations, often not making it clear that these land cessions were simply a weapon of colonization, a mechanism for the dispossession of the Indian peoples of North America, absent all decency and fair play. This, unfortunately, has led several generations of Americans to unquestioningly accept and even admire a process that was, at best, despicable and unworthy of the American nation.

14. Cyrus Kingsbury to Jeremiah Evarts, 8 August 1825, Folder 6, File 47, Cyrus Kingsbury Collection, Western History Collection, University of Oklahoma, Norman.

15. DeRosier, *Removal,* 82; David Folsom to Cyrus Kingsbury, 19 January 1825, Folder 6, Cyrus Kingsbury Collection, Western History Collection, University of Oklahoma, Norman; Angie Debo, *The Rise and Fall of the Choctaw Republic* (Norman: University of Oklahoma Press, 1934), 50; and Foreman, *Indians and Pioneers,* 157–59.

16. Charles J. Kappler, ed. "Treaty with the Choctaw, 1825, Article 7" *Indian Affairs: Laws and Treaties Volume II (Treaties)* (Washington, D.C.: Government Printing Office, 1904.

Online http://digital.library.okstate.edu/kappler/vol2/treaties/cho0211.htm.

17. Elliott Coues, ed., *Expeditions of Zebulon Montgomery Pike* (New York: F. P. Harper, 1895), 2:555 and 590–91.

18. Willard Hughes Rollings, *Prairie Hegemony: An Ethnohistorical Study of the Osage, From Early Times to 1840* (Ph.D. diss., Texas Tech University, 1983). (Reproduction, Ann Arbor, Mich.: University Microfilms International, 1987, 27.)

19. Secretary of War John C. Calhoun exchanged congratulations with Tennessee governor Joseph McMinn in their expert use of bribery, fraud, and double dealings in official U.S. "negotiations" with the Cherokees. McMinn wrote to Calhoun, " . . . I am truly pleased to learn that the usual plans had been taken with the Chiefs in purchasing their friendship, for such has been the course pursued with the natives for time immemorial, and corrupt as it may appear, we are compelled to have to resort to the measure. They have disclosed the secret to me with much gratification." (Joseph McMinn to J. C. Calhoun, Knoxville, 12 April 1818, Office of Indian Affairs, Retired Classified Files, "Special File" no. 131, quoted in Foreman, *Indians and Pioneers*, 68.)

20. Andrew Jackson, Joseph McMinn, and Lewis Meriwether to Secretary of War, 9 July 1817, Andrew Jackson Papers, Library of Congress, 6559.

21. Lowrie, *American State Papers: Indian Affairs* 2:151; Charles Kappler, ed., *Indian Affairs, Laws, and Treaties* (S. Doc. 452, 57th Cong., 1st sess.) (Washington, D.C.: Government Printing Office, 1903), 2:96.

22. *Niles' Weekly Register* (Baltimore), 13:80; Thomas Nuttall, "Journal of Travels into Arkansas Territory, during the Year 1819, with Occasional observations on the manners of the Aborigines," in *Early Western Travels, 1748–1846*, ed. Reuben Gold Thwaites (Cleveland: A. H. Clark Co., 1904–8; reprint, New York: AMS Press, 1966), 13:192 (page citations are to the reprint edition).

23. John Sibley, *A Report from Natchitoches in 1807* (New York: Museum of the American Indian and Heye Foundation, 1922), 12; Foreman, *Indians and Pioneers*, 14–16, 23, 42–43.

24. Foreman, *Indians and Pioneers*, 70–72; Kappler, *Indian Affairs*, 2:96.

25. Foreman, *Indians and Pioneers*, 78.

26. *Niles' Weekly Register,* (Baltimore), vol. 2, 30 March 1823.

27. *Niles' Weekly Register* (Baltimore), vol. 1, 30 March 1822 and vol. 2, 31 March 1823; *Arkansas Gazette,* 19 March 1822, p. 3, col. 1, and 29 April 1823, p. 3, col. 1; Pierre Menard to R. Graham, 3 January 1822, Graham Papers, Missouri Historical Society, St. Louis, Mo.

28. *Missouri Intelligencer,* 24 December 1822, p. 2, col. 3.

29. *Natchitoches Courier,* March 1825, p. 1, col. 1; *Arkansas Gazette,* 26 April 1825, p. 3, col. 1.

30. Kappler, *Indian Affairs,* 2:160–61.

31. Foreman, *Indians and Pioneers,* 180–83.

32. William Clark to John C. Calhoun, 5 September 1823, Graham Papers, Missouri Historical Society, St. Louis, Mo.

33. *Daily National Journal* (Washington), 8 February 1825, p. 3, col. 4; *Arkansas Gazette,* 3 May 1825, p. 3, col. 3; William Clark to Secretary of War, 15 November 1825, Report of Council, "1825 Cherokees of Arkansas and Shawnees," Graham Papers, Missouri Historical Society, St. Louis, Mo.

34. Pierre Menard to Richard Graham, 17 April 1826; Letter from John Campbell, sub-

agent, written at Delaware village, 16 March 1826, Graham Papers, Missouri Historical Society, St. Louis, Mo.

35. Foreman, *Indians and Pioneers,* 204.

36. Ibid., 207; *New York Spectator,* 13 November 1826, p. 1, col. 3.

37. Carolyn Thomas Foreman, "The Cherokee War Path With Annotations," *Chronicles of Oklahoma* 9, no. 3 (September 1931): 233–35.

38. *Illinois Gazette,* 25 October 1828, p. 3, col. 1.

39. Memorial of Arkansas Legislature, 5 November 1829, Adjutant General's Office, Old Records Department, War Department Files, Washington, D.C., quoted in Foreman, *Indians and Pioneers,* 238–40.

40. *Cherokee Phoenix,* 17 March 1830, p. 2, col. 1; *Niles' Weekly Register,* 38:48; *National Intelligencer,* 8 March 1830, p. 3, col. 5.

CHAPTER 5

1. Anthony Winston Dillard, "The Treaty of Dancing Rabbit Creek Between the United States and the Choctaw Indians in 1830," *Alabama Historical Society Transactions* 3 (1899): 99–106.

2. Ibid, 103.

3. Ibid., 28–29.

4. Cyrus Kingsbury to Jeremiah Evarts, 30 January 1830, Kingsbury Collection, Western History Collection, University of Oklahoma, Norman.

5. Arthur H. DeRosier Jr., *The Removal of the Choctaw Indians* (reprint, New York: Harper and Row, 1972), 135.

6. Walter Lowrie and Walter S. Franklin, eds., *American State Papers: Documents, Legislative and Executive, of the Congress of the United States, from the first session of the Fourteenth to the second session of the Nineteenth Congress, inclusive, commencing December 4, 1815, and ending March 3, 1827* (Washington, D.C.: Gales and Seaton).

7. DeRosier, *Removal,* 137.

8. Peter J. Hudson to Grant Foreman, 25 August 1928, pp. 1–4, Grant Foreman Papers, Thomas Gilcrease Institute, Tulsa, Oklahoma; and Jesse O. McKee and Jon A. Schlenker, *The Choctaws: Cultural Evolution of a Native American Tribe* (Jackson: University Press of Mississippi, 1980), 99.

9. Editorial, *Boston Missionary Herald,* 1832, quoted in Gardner Papers, 4026.4558.4, Thomas Gilcrease Institute, Tulsa, Okla.

10. *Report of the Commissioner of Indian Affairs, 1849* (Washington: GPO, 1850), 256.

11. Henry C. Benson, *Life Among the Choctaw Indians and Sketches of the South-West* (New York: Johnson Reprint Corporation, 1970), 31, 32, and 51.

12. Ruth Fowler, interview by author, Oklahoma City, Oklahoma, June 1989; Betsy Tonikha, interview by author, Norman, November 1993; LeAnne Howe, interview by author, Lawrence, Kansas, May 1997.

13. Edwin James, Stephen Harriman Long, and Thomas Say, *Account of an Expedition from Pittsburg to the Rocky Mountains, under the Command of Major Stephen H. Long, from the notes of Major Long, Mr. T. Say, and other gentlemen of the Exploring Party* (Barre, Mass.: Imprint Society, 1972), 55–56; and James Adair, *History of the American Indians: Particularly those Nations adjoining to the Mississippi, East and West Florida, Georgia, South and North Carolina, and Virginia* (1775; reprint, New York: Johnson Reprint Corporation, 1968),

492–93; Peter P. Pitchlynn to Gideon Lincecum, 12 November 1846, Box 1, File 110, Peter P. Pitchlynn Collection, Western History Collection, University of Oklahoma, Norman; and Charles Hudson, *The Southeastern Indians* (Knoxville: University of Tennessee Press, 1976), 368–72.

14. The mound is "on the head waters of Pearl River, and not far from the geographical center of the State of Mississippi. . . . The mound is described as some fifty feet high, covering about three-quarters of an acre, the apex level, with an area of about one fourth of an acre. On the north side of the mound are the remains of a circular earthwork or embankment, that must have been constructed for defensive objects. Many of the Choctaws examined by the Commissioners regard this mound as the mother, or birthplace of the tribe, and more than one claimant declared that he would not quit the country as long as the Nan-a wy-yah remained. It was his mother, and he could not leave her." J. F. H. Claiborne, *Mississippi As a Province, Territory and State with Biographical Notes of Eminent Citizens* (Jackson, Miss.: Power & Barksdale, 1880; reprint, Baton Rouge: Louisiana State University Press, 1964), 519 (page citations are to the reprint edition); John Witthoft, "Green Corn Ceremonialism in the Eastern Woodlands," in *Ethnology of the Southeastern Indians: A Sourcebook* (New York: Garland Publishing, 1985), 15, 33, 70; and Simpson Tubby to John R. Swanton, quoted in John R. Swanton, *Source Material for the Social and Ceremonial Life of the Choctaw Indians* (Birmingham, Ala.: Birmingham Public Library Press, 1993), 100; *"Ohoyo Osh Chisba"* (The unknown woman), in Horatio B. Cushman, *History of the Choctaw, Chickasaw, and Natchez Indians,* (Greenville, Tex.: Headlight Printing House, 1899; reprint, New York: Russell & Russell, 1962), 214–15 (page citations are to the reprint edition); and Buster Jefferson to author, November 1993.

15. Alexander Spoehr, "Changing Kinship Systems, A Study in the Acculturation of the Creeks, Cherokee, and Choctaw," *Anthropological Series,* Field Museum of Natural History, 33 (17 January 1947): 212–13; Fred Eggan, "Historical Changes in the Choctaw Kinship System," *American Anthropologist* 39 (1937): 41, 44.

16. Buster Jefferson, interview by author, Norman, Okla., November 1993; Cyrus Byington, *A Dictionary of the Choctaw Language,* ed. John R. Swanton and Henry S. Halbert, Smithsonian Institution, Bureau of American Ethnology, Bulletin 46 (Brighton, Mich.: Native American Book Publishers, 1990), 10, 14, 230, 488.

17. John M. Hodges, Lukfata, Choctaw Nation, to Loring S. W. Folsom, Caddo, 15 April 1877, Box 4, File 71; Loring Folsom to Peter Pitchlynn, 20 April 1877, Box 4, File 71; Malvina Pitchlynn Folsom, Lukfata, Choctaw Nation, to Peter P. Pitchlynn, Washington City, 2 May 1877, Box 4, File 72; D. L. Kannedy, Eagletown, Choctaw Nation, to Peter P. Pitchlynn, Washington, 28 May 1877, Box 4, File 73; Malvina Pitchlynn Folsom, Caddo Hill, Choctaw Nation, to Peter P. Pitchlynn, 12 July 1877, Box 4, File 74; Malvina Pitchlynn Folsom, Caddo Hill, Choctaw Nation, to Peter P. Pitchlynn, 12 July 1877, Box 4, File 75; Malvina Pitchlynn Folsom to Peter P. Pitchlynn, 7 August 1877, Box 4, File 76; Peter P. Pitchlynn to Caroline V. Lombardi Pitchlynn, 12 October 1877, Box 4, File 78; Loring S. W. Folsom to Peter P. Pitchlynn, 11 November 1877, Box 4, File 79; Loring S. W. Folsom to Peter P. Pitchlynn, 18 November 1877, Box 4, File 80; Malvina Pitchlynn Folsom to Peter P. Pitchlynn, 23 January 1878, Box 4, File 81; Loring S. W. Folsom to Peter P. Pitchlynn, 4 January 1878, Box 4, File 81; Loring S. W. Folsom (Caddo, Choctaw Nation) to Peter P. Pitchlynn, 24 January 1878; Malvina Pitchlynn Folsom to Peter P. Pitchlynn, 19 January 1878, Box 4, File 82; Malvina Pitchlynn

Folsom to Peter P. Pitchlynn, 12 March 1878, Box 4, File 83, Peter P. Pitchlynn Collection, Western History Collection, University of Oklahoma, Norman.

18. Lycurgus P. Pitchlynn to Peter P. Pitchlynn, 31 December 1858, Box 3, File 37; Loring S. W. Folsom to Peter P. Pitchlynn, January 1859, Box 3, File 38; Lycurgus P. Pitchlynn to Peter P. Pitchlynn, 3 January 1859, Box 3, File 39; Lycurgus P. Pitchlynn to Peter P. Pitchlynn, 4 January 1859, Box 3, File 40; Melvina Pitchlynn Folsom to Peter P. Pitchlynn, 10 January 1859, Box 3, File 42, Peter P. Pitchlynn Collection, Western History Collection, University of Oklahoma, Norman; and Cyrus Byington, 30 March 1861, 13 April 1861, and 29 July 1861, Byington Papers, Thomas Gilcrease Institute, Tulsa, Okla.

19. Israel Folsom, New Hope, to Peter P. Pitchlynn, 20 February 1841, 4026.3568.1, Thomas Gilcrease Institute, Tulsa, Okla.; Lycurgus Pitchlynn to Peter P. Pitchlynn, Washington City, 14 July 1841, Jay L. Hargett Collection, Western History Collection, University of Oklahoma, Norman; Edmond Folsom to Peter P. Pitchlynn, 12 August 1832, Box 1, File 30; Peter Folsom and Wart Folsom to Peter P. Pitchlynn, 7 June 1835, Box 1, File 49; McKee Folsom and Chillater to Peter P. Pitchlynn, 15 May 1837, Box 1, File 43; Joseph B. Folsom to Peter P. Pitchlynn, 13 April 1853, Box 2, File 22; James Gamble, Fort Smith, Arkansas, to Peter P. Pitchlynn, 20 July 1857, Box 2, File 103; Sampson Folsom, Doaksville, Choctaw Nation, to *Oni Oshi Ma,* 9 December 1857, Box 3, File 2; Alice Pitchlynn to Peter Pitchlynn, 9 January 1858, Box 3, File 8; Jacob Folsom to Peter P. Pitchlynn, 19 January 1858, Box 3, File 11; Joseph and Nancy Dukes, Norwalk, Choctaw Nation, to Peter Pitchlynn, 21 May 1858, Box 3, File 24; Nathaniel Folsom, Russellville, Kentucky, to Peter P. Pitchlynn, 29 May 1858, Box 3, File 25; Hiram R. Pitchlynn to Peter P. Pitchlynn, 5 February 1860, Box 3, File 57; Sampson Folsom, Doaksville, Choctaw Nation, to Peter P. Pitchlynn, 16 July 1860, Box 3, File 74; Peter P. Howell, Agri College, Maryland, to Peter P. Pitchlynn, October 1860, Box 3, File 83; and Peter P. Pitchlynn to John, 1861, Box 3, File 90, Peter P. Pitchlynn Collection, Western History Collection, University of Oklahoma, Norman.

20. Peter P. Pitchlynn, Washington City, to Lycurgus Pitchlynn, Newark, Delaware, 21 December 1848, Box 2, File 7, Peter P. Pitchlynn Collection, Western History Collection, University of Oklahoma, Norman.

21. Sampson Folsom and James Gamble, Washington, D.C., to James Buchanan, President of the United States, 29 June 1857, Box 2, File 99; Loring S. W. Folsom, Lukfata, Choctaw Nation, to Peter P. Pitchlynn, 2 June 1857, Box 2, File 95; Lycurgus Pitchlynn, Van Buren, Arkansas, to Peter P. Pitchlynn, Washington City, 17 June 1857, Box 2, File 96, and 19 June 1857, Box 2, File 97, Peter P. Pitchlynn Collection, Western History Collection, University of Oklahoma, Norman.

22. John Pitchlynn to Peter P. Pitchlynn, 5 April 1835, Box 1, File 46; Chillater to Peter P. Pitchlynn, 15 May 1837, Box 1, File 53; Rhoda Pitchlynn to Peter P. Pitchlynn, 28 December 1841, Box 1, File 73; Lycurgus Pitchlynn to Peter P. Pitchlynn, 17 June 1857, Box 2, File 97; Lycurgus Pitchlynn to Peter P. Pitchlynn, 11 December 1857, Box 3, File 4; Nathaniel Folsom, Russellville, Kentucky, to Peter P. Pitchlynn, 29 May 1858, Box 3, File 25; Hiram R. Pitchlynn, Greencastle, Indiana, to Peter P. Pitchlynn, 7 February 1860, Box 3, File 57; Caroline C. Webb Pitchlynn, Eagle County, Choctaw Nation, to Peter P. Pitchlynn, 13 July 1860, Box 3, File 71; Peter P. Pitchlynn, Washington, City, to Mary Pitchlynn Garland, 22 November 1871, Box 4, File 52; and Peter Folsom to Sophia C. Pitchlynn, 5 September 1882, Box 4, File 105, Peter P. Pitchlynn Collection, Western History Collection, University of Oklahoma, Norman.

23. Benson, *Life Among the Choctaw Indians,* 34; Hudson, *Southeastern Indians,* 184–86, 190; Buster Jefferson, interview by author, 1993, notes in possession of author.

24. John Pitchlynn to Peter P. Pitchlynn, 7 October 1834, Box 1, File 44, Peter P. Pitchlynn Collection, Western History Collection, University of Oklahoma, Norman; Spoehr, "Changing Kinship Systems," 201, 205, 209; Eggan, "Historical Changes," 37; and Cushman, *History,* 27, 28, 87, 90, 122, 144, and 176.

25. John Pitchlynn to Peter P. Pitchlynn, 10 January 1835, Box 1, File 45; John Pitchlynn to Peter P. Pitchlynn, 30 January 1835, Box 1, File 46; John Pitchlynn to Peter P. Pitchlynn, 5 April 1835, Box 1, File 47, Peter P. Pitchlynn Collection, Western History Collection, University of Oklahoma, Norman.

26. Mary Frances Bonner, interview, 1937, *Indian-Pioneer History Collection,* reel 1, vol. 2, no. 240; and Elijah Conger, interview, 1937, *Indian-Pioneer History Collection,* reel 1, vol. 2, no. 196, Indian Archives, Oklahoma Historical Society, Oklahoma City.

27. Mary Frances Bonner, interview, 1937.

CHAPTER 6

1. Mingo Mushulatubbee et al. to Sec. of War John Eaton, 15 June 1831, U. S. Senate, *Indian Removals* 2:474.

2. Mushualtubbee, Oklabbee, Ispiahhomah, Charles King, James M. King, Hiram King, and Peter King to Andrew Jackson, 23 December 1830, cited in Carolyn Thomas Foreman, "Choctaw Academy," *Chronicles of Oklahoma* 6 (spring, 1924): 475.

3. Loring J. Williams to Peter P. Pitchlynn, 18 August 1835, Box 1, File 50, Peter P. Pitchlynn Collection, Western History Collection, University of Oklahoma, Norman; Benson, "Life Among the Choctaw Indians," 93.

4. Cyrus Kingsbury to Greene, 22 November 1839, Box 2, File 1, Cyrus Kingsbury Collection, Western History Collection, University of Oklahoma, Norman.

5. Henry C. Benson, "Life Among the Choctaw Indians," *Chronicles of Oklahoma* 9 (June, 1926): 90.

6. Loring J. Williams to Peter P. Pitchlynn, 18 August 1835, Box 1, File 50, Peter P. Pitchlynn Collection, Western History Collection, University of Oklahoma, Norman; Benson, "Life Among the Choctaw Indians," 93.

7. Captain Robert Cole to Cyrus Kingsbury, et al., 22 June 1821, Box 9, File 29, Kingsbury Collection, Western History Collection, University of Oklahoma, Norman; and Michael C. Coleman, *Presbyterian Missionary Attitudes toward American Indians, 1837–1893* (Jackson: University Press of Mississippi, 1985), 37.

8. Israel Folsom, New Hope, Choctaw Nation, to Peter P. Pitchlynn, 13 September 1841, Box 1, File 66, Peter P. Pitchlynn Collection, Western History Collection, University of Oklahoma, Norman.

9. Annie Haney, Irwin T. Dodd, interview by author; notes in possession of author, Hugo, Okla., and Oklahoma City.

10. Carolyn Thomas Foreman, "The Choctaw Academy," *Chronicles of Oklahoma,* 6 (1928): 453–80; Charles Kappler, ed., *Indian Affairs, Laws and Treaties* (Washington, D.C.: Government Printing Office, 1929), 2:193; and "Report from the Indian Office," Dept. of War, Office of Indian Affairs, 20 November 1826, *New American State Papers: Indian Affairs* 1:507.

11. David Folsom, Chahta Tamaha to Peter P. Pitchlynn, 26 January 1842, Box 1, File 78;

Israel Folsom to Peter Pitchlynn, 24 September 1841, Box 1, File 68; Jacob Folsom to Peter Pitchlynn, 20 October 1841, Box 1, File 69; Pierre Juzan et al. to Peter P. Pitchlynn, 7 October 1840, Box 1, File 57; and Richard M. Johnson to Peter P. Pitchlynn, 29 January 1841, Box 1, File 59, 31 January 1841, Box 1, File 60, and 7 February 1841, Box 1, File 61, Peter P. Pitchlynn Collection, Western History Collection, University of Oklahoma, Norman.

12. John Pages to Peter P. Pitchlynn, 1841, Box 1, File 58, Peter P. Pitchlynn Collection, Western History Collection, University of Oklahoma, Norman.

13. Jacob Folsom to Peter P. Pitchlynn, 20 October 1841 Box 1, File 69, Peter P. Pitchlynn Collection, Western History Collection, University of Oklahoma, Norman; and Letter Draft, n.d., Folder Un-155, Pitchlynn Collection, Thomas Gilcrease Institute, Tulsa, Okla.

14. Peter J. Hudson to Grant Foreman, 25 August 1928, pp. 1–4, Grant Foreman Papers, Thomas Gilcrease Institute, Tulsa, Okla.

15. Duane Champagne, *Social Order and Political Change*, 185.

16. Ibid.; *Report of the Commissioner of Indian Affairs*, War Department, Office of Indian Affairs, 25 November 1838 (Washington, D.C.: Government Printing Office) 454–55.

17. J. Wall to Peter P. Pitchlynn, Washington City, 11 November 1850, Box 2, File 18; and Thomas Pitchlynn to Peter P. Pitchlynn, 30 March 1851, Box 2, File 19, and 22 December 1852, Box 2, File 21, Peter P. Pitchlynn Collection, Western History Collection, University of Oklahoma, Norman.

18. Armstrong to Herring, 17 September, 1833, Office of Indian Affairs, "Choctaw Agency," in Grant Foreman, *Indian Removal: The Emigration of the Five Civilized Tribes of Indians* (Norman: University of Oklahoma Press, 1932), 97.

19. On 22 November 1833, General Gibson announced that no more Choctaws would be removed under the terms of the treaty, since the three years given to accomplish their dispossession had expired. This left the thousands of Choctaws who were en route without provisions, and upon their arrival, with no assistance at all. See U. S. Senate, "Indian Removal," 23d Cong., 1st sess., 22 November 1833, S. Doc. 512, 1:324.

20. Ibid., 845, 851; and Grant Foreman, *Indian Removal: The Emigration of the Five Civilized Tribes of Indians*, 2d ed. (Norman: University of Oklahoma Press, 1953), 96–99.

21. U.S. Senate, "Indian Removal"

22. Horatio B. Cushman, *History of the Choctaw, Chickasaw, and Natchez Indians* (Greenville, Tex.: Headlight Printing House, 1899), 195.

23. James Mooney, *Calendar History of the Kiowa Indians* (Washington, D. C.: Smithsonian Institution Press, 1979), 260–61; Cushman, *History*, 195–97; and John Pitchlynn, Chickasaw Country, to Peter P. Pitchlynn, 7 October 1834, Box 1, File 44, Peter P. Pitchlynn Collection, Western History Collection, University of Oklahoma, Norman.

24. John Pitchlynn, at home, to Peter P. Pitchlynn, Eagletown, Arkansas, 30 September 1834, Box 1, File 43; and John Pitchlynn, Plymouth, Mississippi, to Peter Pitchlynn, Red River Chaktaw [*sic*] Country, 30 September 1834, Box 1, File 43, Peter P. Pitchlynn Collection, Western History Collection, University of Oklahoma, Norman.

25. Gardner Papers, Thomas Gilcrease Institute, 4026.4557; and U. S. Senate, *Indian Removal*, 1:849.

26. Cushman, *History*, 42.

27. Letter, Cyrus Byington, Stockbridge, 13 July 1842, and 4 August 1841, Gardner Papers, Thomas Gilcrease Institute, 4026.4557.5; Lt. Whipple, quoted in Grant Foreman, ed. *A Pathfinder in the Southwest: The Itinerary of Lt. A. W. Whipple During His Explorations for a Rail-*

way Route from Fort Smith to Los Angeles in the Years 1853 and 1854 (Norman: University of Oklahoma Press, 1941), 35; and Edmond Folsom, Choctaw Nation West, to Peter Pitchlynn Old Nation, Choctaw Agency in Mississippi, 12 August 1832, Box 1, File 30, Peter P. Pitchlynn Collection, Western History Collection, University of Oklahoma, Norman.

28. Loring S. Williams, 1 January 1834, 4026.4557, and Alfred Wright, 14 May 1834, 4026.4557, Gardner Papers, Thomas Gilcrease Institute, Tulsa, Okla.

29. Lavinia Pitchlynn to Peter Pitchlynn, 14 December 1841, Box 1, File 72; Rhoda Pitchlynn to Peter Pitchlynn, 29 December 1841, Box 1, File 73; Rhoda Pitchlynn to Peter Pitchlynn, 5 January 1842, Box 1, File 74, and 15 January 1842, Box 1, File 75, Peter P. Pitchlynn Collection, Western History Collection, University of Oklahoma, Norman.

30. *Report of the Commissioner of Indian Affairs,* 1838, 454–455.

31. *Report of the Commissioner of Indian Affairs,* 25 November 1838, *New American State Papers: Land Cessions* 1:511; see also Cyrus Kingsbury, Mountain Fork, 1838, Gardner Papers, 4206, 4557.2, Thomas Gilcrease Institute, Tulsa, Okla.; and Henry R. Schoolcraft, *Information Respecting History, Condition, and Prospects of Indian Tribes of United States,* (Philadelphia, 1847), 257.

32. Cushman, *History,* 518–19.

33. S. V. R. Ryan to Hon. Lewis Cass, Sec. of War, 24 April 1833, 23d Cong., 1st sess., 1833, S. Doc. 512, "Indian Removal," 1:842; Foreman, *Indian Removal,* 99–102; Choctaw oral traditions, Annie Haney, Irwin T. Dodd, Charlie Jones, and others.

CHAPTER 7

1. Thomas J. Bond (Boggy Depot, Choctaw Nation) to Peter P. Pitchlynn, 25 June 1858, Peter P. Pitchlynn Collection, Western History Collection, University of Oklahoma, Norman.

2. Cyrus Kingsbury to Mr. Treat, June 1857, Box 5, File 52, Kingsbury Collection, Western History Collection, University of Oklahoma, Norman.

3. Wart and Peter Folsom to Peter P. Pitchlynn, 10 June 1835, Box 1, File 49; Israel Folsom to Peter P. Pitchlynn, 27 September 1847, Box 1, File 115, Peter P. Pitchlynn Collection, Western History Collection, University of Oklahoma, Norman.

4. George W. Harkins, Doaksville, Choctaw Nation, to Peter P. Pitchlynn, 12 August 1856, Box 2, File 87, Peter P. Pitchlynn Collection, Western History Collection, University of Oklahoma, Norman.

5. Ibid.

6. Ibid.

7. Horatio B. Cushman, *History of the Choctaw, Chickasaw, and Natchez Indians* (Greenville, Tex.: Headlight Printing House, 1899; reprint, New York: Russell & Russell, 1962), 122, 176 (page citations are to the reprint edition); John Edwards, "The Choctaw Indians in the Middle of the Nineteenth Century," *Chronicles of Oklahoma* 10 (1932): 400, 410.

8. Cyrus Kingsbury to Mr. Treat, June 1857, Box 5, File 52, Kingsbury Collection.

9. Peter P. Pitchlynn to Green and Walker, Attorneys at Law, October 1857, Box 2, File 105; Lycurgus Pitchlynn (Van Buren, Arkansas) to Peter P. Pitchlynn, 17 June 1857, Box 2, File 96, Peter P. Pitchlynn Collection, Western History Collection, University of Oklahoma, Norman.

10. Sampson Folsom and James Gamble, Washington City, to President James Buchanan, 29 June 1857, Box 2, File 99, Peter P. Pitchlynn Collection, Western History Collection, University of Oklahoma, Norman.
11. Peter P. Pitchlynn, Washington City, to Messrs. Walker and Green, Attorneys at Law, Van Buren, Arkansas, October 1857, Box 2, File 105, Peter P. Pitchlynn Collection, Western History Collection, University of Oklahoma, Norman.
12. Jean-Bernard Bossu, *Travels in the Interior of North America, 1751–1762,* trans. and ed. Seymour Feiler (Norman: University of Oklahoma Press, 1961), 169–70; John R. Swanton, *Source Material for the Social and Ceremonial Life of the Choctaw Indians* (Birmingham, Ala.: Birmingham Public Library Press, 1993), 44; Emiziah Bohanan, interview, 1937, *Indian-Pioneer History Collection,* reel 1, vol. 2, no. 228; and Sampson Collin, interview, reel 1, vol. 2, no. 177, Indian Archives, Oklahoma Historical Society, Oklahoma City.
13. Sampson Collin, interview.
14. George Catlin, *Letters and Notes On the Manners, Customs, And Condition of the North American Indians, Written during Eight Year's Travel amongst the Wiles and Tribes of Indians in North America* (1841; reprint, Minneapolis: Ross and Haines, 1965), 2:121–25.
15. James Adair, *History of the American Indians: Particularly those Nations adjoining to the Mississippi, East and West Florida, Georgia, South and North Carolina, and Virginia,* with an introduction by Robert F. Berkhofer Jr., ed. Samuel Cole Williams (New York: Argonaut Press, 1966), 486. Some Choctaw ball plays had mixed-gender teams. This is the likely explanation for the mention of many women being slain in the fight with the Creeks. Some of the women killed may have been on the field of play as competitors. See Grant Foreman, ed., *A Traveler in Indian Territory: The Journal of Ethan Allen Hitchcock, late Major-General in the United States Army* (Cedar Rapids, Iowa: Torch Press, 1930), 158.
16. Peter Folsom and Wart Folsom, Arkansas Territory, to Peter P. Pitchlynn, 7 June 1835, Box 1, File 49, Peter P. Pitchlynn Collection, Western History Collection, University of Oklahoma, Norman.
17. "Report from the Secretary of War on the Subject of Disturbances with the Indians on the Frontier of Arkansas, 1838," Graff Collection, no. 4499, Newberry Library, Chicago; Cyrus Kingsbury to David Greene, 20 July 1843, Box 3, File 8; Diary of Sue McBeth, Goodwater, 11 April 1860, Box 9, File 62, Kingsbury Collection, Western History Collection, University of Oklahoma, Norman.
18. Lycurgus Pitchlynn to Peter Pitchlynn, 22 May 1856, Box 2, File 81; George Harkins to Peter Pitchlynn, 12 August 1856, Box 3, File 87; Lycurgus Pitchlynn to Peter P. Pitchlynn, 4 January 1858, Box 3, File 7, Peter P. Pitchlynn Collection, Western History Collection, University of Oklahoma, Norman.
19. Muriel Wright, "Sarah Ann Harlan: From Her Memoirs of Life in the Indian Territory," *Chronicles of Oklahoma* 39 (1961): 163–64.

CHAPTER 8

1. The account from a Choctaw eyewitness who wrote about the incident in detail to his father-in-law differs in significant facts from the account of William G. McLoughlin, Walter H. Conser, and Virginia Duffy McLoughlin in "The Choctaw Slave Burning: A Crisis in Indian Missions, 1859–1861," in *The Cherokee Ghost Dance: Essays on the Southeastern Indians, 1789–1861* (New York: Mercer, 1984), 343–62. The McLoughlin

account states that the slaves were tortured for days and forced to confess, strongly suggesting that Lucy was innocent. All eyewitness accounts refute this assertion. McLoughlin et al. evidently based their account on the charges made by a disgruntled former employee who was being discharged because of his abolitionist beliefs, which offended some leaders among the Choctaws, and his personal unpopularity. Prior to his firing, this missionary threatened to reveal an "awful" secret that would "ruin the Choctaw Nation" and greatly embarrass the Presbyterian Board of Foreign Missions. His motive was evidently revenge for his discharge. See Lycurgus Pitchlynn to Peter P. Pitchlynn, Eagletown, 3 January 1858 [sic]; Box 3, File 39; L. S. W. Folsom to Peter P. Pitchlynn, January 1859, Box 3, File 38, Peter P. Pitchlynn Collection, Western History Collection, University of Oklahoma, Norman; McLoughlin, Conser, and McLoughlin, "Choctaw Slave Burning," 344.

2. Byington Letters, 30 March 1861, 13 April 1861, and 29 July 1861, Thomas Gilcrease Institute, Tulsa, Okla.

3. M. L. Folsom to Peter P. Pitchlynn, Lukfatah, Choctaw Nation, 10 January 1859, Box 3, File 42; L. S. W. Folsom to Peter P. Pitchlynn, January 1859, Box 3, File 38; Lycurgus P. Pitchlynn to Peter P. Pitchlynn, 31 December 1858, Box 3, File 37; and Lycurgus P. Pitchlynn to Peter P. Pitchlynn, Eagletown, Choctaw Nation, 3 January 1859, Box 3, File 39, Peter P. Pitchlynn Collection, Western History Collection, University of Oklahoma, Norman.

4. Charles K. Whipple, *Relation of the American Board of Commissioners for Foreign Missions to Slavery* (New York: Negro Universities Press, 1969), 202–8, 210, 212, 244–47; and James Frothingham to J. L. Wilson, 25 April 1859, Presbyterian Historical Society (PHS), Philadelphia, Box 10, 2:282.

5. Whipple, *Relation,* 22; and Theda Perdue, *Slavery and the Evolution of Cherokee Society, 1540–1866* (Knoxville: University of Tennessee Press, 1979), 120–25.

6. Michael C. Coleman, *Presbyterian Missionary Attitudes toward American Indians, 1837–1893* (Jackson: University Press of Mississippi, 1985), 59.

Bibliography

Manuscript Collections

American Board of Commissioners for Foreign Missions. Papers. Houghton Library, Harvard University, Cambridge, Mass.

Ayer Collection. The Newberry Library, Chicago.

Belvin, G. N. Papers, 1874–1929. A collection of documents written mostly in English but also many in Choctaw and Creek. Western History Collection, University of Oklahoma, Norman.

Burbank, Elbridge Ayer. *Burbank's Indian Portraits.* Special Collections, Box no. 7, 116–27; 12 drawings in red crayon, Newberry Library, Chicago.

Byington, Cyrus. Papers. Thomas Gilcrease Institute, Tulsa, Okla.

Chickasaw Nation. "Chickasaw Tribal Records." Indian Archives Division, Oklahoma Historical Society, Oklahoma City.

Choctaw Census, 1896, in "A Compilation of Records from the Choctaw Nation, Indian Territory," Microfilm Publication #4, Oklahoma Genealogical Society, 1977.

Choctaw Nation. "Choctaw Tribal Records." Indian Archives Division, Oklahoma Historical Society, Oklahoma City.

Choctaw Nation. Papers, 1868–1936. Western History Collection, University Of Oklahoma, Norman.

Colonial Dames Collection. Papers, 1851–94. Correspondence regarding Choctaw Nation and Spencer Academy. Western History Collection, University of Oklahoma, Norman.

Cook, Benjamin R. Collection. Account books, statements, and receipts from the Hester Mercantile Store, Boggy Depot, Indian Territory. Western History Collection, University of Oklahoma, Norman.

Foreman, Grant. Papers. Oklahoma Historical Society, Oklahoma City. Thousands of pages of source materials regarding the native people of Oklahoma, collected by an eminent Indian historian.

Foreman, Grant Papers. Thomas Gilcrease Institute, Tulsa, Okla. A very large and valuable collection of research and correspondence of Dr. Foreman.

General Council. Proceedings of the General Council of the Indian Territory for 1872, 1873, and 1875. Indian Archives Division, Oklahoma Historical Society, Oklahoma City.

Graff Collection. Newberry Library, Chicago.

Hargett, J. L. Collection. Correspondence regarding missionary work among the Choctaws; diaries, travel accounts, student notebooks. Western History Collection, University of Oklahoma, Norman.

Indian-Pioneer History Collection. 1861–1936. Indian Archives, Oklahoma Historical Society, Oklahoma City. Oral history collection. Interviews during the 1930s of thousands of Oklahomans regarding the settlement of Oklahoma and Indian territories, and the condition and conduct of life there. 80,000 entries.

Jarboe, Mrs. W. C. Manuscript. Western History Collection, University of Oklahoma, Norman.

Kingsbury, Cyrus. Records. Correspondence and reports of Kingsbury, a Presbyterian missionary among the Choctaws, regarding Choctaw "removal" to Indian Territory, the Civil War, and slavery. Western History Collection, University of Oklahoma, Norman.

LeFlore, Carrie. Papers. 1886–92, item 636.Western History Collection, University of Oklahoma, Norman.

Pitchlynn, Peter P. Papers. Thomas Gilcrease Institute, Tulsa, Okla. A rare and important collection of documents and letters pertaining to Pitchlynn and his family, friends, and associates.

Pitchlynn, Peter Perkins. Papers. Western History Collection. University of Oklahoma, Norman. Correspondence (1824–81) of Pitchlynn with prominent citizens and family members in the Choctaw Nation regarding events and troubles within the nation; Pitchlynn's personal journals; Pitchlynn's diary; official reports of the Choctaw Academy; and Pitchlynn family records.

Redwin Trading Company Collection. Records. Collection spans thirty years and reflects the economic conditions of the Choctaw Nation of Indian Territory.

Robertson, Alice. Alice Robertson Collection. Oklahoma Historical Society, Oklahoma City.

Government Records

American State Papers: 2, *Indian Affairs.* 9, *Claims.*

Bureau of Indian Affairs. Letters Received by the Office of Indian Affairs, 1824–81, M234, Record Group 75. National Archives, Washington, D.C.

Bureau of Indian Affairs. Letters Sent by the Office of Indian Affairs, 1824–81, M21, Record Group 75. National Archives, Washington, D.C.

Choctaw Trading House. Records, 1803–24. Microfilm Roll T500, Record Group 75, Records of the Bureau of Indian Affairs.

U.S. Congress. Senate Documents, 23d Cong., 1st sess., no. 512. 5 vols. Correspondence on the subject of the emigration of Indians between 30 November 1831 and 27 December 1833, furnished in answer to a resolution of the Senate of 27 December 1833 in *The Indian Removals,* New York: AMS Press, 1974.

U.S. Secretary of War. Report from the Secretary of War on the subject of disturbances with the Indians on the Frontier of Arkansas, 1838. Graff 4499; Newberry Library, special collection, Chicago.

———. Report of the Commissioner of Indian Affairs. 60 vols. Washington, D.C.: Government Printing Office, 1824–1907.

United States Congress. House. Public Documents of. State Papers. 20th Cong., 1st sess. Vol. 6, no. 233: Information as to Indians that have emigrated west, called for by House resolution March 22, 1828; no. 263: Correspondence relative to Lovely's Purchase, Arkansas, called for by House resolution April 10, 1828. Washington, D.C.: Government Printing Office,

U.S. Congress. House. *Correspondence on the subject of the emigration of the Indians between 30th Nov. 1831, and 27th Dec., 1833, furnished in answer to a resolution of Senate, of 27th Dec., 1833.* 24th Cong., 2d sess., H. Doc. 1, message of president.

———. *Letters from Secretary of War transmitting correspondence relative to settlement of Lovely's Purchase in Territory of Arkansas.* 20th Cong., 1st sess., H. Doc. 263.

———. *Notes of a Military Reconnaissance, from Fort Leavenworth, in Missouri, to San Diego, California, including part of Arkansas, Del Norte, and Gila Rivers, by Lieut. Col. W. H. Emory. Made in 1846-47, with advanced guard of Army of West.* 30th Cong., 1st sess., H. Doc. 41.

———. *Petition of Joseph Bogy praying compensation for spoilations on his property by a numerous party of Choctaw Indians, then at peace with United States, whilst on a trading expedition on Arkansas River, under authority of a license derived from United States.* 24th Cong., 1st sess., H. Doc. 23.

———. *President's message upon the subject of the contemplated removal of Indians to west of Mississippi.* 22d Cong., 1st sess., H. Doc. 116.

———. *Report of the committee on Indian affairs and a bill to provide for establishment of Western Territory, accompanied by a report of commissioners of Indian affairs west, at Fort Gibson.* 23d Cong., 1st sess., H. Doc. 474.

———. *Report of the committee on Indian affairs submitting a bill to provide for establishment of Western Territory, accompanied by a report of commissioners of Indian affairs west, at Fort Gibson.* 23d Cong., 1st sess., H. Doc. 474.

———. *Report of the committee on military affairs, submitting a plan for defense of western frontier, furnished by Major-General Gaines, February 28, 1838.* 25th Cong., 2d sess., H. Doc. 311.

———. *Report of investigating committee of charges of fraud against Samuel Houston and Secretary of War, in rationing of emigrating Indians together with testimony heard by committee.* 22d Cong., 1st sess., H. Doc. 502.

NEWSPAPERS

Arkansas Advocate (Little Rock), 1819-1836.
The Arkansas Gazette (Little Rock), 1823–39.
Arkansas Intelligencer (Van Buren), 1845.
Bishinik (Durant, Choctaw Nation of Oklahoma), 1998–2004.
The Cherokee Advocate (Tahlequah, Cherokee Nation), 1867–79.
Choctaw News (Doaksville), vol.1, October–November 1878.
Choctaw Vindicator (New Boggy, Atoka, Choctaw Nation), 1872.
Daily National Journal (Washington, D.C.), 1824–1832.
Illinois Gazette (Shawneetown, Ill.), 1819–1830.
Indian Citizen (Atoka, Choctaw Nation), October 1895.
Kentucky Gazette (Lexington, Ky.), 1809–1848.
Missionary Herald (Boston), 1819–52.
Mississippi State Gazette (Natchez, Miss.), 1818–1825.
Missouri Intelligencer, (Franklin, Missouri Territory), 1819–1927.
Natchez (Natchez, Mississippi), 1830.

National Intelligencer (Washington, D.C.), 1810–1869.

New York Spectator, 1804–1867.

Niles' Weekly Register (Baltimore), 1833–1854.

ARTICLES

Akers, Donna L. "Robert M. Jones and the Making of the Choctaw Red River Elite." Unpublished manuscript. N.d., 3–8.

Allen, Virginia R. "Medical Practices and Health in the Choctaw Nation, 1831–1885." *Chronicles of Oklahoma* 48 (spring 1970): 60–73.

Andrews, T. F. "Freedmen in Indian Territory: A Post-Civil War Dilemma." *Chronicles of Oklahoma* 4 (1965): 367–76.

Banks, Dean. "Civil War Refugees from Indian Territory in the North, 1861–1864." *Chronicles of Oklahoma* 41 (1963): 286–98.

Benson, Henry C. "Life Among the Choctaw Indians." *Chronicles of Oklahoma* 9 (June 1926): 156–61.

Bilotta, James D. "Manifest Destiny and the Five Civilized Tribes." *Indian Historian* 10, no. 3 (1977): 23–33.

Bolt, Christine. "Return of the Native: Some Reflections on the History of American Indians." *Journal of American Studies* 8, no. 2 (1974): 247–59.

Bonnifield, Paul. "Choctaw Nation on the Eve of the Civil War." *Journal of the West* 12 (July): 386–402.

Brown, Maurice. "A Sociolinguistic Study of the Choctaw Language." *Southern Quarterly* 9 (1970): 41–48.

Brown, Richard Maxwell. "Western Violence: Structure, Values, Myth." *Western Historical Quarterly* (1993): 4–20.

Buckner, H. F. "Burial among the Choctaws." *American Antiquarian and Oriental Journal* 2 (1879): 55–58.

Burnet, William E. "Letters: Removal of the Texas Indians and the Founding of Fort Cobb." *Chronicles of Oklahoma* 38 (autumn 1960): 274–309.

Bushnell, David I., Jr. "Myths of the Louisiana Choctaw." *American Anthropologist* 12 (1910): 526–35.

———. "The Choctaws of St. Tammany." *Louisiana Historical Quarterly* 1 (Spring 1917): 11–20.

Byington, Cyrus. "A Dictionary of the Choctaw Language." *Bulletin of Bureau of American Ethnology* 46 (n.d.): 1–161.

Campbell, T. N. "Medicinal Plants Used by the Choctaw, Chickasaw, and Creek Indians." *Chronicles of Oklahoma* 41 (1951): 285–90.

———. "The Choctaw Afterworld." *Journal of American Folklore* 72 (1959): 146–54.

———. "Choctaw Subsistence: Ethnographic Notes from the Lincecum Manuscript." *Chronicles of Oklahoma* 12 (1959): 9–24.

Carson, James Taylor. "Horses and the Economy and Culture of the Choctaw Indians, 1690–1840." *Ethnohistory* 42, no. 3 (1995): 497–513.

Christian, Emma Ervin. "Memories of My Childhood Days in the Choctaw Nation." *Chronicles of Oklahoma* 9 (1931): 1034–39.

Coleman, Lewis. "Twenty-Five Days to the Choctaw Nation." *Chronicles of Oklahoma* 64 (1986): 4–15.

Conlan, Czarina C. "David Folsom." *Chronicles of Oklahoma* 4 (1926): 340–55.

Cotterill, Robert S. "A Chapter of Panton, Leslie and Company." *Journal of Southern History* 10 (February–November 1944): 287.

Cronon, William, and Richard White. "Indians in the Land." *American Heritage* 37 (1986): 18–25.

Crossett, G. A. "A Vanishing Race." *Chronicles of Oklahoma* 4 (1926): 100–161.

Culbertson, James. "The Fort Towson Road." *Chronicles of Oklahoma* 5 (December 1927): 414–21.

Davis, Edmond. "Early Life among the Five Civilized Tribes." *Chronicles of Oklahoma* 15 (1937): 70–105.

Debo, Angie. "Education in the Choctaw Country after the Civil War." *Chronicles of Oklahoma* 10 (September 1932): 385–91.

———. "Southern Refugees of the Cherokee Nation." *Southwestern Historical Quarterly* 35 (1932): 256–61.

Deloria, Vine, Jr. "Commentary: Research, Redskins, and Reality." *American Indian Quarterly* 15, no. 4 (1991): 457–68.

DeRosier, Arthur H., Jr. "Pioneers with Conflicting Ideals: Christianity and Slavery in the Choctaw Nation." *Journal of Mississippi History* 21 (1959): 174–89.

———. "Negotiations for the Removal of the Choctaw: U.S. Policies of 1820 and 1830." *Chronicles of Oklahoma* 38 (spring 1960): 85–100.

———. "Thomas Jefferson and the Removal of the Choctaw Indians." *Southern Quarterly* 1 (1962): 52–62.

———. "Andrew Jackson and Negotiations for the Removal of the Choctaw Indians." *Historian* 29 (1967): 343–62.

———. "Choctaw Removal of 1831: A Civilian Effort." *Journal of the West* 6 (1967): 237–47.

Dillard, Anthony Winston. "The Treaty of Dancing Rabbit Creek between the United States and the Choctaw Indians in 1830." *Alabama Historical Society Transactions* 3 (1899): 99–106.

Doran, Michael F. "Population Statistics of Nineteenth-Century Indian Territory." *Chronicles of Oklahoma* 53 (winter 1975): 492–578.

———. "Antebellum Cattle Herding in the Indian Territory." *Geographical Review* 66 (1976): 48–58.

Dunkle, W. F. "A Choctaw Indian's Diary." *Chronicles of Oklahoma* 4 (1900): 61–68.

Edmunds, R. David. "Tecumseh, the Shawnee Prophet, and American History: A Reassessment." *Western Historical Quarterly* 14 (July 1983): 261–76.

———. "Coming of Age: Some Thoughts upon American Indian History." *Indiana Magazine of History* 85, no. 4 (1989): 312–21.

———. "Native Americans, New Voices: American Indian History, 1895–1995." *American Historical Review* 100 (June 1995): 717–40.

Edwards, John. "The Choctaw Indians in the Middle of the Nineteenth Century." *Chronicles of Oklahoma* 10 (1932): 329–425.

Eggan, Fred. "Historical Changes in the Choctaw Kinship System." *American Anthropologist* 39 (1937): 34–53.

Estill-Harbour, Emma. "A Brief History of the Red River Country since 1803." *Chronicles of Oklahoma* 16 (1938): 58–85.

Faiman-Silva, Sandra. "Decolonizing the Choctaw Nation: Choctaw Political Economy in the Twentieth Century." *American Indian Culture and Research Journal* 17 (1993): 43.

178 ■ LIVING IN THE LAND OF DEATH

Faragher, John Mack. "The Frontier Trail: Rethinking Turner and Reimagining the American West." American Historical Review 98 (February 1993): 106–17.

Feller, Daniel. "Politics and Society: Toward a Jacksonian Synthesis." Journal of the Early Republic 10 (1990): 135–61.

Fisk, H.N. "Geology of Avoyelks and Rapides Parishes." Louisiana Geological Bulletin no. 18. New Orleans: Louisiana Department of Conservation, 1940.

Flores, Dan. "Bison Ecology and Bison Diplomacy: The Southern Plains from 1800 to 1850." Journal of American History 78 (1991): 465–85.

Forbes, Jack D. "The Manipulation of Race, Caste, and Identity: Classifying Afroamericans, Native Americans, and Red-Black People." Journal of Ethnic Studies 17 (winter 1990): 24–41.

Foreman, Carolyn Thomas. "The Choctaw Academy." Chronicles of Oklahoma 6 (1924): 453–80.

———. "The Cherokee War Path With Annotations." Chronicles of Oklahoma 9, no. 3 (September 1931).

———. "Journal of a Tour in Indian Territory." Chronicles of Oklahoma 10 (1932): 219–56.

Foreman, Grant. "Early Post Offices of Oklahoma." Chronicles of Oklahoma 6 (March 1928): 1–25.

———. "River Navigation in the Early Southwest." Mississippi Valley Historical Review 15 (June 1928): 32–51.

Gaines, George Strother. "Dancing Rabbit Creek Treaty." Historical and Patriotic Series of Alabama State Department of Archives and History 10 (1928): 1–31.

Garrett, Julia Kathryn. "Doctor John Sibley and the Louisiana-Texas Frontier, 1803–1814." Southwestern Historical Quarterly 45 (1942): 286–301.

Gibson, Arrell. "An Indian Territory United Nations: The Creek Council of 1845." Chronicles of Oklahoma 39 (winter 1961): 398–413.

Graebner, Norman Arthur. "Pioneer Agriculture in Oklahoma." Chronicles of Oklahoma 23 (1945): 232–48.

———. "Provincial Indian Society in Eastern Oklahoma." Chronicles of Oklahoma 23 (1945): 323–37.

———. "The Public Land Policy of the Five Civilized Tribes." Chronicles of Oklahoma 23 (1945): 107–337.

Halbert, Henry S. "Okla Hannali, or the Six Towns District of the Choctaws." American Antiquarian and Oriental Journal 15 (1893): 146–49.

———. "A Choctaw Migration Legend." American Antiquarian and Oriental Journal 16 (1894): 215–16.

———. "The Choctaw Creation Legend," Publications of the Mississippi Historical Society 4 (1902): 267–70.

———. "Nanih Waiya, the Sacred Mound of the Choctaws." Publications of the Mississippi Historical Society 2 (1899): 223–34.

———. "Story of the Treaty of Dancing Rabbit Creek." Publications of the Mississippi Historical Society 6 (1902): 373–402.

———. "Courtship and Marriage among the Choctaws of Mississippi." American Naturalist 16 (1906): 222–24.

Hiemstra, William L. "Presbyterian Mission Schools among the Choctaws and Chickasaws 1845–1860." Chronicles of Oklahoma 27 (1949): 33–40.

Hill, Robert T. "The Topography and Geology of the Cross Timbers and Surrounding

Regions in Northern Texas." *American Journal of Science* 33 (1887): 34–49.

Holmes, Jack D. L. "The Choctaws in 1795: A Choctaw Census of 1795, District of Six Villages." *Alabama Historical Quarterly* 30 (1968): 33–48.

Horsman, Reginald. "Well-Trodden Paths and Fresh Byways: Recent Writings on Native American History." *Reviews in American History* 10 (1982): 234–44.

Hosmer, Brian C. "Rescued from Extinction? The Civilizing Program in Indian Territory." *Chronicles of Oklahoma* 68 (1990): 138–53.

Howard, James. "The Southeastern Ceremonial Complex and Its Interpretation." *Missouri Archeological Society Memoirs* 6 (1968): 119–41.

Hoxie, Frederick E. "The Problems of Indian History." *Social Science Journal* 25 (1988): 389–99.

Hudson, Peter. "Recollections of Peter Hudson." *Chronicles of Oklahoma* 10 (1932): 501-19.

———. "A Story of Choctaw Chiefs." *Chronicles of Oklahoma* 17 (1939): 192–249.

Huggard, Christopher J. "Culture Mixing: Everyday Life on Missions among the Choctaws." *Chronicles of Oklahoma* 70 (1992): 432–49.

Hyde, Anne F. "Cultural Filters: The Significance of Perception in the History of the American West." *Western Historical Quarterly* (August 1993): 351–74.

Jordan, H. Glenn. "Choctaw Colonization in Oklahoma." *Chronicles of Oklahoma* 54 (spring 1976): 16–33.

Jorgensen, Joseph G., and Richard O. Clemmer. "America in the Indian's Past: A Review Essay." *Journal of Ethnic Studies* 6 (1975): 65–74.

Kidwell, Clara Sue. "Native Knowledge in the Americas." *Osiris* 1 (1985): 209–28.

———. "Choctaws and Missionaries in Mississippi before 1830." *American Indian Culture and Research Journal* 11 (1987): 51–72.

Kinnard, Lawrence, and Lucia B. Kinnard. "Choctaws West of the Mississippi, 1766–1800." *Southwestern Historical Quarterly* 83 (1980): 349–70.

Kloppenberg, James T. "The Virtues of Liberalism: Christianity, Republicanism, and Ethics in Early American Political Discourse." *Journal of American History* 74, no. 1 (1987): 9–33.

Knight, Oliver. "Fifty Years of Choctaw Law." *Chronicles of Oklahoma* 31 (spring 1953): 76–95.

Lanman, Charles. "Peter Pitchlynn, Chief of the Choctaws." *Atlantic Monthly* 25 (1870): 486–501.

Lewis, Anna. "Diary of a Missionary to the Choctaws." *Chronicles of Oklahoma* 17 (1939): 428–47.

Lewis, Anna. "Oklahoma as a Part of the Spanish Domain." *Chronicles of Oklahoma* 3 (1924): 48-49.

Lewis, David Rich. "Still Native: The Significance of Native Americans in the History of the American Twentieth Century West." *Western Historical Quarterly* 24 (May 1993): 226–41.

Lincecum, Gideon. "Choctaw Traditions about Their Settlement in Mississippi and the Origin of Their Mound." *Publication of the Mississippi Historical Society* 8 (1904): 521–42.

———. "Life of Apushimataha." *Publications of the Mississippi Historical Society* 9 (1905–6): 415–85.

Malone, Michael P. "Beyond the Last Frontier: Toward a New Approach to Western American History." *Western Historical Quarterly* 20, no. 4 (November 1989): 409–28.

Martin, Calvin. "Ethnohistory: A Better Way to Write Indian History." *Western Historical Quarterly* 9, no. 1 (January 1978): 41–56.

———. "The Metaphysics of Writing Indian-White History." *Ethnohistory* 26 (1979): 153–60.

Mathes, Virginia Shirer. "A New Look at the Role of Women in Indian Society." *American Indian Quarterly* 2 (1975): 131–39.

McDermott, John Francis. "Isaac McCoy's Second Exploring Trip in 1828." *Chronicles of Oklahoma* 12 (1936): 400–443.

McKee, Jesse. "The Choctaw Indians: A Geographical Study in Cultural Change." *Southern Quarterly* 9 (1971): 107–41.

McLoughlin, William G. "Cherokee Anti-Mission Sentiment." *Ethnohistory* 21 (1974): 361–70.

———. "Choctaw Slave Burning: A Crisis in Mission Work among the Indians." *Journal of the West* 13 (1974): 113–27.

———. "Red Indians, Black Slavery and White Racism: America's Slaveholding Indians." *American Quarterly* 26 (October 1974): 367–85.

———. "A Note on African Sources of American Indian Racial Myths." *Journal of American Folklore* 89 (1976): 331–35.

———. "Ghost Dance Movements: Some Thoughts on Definition Based on Cherokee History." *Ethnohistory* 37 (1990): 25–44.

Merrell, James H. "Some Thoughts on Colonial Historians and American Indians." *William and Mary Quarterly* 46 (1989): 94–119.

Meserve, John Bartlett. "The Indian Removal Message of President Jackson." *Chronicles of Oklahoma* 14 (March 1936): 63–67.

Methvin, J. J. "Reminiscences of Life among the Indians." *Chronicles of Oklahoma* 5 (1927): 166–79.

Miner, Craig. "The Struggle for an East-West Railway into Indian Territory, 1870–1882." *Chronicles of Oklahoma* 47 (spring 1969): 560–81.

Morrison, James D. "Note from the *Northern Standard*, 1842–1849," *Chronicles of Oklahoma* 19 (1941): 264–81.

———. "The Choctaw Mission of the American Board of Commissioners for Foreign Missions." *Chronicles of Oklahoma* 14 (1947): 166–83.

———. "Problems in the Industrial Progress and Development of the Choctaw Nation." *Chronicles of Oklahoma* 32 (1954): 70–91.

Morrison, William B. "Diary of Rev. Cyrus Kingsbury." *Chronicles of Oklahoma* 3 (June 1925): 152–57.

Newton, Milton B., Jr. "Cultural Preadaptation and the Upland South." *Geoscience and Man* 5 (1974): 143–54.

Nugent, Walter. "Frontiers and Empires in the Late Nineteenth Century." *Western Historical Quarterly* 20 (November 1989): 393–408.

Orr, Kenneth G. "Field Report on the Excavation of Indian Villages in the Vicinity of the Spiro Mounds, LeFlore County, Oklahoma." *Chronicles of Oklahoma* 11 (1939): 8–15.

Ortiz, Alfonzo. "Some Concerns Central to the Writing of 'Indian' History." *Indian Historian* 10 (1977): 17–22.

Parman, Donald L., and Catherine Price. "A 'Work in Progress': The Emergence of Indian History as a Professional Field." *Western Historical Quarterly* 20 (May 1989): 185–96.

Perkins, Elizabeth A. "The Consumer Frontier: Household Consumption in Early Kentucky." *Journal of American History* 78 (1991): 465–85.

Peterson, John T. "Assimilation, Separation, and Out-Migration in an American Indian Group." *American Anthropologist* 74 (1978): 1286–95.

Porter, Kenneth W. "Relations between Negroes and Indians within the Present Limits of the United States." *Journal of Negro History* 17 (1932): 287–366.

Robbins, William G. "The Conquest of the American West: History as Eulogy." *Indian Historian* 10 (1977): 7–13.

———. "Laying Siege to Western History: The Emergence of New Paradigms." *Reviews in American History* 19 (1991): 313–31.

Roberts, Charles. "A Choctaw Odyssey: The Life of Lesa Phillip Roberts." *American Indian Quarterly* 14 (1990): 259–76.

Ross, S. W. "Number of Witches Supposed to Have Lived among Indians in Early Days." *American Indian* 2 (1927): 7.

Rugeley, Terry. "Savage and Statesman: Changing Historical Interpretations of Tecumseh." *Indiana Magazine of History* 85, no. 4 (1989): 289–311.

Schlenker, Jon A. "An Historical Analysis of the Family Life of the Choctaw Indians." *Southern Quarterly* 13 (1975): 323–34.

Schrems, Suzanne H., and Cynthia J. Wolff. "Politics and Libel: Angie Debo and the Publication of *And Still the Waters Run.*" *Western Historical Quarterly* 22 (May 1991): 185–203.

Shalhope, Robert E. "Republicanism, Liberalism, and Democracy: Political Culture in the Early Republic." *Proceedings of the American Antiquarian Society* 102 (1992): 99–152.

Spalding, Armita Scott. "From the Natchez Trace to Oklahoma: Development of Christian Civilization among the Choctaws, 1800–1860." *Chronicles of Oklahoma* 44 (1967): 2–24.

Spoehr, Alexander. "Changing Kinship Systems, A Study in the Acculturation of the Creeks, Cherokee, and Choctaw," *Anthropological Series,* Field Museum of Natural History, 33 (17 January 1947).

Strickland, Rennard J., and William M. Strickland. "The Court and the Trail of Tears." *Supreme Court Historical Society 1979 Yearbook* (1979): 20–30.

Strickland, William M. "The Rhetoric of Removal and the Trail of Tears: Cherokee Speaking against Jackson's Removal Policy." *Southern Speech Communication Journal* 47 (1982): 292–309.

Swanton, John R.. "Social Organization and Social Usages of the Indians of the Creek Confederacy." *Bureau of American Ethnology Annual Report* 42 (1928): 486–501.

———. "Historic Use of the Spear-Thrower in Southeastern North America," *American Antiquity* 4 (1938): 36–58.

———. "Sun Worship in the Southeast," *American Anthropologist* 30 (1928): 206–224.

Synderfaard, Rex. "The Final Move of the Choctaws." *Chronicles of Oklahoma* 52 (summer 1974): 207–19.

Usner, Daniel H., Jr. "Food from Nature: Learning from the Choctaw of the Eighteenth–Century South." *Southern Exposure* 11 (1983): 66–69.

———. "American Indians on the Cotton Frontier: Changing Economic Relations with Citizens and Slaves in the Mississippi Territory." *Journal of American History* 72 (1985): 297–317.

Vaughn, Alden T. "From White Man to Redskin: Changing Anglo-American Perceptions of the American Indian." *American Historical Review* 87 (1982): 917–53.

Wade, John Williams. "The Removal of the Mississippi Choctaws." *Publications of the Mississippi Historical Society* 8 (1904): 397–426.

Watkins, John A. "The Choctaws in Mississippi." *American Antiquarian and Oriental Journal* 16 (1894): 69–77.

West, R. T. "Pushmataha's Travels." *Chronicles of Oklahoma* 37 (summer 1959): 162–74.

White, Richard. "What Chigabe Knew: Indians, Household Government, and the State."

William and Mary Quarterly 52 (1995): 151–56.

Wilentz, Sean. "On Class and Politics in Jacksonian America." *Reviews in American History* 10 (1982): 45–63.

Winsor, H. M. "Chickasaw-Choctaw Removal Relations with the United States, 1830–1880." *Journal of the West* 12 (1973): 356–71.

Worster, Donald. "Transformations of the Earth: Toward an Agroecological Perspective in History." *Journal of American History* 76 (March 1990):1087–1106.

Wright, J. B. "Ranching in the Choctaw and Chickasaw Nations." *Chronicles of Oklahoma* 37 (fall 1959): 294–300.

Wright, Muriel. "Choctaws." *Chronicles of Oklahoma* 25 (1828): 178–83.

———. "Early Navigation and Commerce along the Arkansas and Red Rivers in Oklahoma." *Chronicles of Oklahoma* 8 (March 1927): 65–88.

———. "Old Boggy Depot." *Chronicles of Oklahoma* 5 (1927): 4–17.

———. "The Removal of the Choctaws to the Indian Territory, 1830–1833." *Chronicles of Oklahoma* 4 (1928): 103–28.

———. "Brief Outline of the Choctaw and the Chickasaw Nations in the Indian Territory, 1830–1833." *Chronicles of Oklahoma* 7 (December 1929): 388–413.

———. "Historic Spots in the Vicinity of Tuskahoma." *Chronicles of Oklahoma* 9 (March 1931): 27–42.

———. "A Brief Review of the Life of Doctor Eliphalet Nott Wright." *Chronicles of Oklahoma* 10 (1932): 267–86.

———. "Historic Places on the Old Stage Line from Fort Smith to Red River." *Chronicles of Oklahoma* 11 (1933): 798–822.

———. "The Butterfield Overland Mail One Hundred." *Chronicles of Oklahoma* 35 (1957): 55–71.

———. "Sarah Ann Harlan: From Her Memoirs of Life in the Indian Territory." *Chronicles of Oklahoma* 39 (1961): 158–79.

Young, F. B. "Notices of the Choctaw and Choktah Tribe." *Edinburgh Journal of Natural and Geographical Science* 2 (1830): 13–17.

Young, Mary. "Indian Removal and Land Allotment: The Civilized Tribes and Jacksonian Justice." *American Historical Review* 64 (1958): 31–45.

BOOKS

Abel, Annie H. "Proposals for an Indian State, 1778–1878." In *Annual Report of the American Historical Association for the Year 1907.* Washington, D.C.: Government Printing Office, 1907, 1:87–102.

Abel, Annie Heloise. *The American Indian under Reconstruction.* Cleveland: Arthur H. Clark Company, 1925.

———. *The American Indian as Participant in the Civil War.* New York: Johnson Reprint Corporation, 1970.

———. *The History of Events Resulting in Indian Consolidation West of the Mississippi.* New York: AMS Press, 1972.

———. *The American Indian as Slaveholder and Secessionist.* Bison Book ed. Lincoln: University of Nebraska Press, 1992.

An Account of Louisiana: Being an Abstract of Documents in the Offices of the Departments of State and of the Treasury. Philadelphia: John Conrad, 1803.

Adair, James. *History of the American Indians: Particularly those Nations adjoining to the Missis-sippi East and West Florida, Georgia, South and North Carolina, and Virginia*, with an intro. by Robert F. Berkhofer Jr. 1775; reprint, New York: Johnson Reprint Corporation, 1968.

Adair, James. *History of the American Indians: Particularly those Nations adjoining to the Mississippi, East and West Florida, Georgia,*

South and North Carolina, and Virginia, with an introduction by Robert f. Berkhofer, Jr., ed. Samuel Cole Williams. New York: Argonaut Press, 1966.

Adair, James. *Adair's History of the American Indians*. Edited by Samuel

Cole Williams. Johnson City, Tenn., 1775; New York: Promontory Press, 1974.

Adams, J. Q. *Memoirs of, edited by Charles Francis Adams*. 12 vols. Philadelphia: J. B. Lippincott & Co., 1877.

Aldridge, Reginald. *Ranch Notes in Kansas, Colorado, The Indian Territory, and Northern Texas*. London: Longmans, Green, and Co., 1884.

Anderson, Terry L., and Peter J. Hill, eds. *The Political Economy of the American West*. Lanham, Md.: Rowman & Littlefield Publishers, 1994.

Bailey, L. R. *Indian Slave Trade in the Southwest*. Los Angeles: Westerlore Press, 1966.

Bailey, M. Thomas. *Reconstruction in Indian Territory: A Story of Avarice, Discrimination, and Opportunism*. Port Washington, N.Y.: National University Publications, 1972.

Baird, W. David. *Peter Pitchlynn: Chief of the Choctaws*. Norman: University of Oklahoma Press, 1972.

Bamforth, Douglas B. *Ecology and Human Organization on the Great Plains*. New York: Plenum Press, 1988.

Bartram, William. *Travels through North and South Carolina, Georgia, East and West Florida*. Charlottesville: University Press of Virginia, 1972.

Bassett, John Spencer, ed. *Correspondence of Andrew Jackson*. Washington, D.C.: Carnegie Institution of Washington, 1928.

Beadle, J. H. *Western Wilds and the Men Who Redeem Them*. Cincinnati: Jones Brothers and Co., 1881.

Benson, Henry C. *Life Among the Choctaw Indians and Sketches of the South-West*. 1860; reprint, New York: Johnson Reprint Corporation, 1970.

Benton, Thomas H. *Thirty Years' View*. 2 vol. New York: n.p., 1854.

Blouet, Brian W., and Frederick C. Luebke, eds. *The Great Plains in Transition: Environment and Culture*. Lincoln: University of Nebraska Press, 1979.

Bossu, Jean-Bernard. *Travels in the Interior of North America, 1751–1762*. Translated and edited by Seymour Feiler. Norman: University of Oklahoma Press, 1961.

Bourne, Edward Gaylord, ed. *Narratives of the Career of Hernando de Soto in the conquest of Florida, as told by a knight of Elvas; and in a relation by Luys Hernandez de Biedma, factor of the expedition, tr. by Buckingham Smith, together with an account of de Soto's expedition based on the diary of Rodrigo Ranjel, his private secretary translated from Oviedo's Historia general u naturel de las Indias*. New York: Allerton Book Company, 1922; reprint, New York: AMS Press, 1973.

Brinton, P. G., and Cyrus Byington, eds. *Grammar of the Choctaw Language by the Reverend Cyrus Byington. Edited from the Original Manuscript in the Library of the American Philosophical Society by P. B. D. Brinton*. Philadelphia: McCalla & Stavely, 1870.

Burkhalter, Lois Wood. *Gideon Lincecum, 1793–1874*. Austin: University of Texas Press, 1965.

Burton, Jeffrey. *Indian Territory and the United States, 1866–1906: Courts, Government, and the*

Movement for Oklahoma Statehood. Norman: University of Oklahoma Press, 1995.

Bushnell, David I., Jr. *The Choctaw of Bayou Lacomb, St. Tammany Parish, Louisiana*. Washington, D.C.: Government Printing Office, 1909.

Byington, Cyrus. *Holisso Anumpa Tosholi: An English and Choctaw Definer; for the Choctaw Academies and Schools*. New York: American Board of Commissioners for Foreign Missions, 1852.

———. *A Dictionary of the Choctaw Language*. Edited by John R. Swanton and Henry S. Halbert. Smithsonian Institution, Bureau of American Ethnology, Bulletin 46, 1915. Brighton, Mich.: Native American Book Publishers, 1990.

———. *Chahta Almanac for the Year of Our Lord 1839*. Park Hill, Okla.: Mission Press, 1939.

Calhoun, John C. *The Papers of John C. Calhoun*. Edited by W. Edwin Hemphill. 19 vol. Columbia: University of South Carolina Press, 1957.

Carmody, Denise Lardner, and John Tully Carmody. *Native American Religions: An Introduction*. New York: Paulist Press, 1993.

Carter, Cecile Elkins. *Caddo Indians: Where We Come From*. Norman: University of Oklahoma Press, 1995.

Catlin, George. *Letters and Notes on the manners, customs, and condition of the north American Indians, written during eight years' travel amongst wildest tribes of Indians in North America*. Philadelphia: Willis P. Hazard, 1857.

———. *Letters and Notes on the Manners, Customs, and Condition of the North American Indians*. 1841. Reprint, Minneapolis: Ross & Haines, 1965.

Champagne, Duane. *Social Order and Political Change: Constitutional Governments among the Cherokee, the Choctaw, the Chickasaw, and the Creek*. Stanford, Calif.: Stanford University Press, 1992.

Chepesiuk, Ron, and Arnold Shankman, eds. *American Indian Archival Material: A Guide to Holdings in the Southeast*. Westport, Conn.: Greenwood Press, 1982.

Claiborne, J. F. H. *Mississippi As a Province, Territory and State with Biographical Notes of Eminent Citizens*. Jackson, Miss.: Power & Barksdale, 1880; reprint, Baton Rouge: Louisiana State University Press, 1964.

Clayton, Lawrence A., Vernon James Knight Jr., and Edward C. Moore, eds., *The DeSoto Chronicles: The Expedition of Hernando de Soto to North America in 1539–1543*. Tuscaloosa: University of Alabama Press, 1993.

Coker, William S., and Thomas D. Watson. *Indian Traders of the Southeastern Spanish Borderlands: Panton, Leslie & Company and John Forbes & Company, 1783–1847*. Pensacola: University of West Florida Press, 1986.

Coleman, Michael C. *Presbyterian Missionary Attitudes toward American Indians, 1837–1893*. Jackson: University Press of Mississippi, 1985.

Coman, Katharine. *Economic Beginnings of the Far West*. 2 vol. New York: Augustus M. Kelley, 1912; reprint, New York: AMS Press, 1969.

Commissioner of Indian Affairs. *Indian Treaties Between the United States and the Indian Tribes, 1778–1837*. Washington, D.C.: Langtree & O'Sullivan, 1837.

Committee of Investigation. *Reports of the Committee of Investigation sent in 1873 by the Mexican Government to the frontier of Texas*. New York: Baker and Godwin, 1875.

Cotterill, R. S. *The Southern Indians: The Story of the Civilized Tribes before Removal*. Norman: University of Oklahoma Press, 1954.

Coues, Elliott, ed. *Expeditions of Zebulon Montgomery Pike*. 3 vol. New York: F. P. Harper, 1895.

———. *Journal of Jacob Fowler, narrating an adventure from Arkansas through the Indian Territory,*

Oklahoma, Kansas, Colorado, and New Mexico, to the source of Rio Grande del Norte, 1821–1822. New York: F.P. Harper, 1898.

Cox, Isaac Joslin. "Exploration of the Louisiana Frontier, 1803–1806." In *Annual Report of the American Historical Association for the Year 1904.* Washington, D.C.: Government Printing Office, 1905.

Cralle, Richard K., ed. *Reports and Public Letters of John C. Calhoun.* New York: D. Appleton & Co., 1888.

Cronon, William. *Changes in the Land: Indians, Colonists, and the Ecology of New England.* New York: Hill and Wang, 1983.

Cushman, Horatio B. *History of the Choctaw, Chickasaw, and Natchez Indians.* Greenville, Tex.: Headlight Printing House, 1899; reprint, New York: Russell & Russell, 1962.

Danky, James P., and Maureen E. Hady, eds. *Native American Periodicals and Newspapers 1828–1982: Bibliography, Publishing Record, and Holdings.* Westport, Conn.: Greenwood Press, 1984.

Debo, Angie. *The Rise and Fall of the Choctaw Republic.* Norman: University of Oklahoma Press, 1934.

———. *And Still the Waters Run: The Betrayal of the Five Civilized Tribes.* Princeton ed. Princeton, N.J.: Princeton University Press, 1940.

———. *Oklahoma: Footloose and Fancy-Free.* Norman: University of Oklahoma Press, 1949.

———. *The Five Civilized Tribes of Oklahoma: Report on Social and Economic Conditions.* Philadelphia: Indian Rights Association, 1951.

———. *A History of the Indians of the United States.* Norman: University of Oklahoma Press, 1970.

De Bow, J. D. B. *Industrial Resources of the Southern and Western States.* 3 vol. New Orleans: Office of DeBow's Review, 1852.

DePratter, Chester B., ed. *The Late Prehistoric Southeast: A Source Book.* New York: Garland Publishing, 1986.

DeRosier, Arthur H., Jr. *The Removal of the Choctaw Indians.* Knoxville: University of Tennessee Press, 1970; New York: Harper & Row, 1972.

DeWees, William B., and Clara Cardelle, comp. *Letters from an Early Settler of Texas.* Louisville, Ky.: Morton & Griswold, 1852.

Dobyns, Henry F. "Indians in the Colonial Spanish Borderlands." In *Indians in American History: An Introduction,* edited by Frederick E. Hoxie, 67–93. Arlington Heights, Ill.: Harlan Davidson, 1988.

Dodge, Richard I. *The Plains of the Great West.* New York: G. P. Putnam's Sons, 1877.

Dowd, Gregory. *A Spirited Resistance: The North American Indian Struggle for Unity.* Baltimore: Johns Hopkins University Press, 1992.

Duke, Philip, and Michael C. Wilson, eds. *Beyond Subsistence: Plains Archeology and the Postprocessual Critique.* Tuscaloosa: University of Alabama Press, 1995.

Rowland, Dunbar. *History of Mississippi, Heart of the South.* Chicago: S. J. Clarke Publishing Company, 1925.

Dunbar, William. *Exploration of Red River. American State Papers: Indian Affairs* 1:721–43.

Duncan, David Ewing. *Hernando de Soto: A Savage Quest in the Americas.* New York: Crown Publishers, 1995.

Edmunds, R. David. "National Expansion from the Indian Perspective." In *Indians in American History: An Introduction,* edited by Frederick E. Hoxie, 159–77. Arlington Heights, Ill.: Harlan Davidson, 1988.

Eggan, Fred. *The American Indian: Perspectives for the Study of Social Change*. Chicago: Aldine Publishing Company, 1966.

Espenshade, Edward B., Jr., and Joel L. Morrison, eds. *Goode's World Atlas*. 14th ed. Chicago: Rand McNally & Co., 1974.

Evarts, Jeremiah. *Essays of the Present Crisis in the Condition of the American Indians*. Boston: Perkins & Marvin, 1829.

Evarts, Jeremiah, ed. *Speeches on the Passage of the Bill for the Removal of the Indians*. Boston and New York: Perkins & Marvin, 1830.

Fischer, LeRoy H., ed. *The Civil War Era in Indian Territory*. Los Angeles: Lorrin L. Morrison, 1974.

Flickinger, Robert Elliott. *The Choctaw Freedmen and the Story of Oak Hill Industrial Academy– Valliant, McCurtain County, Oklahoma Now Called the Alice Lee Elliott Memorial: Including the early history of the Five Civilized Tribes of Indian Territory the Presbytery of Kiamichi, Synod of Canadian, and the Bible in the Free Schools of the American Colonies, but suppressed in France, previous to the American and French Revolutions*. Fonda, Iowa: Journal and Times Press, 1914.

Flint, Timothy. *Recollections of the Last Ten Years*. Boston: Cummings, Hilliard and Co., 1826.

———. *History and Geography of Mississippi Valley*. Cincinnati: E. H. Flint and L. R. Lincoln, 1832.

Flores, Dan L., ed. *Jefferson & Southwestern Exploration: The Freeman & Curtis Accounts of the Red River Expedition of 1806*. Norman: University of Oklahoma Press. 1984.

Folsom, Joseph P. *Constitution and Laws of The Choctaw Nation: Together with the Treaties of 1855, 1865, and 1866*. New York: Wm. P. Lyon & Son, 1869.

Ford, Paul Leicester. *The Works of Thomas Jefferson*. 12 volumes. New York: G. P. Putnam's Sons, 1904-5.

Foreman, Carolyn Thomas. *Oklahoma Imprints, 1835–1907*. Norman: University of Oklahoma Press, 1936.

Foreman, Grant. *Pioneer Days in the Early Southwest*. Cleveland: Arthur H. Clark Company, 1926.

———. *Indian Removal: The Emigration of the Five Civilized Tribes of Indians*. Norman: University of Oklahoma Press, 1932.

———. *Advancing the Frontier: 1830–1860*. Norman: University of Oklahoma Press, 1933.

———. *Indians and Pioneers: The Story of the American Southwest before 1830*. 1936. Reprint, Norman: University of Oklahoma Press, 1967.

Foreman, Grant, ed. *A Traveler in Indian Territory: The Journal of Ethan Allen Hitchcock, late Major-General in the United States Army*. Cedar Rapids, Iowa: The Torch Press, 1930.

———. *Marcy and the Gold Seekers: The Journal of Captain R. B. Marcy, with an Account of the Gold Rush Over the Southern Route*. Norman: University of Oklahoma Press, 1939.

———. *A Pathfinder in the Southwest: The Itinerary of Lt. A. W. Whipple During His Explorations for a Railway Route from Fort Smith to Los Angeles in the Years 1853 & 1854*. Norman: University of Oklahoma Press, 1941.

Fundaburk, Emma Lila, ed. *Southeastern Indians: Life Portraits, A Catalogue of Pictures 1564–1860*. Metuchen, N.J.: Scarecrow Reprint Company, 1958.

Galloway, Patricia. "Confederacy as a Solution to Chiefdom Dissolution: Historical Evidence in the Choctaw Case." In *The Forgotten Centuries: Indians and Europeans in the American South, 1521–1704*, edited by Charles Hudson and Carmen Chavez-Tesser, 393–417. Athens: University of Georgia Press, 1994.

Galloway, Patricia. *Choctaw Genesis, 1500–1700*. Lincoln: University of Nebraska Press, 1995.

Garcilaso de la Vega, G. S. *The Florida of the Inca*. Austin: University of Texas Press, 1951.

Gayarre, Charles. *History of Louisiana*. Vol. 3, *American Domination to 1860*. New York: W. J. Widdleton, 1866.

Goode, William H. *Outposts of Zion, With Limnings of Mission Life*. Cincinnati: Poe and Hitchcock, 1863.

Gould, Charles N. *Geography of Oklahoma*. Ardmore, Okla.: Bunn Brothers, 1909.

Grant, Madison. *The Passing of the Great Race, or the Racial Bias of European History*. New York: C. Scribner, 1916.

Gregg, Josiah. *Commerce of Prairies; or journal of a Santa Fe trader, during eight expeditions across great western prairies, and a residence of nearly nine years in Northern Mexico, 1831–1839*. 1845; reprint, Cleveland: Arthur H. Clark Company, 1905.

Halbert, H. S. "District Divisions of the Choctaw Nation." In *Report of the Alabama Historical Commission to the Governor of Alabama*, edited by Thomas McAdory Owen, 375–85. Montgomery, Ala.: Brown Printing Co., 1901.

———. "Nanih Waiya, The Sacred Mound of the Choctaws," In *A Choctaw Sourcebook*, edited with an introduction by John H. Peterson Jr., 222–34, New York: Garland Publishing, 1983.

Hall, James. *The West: Its commerce and navigation*. Cincinnati: H. W. Derby & Co., 1848.

Hall, Ted Byron. *Oklahoma: Indian Territory*. Fort Worth, Tex.: American Reference Publishers, 1971.

Harman, S. W. *Hell on the Border; He Hanged Eighty-Eight men. A History of the Great United States Criminal Court at Fort Smith, Arkansas, and of Crime and Criminals in the Indian Territory, and the Trial and Punishment Thereof Before His Honor Judge Isaac C. Parker, "The Terror of Law-Breakers," And by the Courts of Said Territory, Embracing the Leading Sentences and Charges to Grand and Petit Juries Delivered by the World Famous Jurist—His Acknowledged Masterpieces, Besides Much other legal lore of untold value to Attorneys and of Interest to Readers in Every Walk of Life—a Book for the Millions—Illustrated with over 50 Fine Half Tones*. Fort Smith, Ark: Phoenix Publishing Company, 1898.

Hauptman, Laurence M. *Between Two Fires: American Indians in the Civil War*. New York: Free Press, 1995.

Hempstead, Fay. *A Pictorial History of Arkansas from the Earliest Times to 1890*. St. Louis: H. W. Derby & Co., 1890.

Hess, Karl, Jr. *Visions upon the Land: Man and Nature on the Western Range*. Washington, D.C.: Island Press, 1992.

Hodgson, Adam. *Letters from North America, Written During a Tour in the United States and Canada*. London: Hurst Robinson & Co., 1824.

Hoig, Stan. *Tribal Wars of the Southern Plains*. Norman: University of Oklahoma Press, 1993.

Horsman, Reginald. *Race and Manifest Destiny*. Cambridge: Harvard University Press, 1981.

Howard, James H., and Victoria Lindsay Levine. *Choctaw Music and Dance*. Norman: University of Oklahoma Press, 1990.

Howard, James H., and Willie Lena. *Oklahoma Seminoles: Medicines, Magic, and Religion*. Norman: University of Oklahoma Press, 1984.

Howeland, Mrs. E. P. *A Tale of Home and War*. Portland, Maine: Brown Thurston & Co., 1888.

Hudson, Charles M. *The Southeastern Indians*. Knoxville: University of Tennessee Press, 1976.

———, ed. *Four Centuries of Southern Indians*. Athens: University of Georgia Press, 1975.

———. *Ethnology of the Southeastern Indians: A Sourcebook*. New York: Garland Publishing, 1985.

Hoxie, Frederick E. "The Problems of American History." In *Major Problems in American*

Indian History, edited by Albert L. Hurtado and Peter Iverson, 33–43. Lexington, Mass.: D.C. Heath and Company, 1994.

Hudson, Charles M., and Carmen Chaves Tesser, eds. *The Forgotten Centuries: Indians and Europeans in the American South, 1521–1704*. Athens: University of Georgia Press, 1994.

Hulbert, Archer Butler. *Redmen's Roads: The Indian Thoroughfares of the Central West*. Columbus, Ohio: F. J. Heer & Co., 1900.

Hunt, R. Douglas. *Indian Agriculture in America: Prehistory to the Present*. Lawrence: University Press of Kansas, 1987.

Hutchinson, A., ed. *Code of Mississippi being an analytical compilation of the public and government statutes of the Territory and State, with Tabular References to the Local and Private Acts, from 1789 to 1848*. Jackson, Miss.: Price and Fall, 1848.

Irving, Washington. *A Tour on the Prairies*. Norman: University of Oklahoma, 1956.

Jackson, A. P., and E. C. Cole. *Oklahoma! Politically and Topographically Described. History and Guide to the Indian Territory. Biographical Sketches of Capt. David L. Payne, W. L. Couch, Wm. H. Osborn, and Others*. Kansas City, Mo.: Ramsey, Millett & Hudson, 1885.

James, Edwin. *Account of an Expedition from Pittsburgh to the Rocky Mountains Performed in the Years 1819, 1820*. Vol. 4, *Early Western Travels, 1748-1846*, ed. Reuben Gold Thwaites. New York: AMS Press, 1966.

James, Edwin, Stephen Harriman Long, and Thomas Say. *Account of an Expedition From Pittsburgh to the Rocky Mountains, under the command of Major Stephen H. Long, from the notes of Major Long, Mr. T. Say, and other gentlemen of the exploring party*. Barre, Mass.: Imprint Society. 1972.

Jefferson, Thomas. *Account of Louisiana*. Philadelphia: John Conrad, 1803.

Jefferson, Thomas, and William Dunbar, eds. *Documents relating to purchase and exploration of Louisiana*. Boston: American Philosophical Society, 1904.

Jones, Charles C., Jr. *Antiquities of the Southern Indians, Particularly of the Georgia Tribes*. New York: AMS Press, 1973.

Jordan, Terry G., and Matti Kaups. *The American Backwoods Frontier: An Ethnic and Ecological Interpretation*. Baltimore: Johns Hopkins University Press, 1989.

Journal of the Sixth Annual Session of the General Council of the Indian Territory composed of Delegates duly elected from the Indian tribes legally resident therein, assembled in council at Okmulgee, Indian Territory, from the 3d to the 15th (inclusive) of May, 1875, Under the Provision of the Twelfth Article of the Treaty made and concluded at the City of Washington in the year 1866, between the United States and the Cherokee Nation and similar Treaties between the United States and the Choctaw and Chickasaw, Muscogee and Seminole Tribes of Indians, of same date. Lawrence, Kans.: Republican Journal Steam Printing Establishment, 1875.

Kappler, Charles, ed. *Indian Affairs, Laws, and Treaties*. 30 vol. Washington, D.C.: Government Printing Office, 1929.

Kidwell, Clara Sue. *Choctaws and Missionaries in Mississippi, 1818–1918*. Norman: University of Oklahoma Press, 1995.

Kilpatrick, Jack Frederick, and Anna Gritts Kilpatrick. *Notebook of a Cherokee Shaman*. Smithsonian Contributions to Anthropology, vol. 2–6. Washington, D.C.: Smithsonian Institution Press, 1970.

Kindscher, Kelly. *Medicinal Wild Plants of the Prairie: An Ethnobotanical Guide*. Lawrence: University Press of Kansas, 1992.

King, Edward. *The Great South: A Record of Journeys in Louisiana, Texas, The Indian Territory, Missouri, Arkansas, Mississippi, Alabama, Georgia, Florida, South Carolina, North Carolina,*

Tennessee, Virginia, West Virginia, and Maryland. Vol. 1. New York: Burt Franklin, 1969.

King, Henry, ed. *Magazine Articles on the Indians.* 1870.

Kniffen, Fred B., Hiram F. Gregory, and George A. Stokes. *The Historic Indian Tribes of Louisiana: From 1542 to the Present.* Baton Rouge: Louisiana State University Press, 1987.

Korp, Maureen. *The Sacred Geography of the American Mound Builders.* Lewiston, N.Y.: Edward Mellen Press, 1990.

Kremm, Thomas W., ed. *Guide to Oklahoma State Archives.* Vol. 1. Oklahoma City: Archives and Records Division, Oklahoma Department of Libraries, 1980.

Kvasnicka, Robert M., and Herman J. Viola, eds. *The Commissioners of Indian Affairs, 1824–1977.* Lincoln: University of Nebraska Press, 1979.

Lamm, Richard D., and Michael McCarthy. *The Angry West: A Vulnerable Land and Its Future.* Boston: Houghton Mifflin Co, 1982.

Lancaster, Jane F. *Removal Aftershock: The Seminoles' Struggle to Survive in the West, 1836–1866.* Knoxville: University of Tennessee Press, 1994.

Lankford, George, ed. *Native American Legends: Southeastern Legends— Tales from the Natchez, Caddo, Biloxi, Chickasaw, and Other Nations.* Little Rock, Ark.: August House, 1987.

Lawson, Merlin Paul. *The Climate of the Great American Desert: Reconstruction of the Climate of Western Interior United States, 1800–1850.* Lincoln: University of Nebraska Press, 1974.

Leopold, Aldo. *A Sand County Almanac.* New York: Oxford University Press, 1979.

Lewis, Anna. *Chief Pushmataha, American Patriot.* New York: Exposition Press, 1959.

Lincecum, Jerry Bryan, and Edward Hake Phillips, eds. *Adventure of a Frontier Naturalist: The Life and Times of Dr. Gideon Lincecum.* College Station, Tex.: Texas A&M Press, 1994.

Lipscomb, Andrew A., and Albert Ellery Bergh, eds. *The Writings of Thomas Jefferson Memorial Edition Containing his Autobiography, Notes on Virginia, Parliamentary Manual, Official Papers, Messages and Addresses, and other Writings, Official and Private, now Collected and Published in their Entirety for the first time Including all of the Original Manuscripts, Deposited in the Department of State and Published in 1853 by order of the Joint Committee of Congress with Numerous Illustrations and A Comprehensive Analytical Index.* Vol. 10, 11, 12. Washington, D.C.: Thomas Jefferson Memorial Association of the United States, 1904.

Littlefield, Daniel F., Jr. *The Chickasaw Freedmen.* Westport, Conn.: Greenwood Press, 1980.

Loomis, A. W. *Scenes in Indian Country.* Philadelphia: Presbyterian Board of Publication, 1859.

Loewen, James W. *Lies My Teacher Told Me: Everything Your American History Textbook Got Wrong.* New York: Simon & Schuster, 1995.

Marcy, Randolph B and J. H. Simpson. *Route from Ft. Smith to Santa Fe.* Washington, D.C.: United States Army Corps of Engineers, 1850.

———. *The Prairie Traveler. A Handbook for Overland Expeditions. With Maps, Illustrations, and Itineraries of the Principle Routes between the Mississippi and the Pacific.* New York: Harper & Brothers, 1859.

———. *Thirty Years of Army Life on the Border.* New York: Harper & Brothers, 1866.

Marcy, Randolph, and George B. McClellan. *Exploration of the Red River of Louisiana, in the year 1852.* Senate, 32d Cong., 2d sess., S. Rept. 54, 1853.

Martin, Calvin. "Ethnohistory: A Better Way to Write Indian History." In *Major Problems in American Indian History,* edited by Albert L. Hurtado and Peter Iverson, 23–33. Lexington, Mass.: D.C. Heath & Co., 1994.

Martin, Joel W. *Sacred Revolt: The Muskogee's Struggle for a New World.* Boston: Beacon Press, 1991.

Mayhall, Mildred P. *The Kiowas*. Norman: University of Oklahoma Press, 1962.

McCoy, Isaac. *History of the Baptist Indian Missions*. New York: Johnson Reprint Corporation, 1970.

McCoy, Joseph G. *Historic Sketches of the Cattle Trade of the West and Southwest*. Kansas City: Ramsey, Millett and Hudson, 1874.

McCurtain County Historical Society. *McCurtain County: A Pictorial History*. McCurtain County Historical Society: Idabel, Okla., 1982.

McKee, Jesse O., and Jon A. Schlenker. *The Choctaws: Cultural Evolution of a Native American Tribe*. Jackson: University Press of Mississippi, 1980.

McKenney, Thomas L. *Memoirs, official and personal with sketches of travels among northern and southern Indians; embracing a war excursion, and descriptions of scenes along western borders*. 2d ed. New York: Paine and Burgess, 1846.

McLemore, Richard Aubrey, ed. *A History of Mississippi*. Hattiesburg: University & College Press of Mississippi, 1973.

McLoughlin, William G., and Walter H. Conser. *The Cherokees and Christianity, 1794–1870: Essays on Acculturation and Cultural Persistence*. Athens: University of Georgia Press, 1994.

McLoughlin, William G., Walter H. Conser Jr., and Virginia Duffy McLoughlin. *The Cherokee Ghost Dance: Essays on the Southeastern Indians, 1789–1861*. New York: Mercer University Press, 1984.

Meinig, D. W. *The Shaping of America: A Geographical Perspective on 500 Years of History*. 2 vol. New Haven, Conn.: Yale University Press, 1993.

Meredith, Howard. *Dancing on Common Ground: Tribal Cultures and Alliances on the Southern Plains*. Lawrence: University Press of Kansas, 1995.

Mereness, Newton D., ed. *Travels in the American Colonies*. New York: MacMillan Company, 1916.

Milligan, Dorothy. *The Indian Way: Choctaws*. Wichita Falls, Tex.: Nortex Press, 1977.

Miner, H. Craig. *The Corporation and the Indian: Tribal Sovereignty and Industrial Civilization in Indian Territory, 1865–1907*. Columbia: University of Missouri Press, 1976.

Mooney, James. *Calendar History of the Kiowa Indians*. Washington, D.C.: Smithsonian Institute Press, 1979.

Mooney, James, and Frans M. Olbrechts. *The Swimmer Manuscript: Cherokee Sacred Formulas and Medicinal Prescriptions*. Washington, D.C.: Government Printing Office, 1932.

Morris, John W., Charles R. Goins, and Edwin C. McReynolds. *Historical Atlas of Oklahoma*. 3d ed. Norman: University of Oklahoma Press, 1965.

Morrison, James D. *The Social History of the Choctaw Nation, 1865–1907*. Durant, Okla.: Creative Infomatics, 1987.

Morse, Jedediah. *A Report to the Secretary of War of the United States, on Indian Affairs, Comprising a Narrative of a Tour Performed in the Summer of 1820, under a Commission from the President of the United States, for the Purpose of Ascertaining for the Use of the Government, the Actual State of the Indian Tribes in Our Country*. New Haven, Conn.: Davis and Force, 1822.

Murrow, J. S. *The Indian's Side*. Atoka, Okla.: Atoka Press, 1916.

Nagel, Joane. *American Indian Ethnic Renewal: Red Power and the Resurgence of Identity and Culture*. New York: Oxford University Press, 1996.

Noyes, Stanley. *Los Comanches: The Horse People, 1751–1845*. Albuquerque: University of New Mexico Press, 1993.

Nuttall, Thomas. *A Journey of Travels into Arkansas Territory, during the year 1819, with Occasional observations on the manners of the Aborigines*. Vol. 13 of 32 in *Early Western*

Travels, 1748–1846, ed. Reuben Gold Thwaites. New York: AMS Press, 1966.

O'Beirne, Harry F., and Edward S. O'Beirne. *The Indian Territory: Its Chiefs, Legislators, and Leading men.* St. Louis: C. B. Woodward Company, 1892.

Painter, Charles Cornelius Coffin. *The Condition of Affairs in Indian Territory and California.* New York: AMS Press, 1976.

Payne, John Howard. "The Green Corn Dance." In *Ethnology of the Southeastern Indians: A Sourcebook,* edited by Charles M. Hudson, 170–95. New York: Garland Publishing, 1932.

Perdue, Theda-. *Slavery and the Evolution of Cherokee Society, 1540–1866.* Knoxville: University of Tennessee Press, 1979.

————, ed. *Nations Remembered: An Oral History of the Cherokees, Chickasaws, Choctaws, Creeks, and Seminoles in Oklahoma, 1865–1907.* Norman: University of Oklahoma Press, 1993.

Peterson, John H., Jr., ed. *A Choctaw Source Book.* New York: Garland Publishing, 1985.

————. *Persistence of Pattern in Mississippi Choctaw Culture.* Jackson, Miss.: Mississippi Department of Archives and History, 1987.

Pickett, Albert James. *History of Alabama and Incidentally of Georgia and Mississippi from the Earliest Period.* Vol. 2. Birmingham, Ala.: Webb Book Co. 1900.

Pike, Albert. *Prose Sketches and Poems, Written in the Western Country.* Boston: Light and Horton, 1834.

Pike, Major Zebulon Montgomery. *An Account of the Expeditions to the Sources of the Mississippi and through the Western parts of Louisiana, to the sources of the Arkansas, Kansas, La Platte, and Pierre Jaun, Rivers; Performed by order of the Government of the United States During the Years 1805, 1806, and 1807. And a Tour Through the Interior Parts of New Spain, When conducted through these provinces, by order of the Captain-General in the Year 1807.* Philadelphia: C. A. Conrad & Co., 1810.

Pike, Zebulon Montgomery. *The Expeditions of Zebulon Montgomery Pike to the Headwaters of the Mississippi River through Louisiana Territory, and in New Spain, during the years 1805-6-7.* Elliott Coues, ed. Reprint, Minneapolis: Ross & Haines, 1965.

Powell, John Wesley. *Report on the Lands of the Arid Region.* Washington, D.C.: Government Printing Office, 1878.

Prucha, Francis Paul. *The Great Father: The United States Government and the American Indians.* Lincoln: University of Nebraska Press, 1984.

Rader, Brian F. *The Political Outsiders: Blacks and Indians in a Rural Oklahoma County.* San Francisco: R & E Research Associates, 1978.

Randolph, Thomas Jefferson, ed. *Memoir, Correspondence and Miscellanies, from the Papers of Thomas Jefferson.* 4 vol. Charlottesville, Va.: F. Carr & Co., 1829.

Reeves, Carolyn Keller, ed. *The Choctaw before Removal.* Jackson: University Press of Mississippi, 1985.

Remini, Robert. *The Age of Jackson.* Columbia: University of South Carolina Press, 1972,

Richardson, James D. *Messages and Papers of the Presidents, 1789–1817.* Washington, D.C.: Government Printing Office, 1896–99.

Risser, Paul G., E. C. Birney, H. D. Blocker, S. W. May, W. J. Parton, and J. A. Wiens. *The True Prairie Ecosystem.* Stroudsburg, Penn.: Hutchinson Ross Publishing Company, 1981.

Rogin, Michael Paul. *Fathers and Children: Andrew Jackson and the Subjugation of the American Indian.* New York: Knopf, 1975.

Rollings, Willard H. *The Osage: An Ethnohistorical Study of Hegemony on the Prairie-Plains.* Columbia: University of Missouri Press, 1992.

Rollings, Willard H. "Living in a Graveyard: Native Americans in Colonial Arkansas," in *Cultural Encounters in the Early South: Indians and Europeans in Arkansas.* Compiled by Jeannie Whayne, 38–60. Fayetteville: University of Arkansas Press, 1995.

Rollings, Ward Hughes. "Prairie Hegemony: An Ethnohistorical Study of the Osage from Early Times to 1840" (Ph.D. Diss., Texas Tech University, 1983.) Reproduction, Ann Arbor University Microfilms International. 1987.

Rowland, Dunbar, ed. *The Mississippi Territorial Archives 1798–1803: Executive Journals of Governor Winthrop Sargent and Governor William Charles Cole Claiborne.* Vol. 1. Nashville: Press of Brandon Printing Company, 1905.

Sattler, Richard A. "Remnants, Renegade, and Runaways: Seminole Ethnogenesis Reconsidered." In *History, Power, and Identity: Ethnogenesis in the Americas, 1492–1992,* edited by Jonathan D. Hill, 36–69. Iowa City: University of Iowa Press, 1996.

Satz, Ronald N. *American Indian Policy in the Jacksonian Era.* Lincoln: University of Nebraska Press, 1975.

Schoolcraft, Henry R. *A View of the Lead Mines of Missouri; including some observations on the mineralogy, geology, geography, antiquities, soil, climate, population, and productions of Missouri and Arkansas, and Other Sections of the Western country.* New York: Charles Wiley & Co., 1819.

———. *Information Respecting the History, Condition and Prospects of the Indian Tribes of the United States.* Philadelphia: Lippincott, Grambo & Co, 1847.

Searcy, Margaret Zehmer. "Choctaw Subsistence, 1540–1830: Hunting, Fishing, Farming, and Gathering." In *The Choctaw Before Removal,* edited by Carolyn Keller Reeves, 32–54. Jackson: University Press of Mississippi, 1985.

Sellers, Charles. *The Market Revolution: Jacksonian America, 1815–1846.* New York: Oxford University Press, 1991.

Shirley, Glenn. *Law West of Fort Smith: A History of Frontier Justice in the Indian Territory, 1834–1896.* Lincoln: University of Nebraska Press, 1968.

Sibley, John. *Explorations of Red River and Washita River, 1803–04. American State Papers: Indian Affairs* 1:721–43.

———. *A Report from Natchitoches in 1807.* New York: Museum of the American Indian and Heye Foundation, 1922.

Simpson, James H. *Report from the secretary of war, communicating the report and map of the route from Ft. Smith, Ark, to Santa Fe, New Mexico, made by Lt. Simpson.* Washington, D.C.: Government Printing Office, 1849.

Snell, Joseph W., ed. *Guide to the Microfilm Edition of the Isaac McCoy Papers 1808–1874 in the Kansas State Historical Society.* Topeka: Kansas State Historical Society, 1967.

Southwestern Brand Book! Containing the Marks and Brands! of the Cattle and Horse Registers of Southwestern Kansas, the Indian Territory and the Panhandle of Texas for the Roundup of 1883. Barbour County, Kans.: Medicine Lodge Cresset, 1883.

Spicer, Edward H. *Perspectives in American Indian Culture Change.* Chicago: University of Chicago Press, 1961.

Spoehr, Alexander. *Changing Kinship Systems: A Study in the Acculturation of the Creeks, Cherokee, and Choctaw.* Chicago: Field Museum of Natural History, 1947.

Stephanson, Anders. *Manifest Destiny: American Expansionism and the Empire of Right.* New York: Wang and Hill, 1995.

Stoddard, Major Amos. *Sketches, Historical, and Descriptive of Louisiana.* Philadelphia: Matthew Carey, 1812.

Strickland, Rennard. *The Indians in Oklahoma*. Norman: University of Oklahoma Press, 1980.

Swanton, John R. *Early History of the Creek Indians and Their Neighbors*. Washington, D.C.: Government Printing Office, 1922.

———. "Aboriginal Culture of the Southeast." In *Ethnology of the Southeastern Indians: A Source Book*, edited by Charles M. Hudson, 677–726. New York: Garland Publishing, 1928.

———. "Sun Worship in the Southeast." In *Ethnology of the Southeastern Indians*, edited by Charles M. Hudson, 206–13. New York: Garland Publishing, 1928.

———, ed. *Source Material for the Social and Ceremonial Life of the Choctaw Indians*. Washington, D.C.: Government Printing Office, 1931.

———, ed. *Source Material on the History and Ethnology of the Caddo Indians*. Washington, D.C.: Government Printing Office, 1942.

———, ed. *The Indians of the Southeastern United States*. Washington, D.C.: Government Printing Office, 1946.

Swanton, John R., and Henry S. Halbert, eds. *A Dictionary of the Choctaw Language*. Washington, D.C.: Government Printing Office, 1915.

Sweet, William Warren, ed. *Religion on the American Frontier: The Presbyterians, 1783–1840*. Vol. 2. New York: Harper & Brothers Publishers, 1936.

Thoburn, Joseph B., and Muriel H. Wright. *Oklahoma: A History of the State and Its People..* 4 vol. New York: Lewis Historical Publishing Co., 1929.

Thompson, John. *Closing the Frontier: Radical Response in OK, 1889–1923*. Norman: University of Oklahoma Press, 1986.

Thornton, Russell. *American Indian Holocaust and Survival: A Population History Since 1492*. Norman: University of Oklahoma Press, 1987.

Thwaites, Reuben Gold, ed. *Early Western Travels, 1748–1846*. London ed. 39 vol. New York: AMS Press, 1966.

Tomer, John S., and Michael J. Brodhead, eds. *A Naturalist in Indian Territory*. Norman: University of Oklahoma Press, 1992.

Tooker, Elizabeth, ed. *Native North American Spirituality of the Eastern Woodlands: Sacred Myths, Dreams, Visions, Speeches, Healing Formulas, Rituals and Ceremonials*. New York: Paulist Press, 1979.

Trafzer, Clifford E. *The Kit Carson Campaign: The Last Great Navajo War*. Norman: University of Oklahoma Press, 1982.

———. *Death Stalks the Yakima: Epidemiological Transitions and Mortality on the Yakima Indian Reservation, 1888–1964*. East Lansing: Michigan State University Press, 1997.

Tyson, Carl Newton. *The Red River in Southwestern History*. Norman: University of Oklahoma Press, 1981.

U.S. Census Office. *Extra Census Bulletin: The Five Civilized Tribes in Indian Territory: The Cherokee, Choctaw, Creek, and Seminole Nations*. Washington, D.C.: U.S. Census Printing Office, 1894.

U.S. Congress. *Letter from the Secretary of the Interior*. Washington, D.C.: Government Printing Office, 1890.

———. *Speeches on the Passage of the Bill for the Removal of the Indians, Delivered in the Congress of the United States, April and May 1830*. Millwood, N.Y.: Kraus Reprint Co., 1973.

U.S. Department of the Interior. *The Five Civilized Tribes in Indian Territory: The Cherokee, Chickasaw, Choctaw, Creek, and Seminole Nations*. Washington, D.C.: United States Census Printing Office, 1895.

U.S. Department of the Interior. *Interior Department Territorial Papers: Oklahoma 1889–1912.* Washington, D.C.: National Archives and Records Service, 1972.

U.S. Department of the Interior. *The Choctaw Nation: Its Resources and Development Potential.* Billings, Mont: U.S. Department of the Interior, 1973.

U.S. Department of the Interior. *Restoring America's Wildlife 1937–1987.* Washington, D.C.: Government Printing Office, 1987.

Unrau, William E. *Mixed Bloods and Tribal Dissolution: Charles Curtis and the Quest for Indian Identity.* Lawrence: University Press of Kansas, 1989.

———. *White Man's Wicked Water: The Alcohol Trade and Prohibition in Indian Country, 1802– 1892.* Lawrence: University Press of Kansas, 1996.

Waldman, Carl. *Atlas of the North American Indian.* New York: Facts on File, 1985.

Wallerstein, Immanuel M. *The Modern World System.* New York: Academic Press, 1989.

Ward, Dillis B. *Across the Plains in 1853.* Seattle: Bull Brothers, 1911.

Ward, Geoffrey C., with Rick Burns and Ken Burns. *The Civil War: An Illustrated History.* New York: Alfred A. Knopf, 1990.

Warren, Lt. G. K. *Reports of Explorations and Surveys to ascertain the most practicable and economical route for a Railroad from the Mississippi River to the Pacific Coast.* Washington, D.C.: United States Topographical Survey, 1861.

Watkins, Ben. *Complete Choctaw Definer: English with Choctaw Definition.* Van Buren, Ark.: J. W. Baldwin, 1892.

Webb, Walter Prescott. *The Great Plains.* Lincoln: University of Nebraska Press, 1981.

Whipple, Charles K. *Relation of the American Board of Commissioners for Foreign Missions to Slavery.* 1861. Reprint, New York: Negro Universities Press, 1969.

White, Richard. *The Roots of Dependency: Subsistence, Environment, and Social Change among the Choctaws, Pawnees, and Navajos.* Lincoln: University of Nebraska Press, 1983.

Witthoft, John. "Green Corn Ceremonialism in the Eastern Woodlands." In *Ethnology of the Southeastern Indians: A Sourcebook,* edited by Charles M. Hudson, 1–91. New York: Garland Publishing, 1949.

Whorf, Benjamin Lee. "The Relation of Habitual Thought and Behaviour to Language," in *Language, Culture, and Personality* by Leslie Spier et al. Menasha, Wis.: Sapir Memorial Publication Fund, 1941.

———. "An American Model of the Universe." In *Teachings from the American Earth,* edited by Dennis Tedlock and Brenda Tedlock, 122. New York: Liverwright, 1976.

Wilbarger, J. W., ed. *Indian Depredations in Texas: Reliable Accounts of Battles, Wars, Adventures, Forays, Murders, Massacres, Etc., Etc., Together with Biographical Sketches of Many of the Most Noted Indian Fighters and Frontiersmen of Texas.* Facsimile reproduction ed., Austin, Tex.: Eakin Press, 1889.

Williams, L. S. *Family Education and Government: A Discourse in the Choctaw Language.* Printed for the American Board of Commissioners for Foreign Missions. Carrollton, Miss.: Crocker & Brewster, 1835.

Wiltshire, Betty C., ed. *Register of Choctaw Emigrants to the West, 1831 and 1832.* Carrollton, Miss.: Olde Times Publishing Co., 1993.

Worster, Donald. *Dust Bowl: The Southern Plains in the 1930s.* New York: Oxford University Press, 1979.

Worster, Donald. *Under Western Skies: Nature and History in the American West.* New York: Oxford University Press. 1992.

Wright, Alfred, and Cyrus Byington, eds. *A Spelling Book, Written in the Chahta Language with an English Translation; Prepared and Published Under the Direction of the Missionaries in the Chahta Nation with the Aid of Captain David Folsom, Interpreter.* Cincinnati: Morgan, Lodge, and Fisher, 1825.

Wright, Alfred and Cyrus Byington. *Chahta holisso Ai isht la ummona.* Boston: American Board of Commissioners for Foreign Missions, 1835.

Wright, Henry A., and Arthur W. Bailey. *Fire Ecology: United States and Southern Canada.* New York: John Wiley & Sons, 1982.

Wright, J. Leitch Jr. *The Only Land They Knew: The Tragic Story of the American Indians in the Old South.* New York: Free Press, 1981.

Wright, Muriel H. *A Guide to the Indian Tribes of Oklahoma.* Norman: University of Oklahoma Press, 1951.

Yoakum, H. *History of Texas from its first settlement in 1685 to its annexation to the United States in 1846.* Vol. 2. New York: Redfield, 1856.

Young, Mary. *Redskins, Ruffleshirts, and Rednecks: Indian Allotments in Alabama and Mississippi, 1830–1860.* Norman: University of Oklahoma Press, 1970.

Index